FORD
ZEPHYR·ZODIAC
EXECUTIVE
Mk.III & IV
1962-1971

Compiled by
R.M. Clarke

ISBN 1 85520 0643

Distributed by
Brooklands Book Distribution Ltd.
'Holmerise', Seven Hills Road,
Cobham, Surrey, England
Printed in Hong Kong

BROOKLANDS BOOKS

BROOKLANDS ROAD TEST SERIES
AC Ace & Aceca 1953-1983
Alfa Romeo Alfasud 1972-1984
Alfa Romeo Alfetta Coupes GT. GTV. GTV6 1974-1987
Alfa Romeo Giulia Berlinas 1962-1976
Alfa Romeo Giulia Coupes 1963-1976
Alfa Romeo Giulietta Gold Portfolio 1954-1965
Alfa Romeo Spider 1966-1990
Allard Gold Portfolio 1937-1958
Alvis Gold Portfolio 1919-1969
American Motors Muscle Cars 1966-1970
Aston Martin Gold Portfolio 1972-1985
Austin Seven 1922-1982
Austin A30 & A35 1951-1962
Austin Healey 100 & 100/6 Gold Portfolio 1952-1959
Austin Healey 3000 Gold Portfolio 1959-1967
Austin Healey 'Frogeye' Sprite Col No.1 1958-1961
Austin Healey Sprite 1958-1971
Avanti 1962-1983
BMW Six Cylinder Coupes 1969-1975
BMW 1600 Col. 1 1966-1981
BMW 2002 1968-1976
Bristol Cars Gold Portfolio 1946-1985
Buick Automobiles 1947-1960
Buick Muscle Cars 1965-1970
Buick Riviera 1963-1978
Cadillac Automobiles 1949-1959
Cadillac Automobiles 1960-1969
Cadillac Eldorado 1967-1978
High Performance Capris Gold Portfolio 1969-1987
Chevrolet Camaro SS & Z28 1966-1973
Chevrolet Camaro & Z-28 1973-1981
High Performance Camaros 1982-1988
Camaro Muscle Cars 1966-1972
Chevrolet 1955-1957
Chevrolet Corvair 1959-1969
Chevrolet Impala & SS 1958-1971
Chevrolet Muscle Cars 1966-1971
Chevelle and SS 1964-1972
Chevy Blazer 1969-1981
Chevy EL Camino & SS 1959-1987
Chevy II Nova & SS 1962-1973
Chrysler 300 1955-1970
Citroen Traction Avant Gold Portfolio 1934-1957
Citroen DS & ID 1955-1975
Citroen SM 1970-1975
Citroen 2CV 1949-1988
Shelby Cobra Gold Portfolio 1962-1969
Cobras & Replicas 1962-1983
Chevrolet Corvette Gold Portfolio 1953 1962
Corvette Stingray Gold Portfolio 1963-1967
High Performance Corvettes 1983-1989
Daimler SP250 Sport & V-8250 Saloon Gold Portfolio 1959-1969
Datsun 240Z 1970-1973
Datsun 280Z & ZX 1975-1983
De Tomaso Collection No.1 1962-1981
Dodge Charger 1966-1974
Dodge Muscle Cars 1967-1970
Excalibur Collection No.1 1952-1981
Facel Vega 1954-1964
Ferrari Cars 1946-1956
Ferrari Cars 1973-1977
Ferrari Dino 1965-1974
Ferrari Dino 308 1974-1979
Ferrari 308 & Mondial 1980-1984
Ferrari Collection No.1 1960-1970
Fiat-Bertone X1/9 1973-1988
Fiat Pininfarina 124 + 2000 Spider 1968-1985
Ford Automobiles 1949-1959
Ford Bronco 1966-1977
Ford Bronco 1978-1988
Ford Consul. Zephyr Zodiac MkI & II 1950-1962
Ford Cortina 1600E & GT 1967-1970
Ford Fairlane 1955-1970
Ford Falcon 1960-1970
Ford GT40 Gold Portfolio 1964-1987
Ford RS Escorts 1968-1980
Ford Zephyr Zodiac Executive MkIII & MkIV 1962-1971
High Performance Escorts Mk1 1968-1974
High Performance Escorts Mk II 1975-1980
High Performance Mustangs 1982-1988
Holden 1948-1962
Honda CRX 1983-1987
Hudson & Railton 1936-1940
Jaguar and SS Gold Portfolio 1931-1951
Jaguar Cars 1957-1961
Jaguar Cars 1961-1964
Jaguar Mk2 1959-1969
Jaguar E-Type Gold Portfolio 1961-1971
Jaguar E-Type 1966-1971
Jaguar E-Type V-12 1971-1975
Jaguar XKE Collection No.1 1961-1974
Jaguar XJ6 1968-1972
Jaguar XJ6 Series II 1973-1979
Jaguar XJ6 & XJ12 Series III 1979-1985
Jaguar XJ12 1972-1980
Jaguar XJS Gold Portfolio 1975-1988
Jaguar XK120.XK140.XK150 Gold Portfolio 1948-1960
Jeep CJ5 & CJ6 1960-1976
Jeep CJ5 & CJ7 1976-1986
Jensen Cars 1946-1967
Jensen Cars 1967-1979
Jensen Interceptor Gold Portfolio 1966-1986
Jensen Healey 1972-1976
Lamborghini Cars 1964-1970
Lamborghini Cars 1970-1975
Lamborghini Countach Col No.1 1971-1982
Lamborghini Countach & Urraco 1974-1980
Lamborghini Countach & Jalpa 1980-1985
Lancia Stratos 1972-1985
Land Rover 1948-1973 - A Collection
Land Rover Series II & IIa 1958-1971
Land Rover Series III 1971-1985
Land Rover 90 & 110 1983-1989
Lincoln Gold Portfolio 1949-1960
Lincoln Continental 1961-1969
Lotus and Caterham Seven Gold Portfolio 1957-1989
Lotus Cortina Gold Portfolio 1963-1970
Lotus Elan Gold Portfolio 1962-1974
Lotus Elan Collection No.2 1963-1972
Lotus Elite 1957-1964
Lotus Elite & Eclat 1974-1982
Lotus Turbo Esprit 1980-1986
Lotus Europa 1966-1975
Lotus Europa Collection No.1 1966-1974
Lotus Seven Collection No.1 1957-1982

Marcos Cars 1960-1988
Maserati 1965-1970
Maserati 1970-1975
Mazda RX-7 Collection No.1 1978-1981
Mercedes 190 & 300SL 1954-1963
Mercedes 230/250/280SL 1963-1971
Mercedes Benz SLs & SLCs Gold Portfolio 1971-1989
Mercedes Bens Cars 1949-1954
Mercedes Bens Cars 1954-1957
Mercedes Bens Cars 1957-1961
Mercedes Bens Competition Cars 1950-1957
Mercury Muscle Cars 1966-1971
Metropolitan 1954-1962
MG TC 1945-1949
MG TD 1949-1953
MG TF 1953-1955
MG Cars 1959-1962
MGA Roadsters 1955-1962
MGA Collection No.1 1955-1982
MGB Roadsters 1962-1980
MGB GT 1965-1980
MG Midget 1961-1980
Mini Cooper Gold Portfolio 1961-1971
Mini Moke 1964-1989
Mini Muscle Cars 1961-1979
Mopar Muscle Cars 1964-1967
Mopar Muscle Cars 1968-1971
Morgan Three-Wheeler Gold Portfolio 1910-1952
Morgan Cars 1960-1970
Morgan Cars Gold Portfolio 1968-1989
Morris Minor Collection No.1
Mustang Muscle Cars 1967-1971
Oldsmobile Automobiles 1955-1963
Old's Cutlass & 4-4-2 1964-1972
Oldsmobile Muscle Cars 1964-1971
Oldsmobile Toronado 1966-1978
Opel GT 1968-1973
Packard Gold Portfolio 1946-1958
Pantera Gold Portfolio 1970-1989
Plymouth Barracuda 1964-1974
Plymouth Muscle Cars 1966-1971
Pontiac Tempest & GTO 1961-1965
Pontiac GTO 1964-1970
Pontiac Firebird 1967-1973
Pontiac Firebird and Trans-Am 1973-1981
High Performance Firebirds 1982-1989
Pontiac Fiero 1984-1988
Pontiac Muscle Cars 1966-1972
Porsche 356 1952-1965
Porsche Cars in the 60's
Porsche Cars 1960-1964
Porsche Cars 1964-1968
Porsche Cars 1968-1972
Porsche Cars 1972-1975
Porsche Turbo Collection No.1 1975-1980
Porsche 911 1965-1969
Porsche 911 1970-1972
Porsche 911 1973-1977
Porsche 911 Carrera 1973-1977
Porsche 911 Turbo 1975-1984
Porsche 911 SC 1978-1983
Porsche 914 Gold Portfolio 1969-1976
Porsche 914 Collection No.1 1969-1983
Porsche 924 Gold Portfolio 1975-1988
Porsche 928 1977-1989
Porsche 944 1981-1985
Range Rover Gold Portfolio 1970-1988
Reliant Scimitar 1964-1986
Riley 11/2 & 21/2 Litre Gold Portfolio 1945-1955
Rolls Royce Silver Cloud 1955-1965
Rolls Royce Silver Shadow 1965-1981
Rover P4 1949-1959
Rover P4 1955-1964
Rover 3 & 3.5 Litre 1958-1973
Rover 2000 + 2200 1963-1977
Rover 3500 1968-1977
Rover 3500 & Vitesse 1976-1986
Saab Sonett Collection No.1 1966-1974
Saab Turbo 1976-1983
Shelby Mustang Muscle Cars 1965-1970
Stubebaker Gold Portfolio 1947-1966
Stubebaker Hawks & Larks 1956-1963
Sunbeam Tiger & Alpine Gold Portfolio 1959-1967
Thunderbird 1955-1957
Thunderbird 1958-1963
Thunderbird 1964-1976
Toyota Land Cruiser 1956-1984
Toyota MR2 1984-1988
Triumph 2000. 2.5. 2500 1963-1977
Triumph GT6 1966-1974
Triumph Spitfire 1962-1980
Triumph Spitfire Col No.1 1962-1982
Triumph Stag 1970-1980
Triumph Stag Collection No.1 1970-1984
Triumph TR2 & TR3 1952-60
Triumph TR4-TR5-TR250 1961-1968
Triumph TR6 1969-1976
Triumph TR6 Collection No.1 1969-1983
Triumph TR7 & TR8 1975-1982
Triumph Herald 1959-1971
Triumph Vitesse 1962-1971
TVR Gold Portfolio 1959-1988
Volkswagen Cars 1936-1956
VW Beetle Collection No.1 1970-1982
VW Golf GTi 1976-1986
VW Karmann Ghia 1955-1982
VW Kubelwagen 1940-1975
VW Scirocco 1974-1981
VW Bus. Camper. Van 1954-1967
VW Bus. Camper. Van 1968-1979
VW Bus. Camper. Van 1979-1989
Volvo 120 1956-1970
Volvo 1800 1960-1973

BROOKLANDS ROAD & TRACK SERIES
Road & Track on Alfa Romeo 1949-1963
Road & Track on Alfa Romeo 1964-1970
Road & Track on Alfa Romeo 1971-1976
Road & Track on Alfa Romeo 1977-1989
Road & Track on Aston Martin 1962-1984
Road & Track on Auburn Cord and Duesenburg 1952-1984
Road & Track on Audi & Auto Union 1952-1980
Road & Track on Audi 1980-1986
Road & Track on Austin Healey 1953-1970
Road & Track on BMW Cars 1966-1974

Road & Track on BMW Cars 1975-1978
Road & Track on BMW Cars 1979-1983
Road & Track on Cobra, Shelby & GT40 1962-1983
Road & Track on Corvette 1953-1967
Road & Track on Corvette 1968-1982
Road & Track on Corvette 1982-1986
Road & Track on Datsun Z 1970-1983
Road & Track on Ferrari 1950-1968
Road & Track on Ferrari 1968-1974
Road & Track on Ferrari 1975-1981
Road & Track on Ferrari 1981-1984
Road & Track on Fiat Sports Cars 1968-1987
Road & Track on Jaguar 1950-1960
Road & Track on Jaguar 1961-1968
Road & Track on Jaguar 1968-1974
Road & Track on Jaguar 1974-1982
Road & Track on Jaguar 1983-1989
Road & Track on Lamborghini 1964-1985
Road & Track on Lotus 1972-1981
Road & Track on Maserati 1952-1974
Road & Track on Maserati 1975-1983
Road & Track on Mazda RX7 1978-1986
Road & Track on Mercedes 1952-1962
Road & Track on Mercedes 1963-1970
Road & Track on Mercedes 1971-1979
Road & Track on Mercedes 1980-1987
Road & Track on MG Sports Cars 1949-1961
Road & Track on MG Sprots Cars 1962-1980
Road & Track on Mustang 1964-1977
Road & Track on Nissan 300-ZX & Turbo 1984-1989
Road & Track on Peugeot 1955-1986
Road & Track on Pontiac 1960-1983
Road & Track on Porsche 1961-1967
Road & Track on Porsche 1968-1971
Road & Track on Porsche 1972-1975
Road & Track on Porsche 1975-1978
Road & Track on Porsche 1979-1982
Road & Track on Porsche 1982-1985
Road & Track on Porsche 1985-1988
Road & Track on Rolls Royce & B'ley 1950-1965
Road & Track on Rolls Royce & B'ley 1966-1984
Road & Track on Saab 1955-1985
Road & Track on Toyota Sports & GT Cars 1966-1984
Road & Track on Triumph Sports Cars 1953-1967
Road & Track on Triumph Sports Cars 1967-1974
Road & Track on Triumph Sports Cars 1974-1982
Road & Track on Volkswagen 1951-1968
Road & Track on Volkswagen 1968-1978
Road & Track on Volkswagen 1978-1985
Road & Track on Volvo 1957-1974
Road & Track on Volvo 1975-1985
Road & Track - Henry Manney at Large and Abroad

BROOKLANDS CAR AND DRIVER SERIES
Car and Driver on BMW 1955-1977
Car and Driver on BMW 1977-1985
Car and Driver on Cobra, Shelby & Ford GT 40 1963-1984
Car and Driver on Corvette 1956-1967
Car and Driver on Corvette 1968-1977
Car and Driver on Corvette 1978-1982
Car and Driver on Corvette 1983-1988
Car and Driver on Datsun Z 1600 & 2000 1966-1984
Car and Driver on Ferrari 1955-1962
Car and Driver on Ferrari 1963-1975
Car and Driver on Ferrari 1976-1983
Car and Driver on Mopar 1956-1967
Car and Driver on Mopar 1968-1975
Car and Driver on Mustang 1964-1972
Car and Driver on Pontiac 1961-1975
Car and Driver on Porsche 1955-1962
Car and Driver on Porsche 1963-1970
Car and Driver on Porsche 1970-1976
Car and Driver on Porsche 1977-1981
Car and Driver on Porsche 1982-1986
Car and Driver on Saab 1956-1985
Car and Driver on Volvo 1955-1986

BROOKLANDS PRACTICAL CLASSICS SERIES
PC on Austin A40 Restoration
PC on Land Rover Restoration
PC on Metalworking in Restoration
PC on Midget/Sprite Restoration
PC on Mini Cooper Restoration
PC on MGB Restoration
PC on Morris Minor Restoration
PC on Sunbeam Rapier Restoration
PC on Triumph Herald/Vitesse
PC on Triumph Spitfire Restoration
PC on VW Beetle Restoration
PC on 1930s Car Restoration

BROOKLANDS MOTOR & THOROGHBRED & CLASSIC CAR SERIES
Motor & T & CC on Ferrari 1966-1976
Motor & T & CC on Ferrari 1974-1984
Motor & T & CC on Lotus 1979-1983

BROOKLANDS MILITARY VEHICLES SERIES
Allied Mil. Vehicles No.1 1942-1945
Allied Mil. Vehicles No.2 1941-1946
Dodge Mil. Vehicles Col. 1 1940-1945
Military Jeeps 1941-1945
Off Road Jeeps 1944-1971
Hail to the Jeep
US Military Vehicles 1941-1945
US Army Military Vehicles WW2-TM9-2800

BROOKLANDS HOT ROD RESTORATION SERIES
Auto Restoration Tips & Techniques
Basic Bodywork Tips & Techniques
Basic Painting Tips & Techniques
Camaro Restoration Tips & Techniques
Custom Painting Tips & Techniques
Engine Swapping Tips & Techniques
How to Build a Street Rod
Mustang Restoration Tips & Techniques
Performance Tuning - Chevrolets of the '60s
Performance Tuning - Ford of the '60s
Performance Tuning - Mopars of the '60s
Performance Tuning - Pontiacs of the '60s

BROOKLANDS BOOKS

CONTENTS

5	Ford Zodiac Mk III	*Motor*	April 18	1962
9	Ford Zephyr 4 Manual and Automatic Road Test	*Autocar*	April 27	1962
14	The Ford Zodiac Mk III Road Test	*Motor*	April 18	1962
18	The New Mark III Fords	*Cars Illustrated*	May	1962
20	Two New Zephyrs	*Motor*	May 2	1962
24	Ford Zodiac Mk III Road Test	*Cars Illustrated*	July	1962
27	Is This Ford's Best Car? Road Test	*Wheels*	Oct.	1962
31	Ford Zephyr 6 Estate Car Road Test	*Autocar*	May 24	1963
36	Ford Zodiac Mk III	*Car South Africa*	Nov.	1964
38	Ford Executive Zodiac Road Test	*Autocar*	April 9	1965
44	Zephyr 4 Spot Check	*Motor*	Sept. 18	1966
46	The Ford Zephyr Six and Zodiac Mk III Spot Check	*Motor*	Mar. 26	1966
48	Zephyr/Zodiac Mk III Car Owner Report	*Car South Africa*	March	1966
50	Zodiac to Sofia	*Autocar*	Dec. 4	1964
53	Unveiled in Tunisia – Ford's New V6	*Car and Car Conversions*	May	1966
55	Flexible Five-Seater – Zodiac Mk IV Road Test	*Motor*	April 23	1966
61	Zephyr 6 Mk IV Road Test	*Autocar*	April 22	1966
67	Zodiac Automatic Driving Impression	*Car & Car Conversions*	May	1966
68	Zephyr and Zodiac go V6	*Sporting Motorist*	May	1966
70	Enter the V6	*Modern Motor*	June	1966
72	V6 Zodiac with Meissner V Camshaft	*Car South Africa*	Sept.	1966
74	Ford Zephyr V6 12,000 Mile Report	*Motor*	April 22	1967
80	Ford Zephyr De Luxe Road Test	*Autocar*	Aug. 15	1968
84	1966 Ford Zephyr Used Car Test	*Autocar*	Oct. 10	1968
87	Freight Express – Ford Zodiac Estate Road Test	*Motor*	Aug. 30	1969
92	Ford Status Symbol – Executive Road Test	*Motor*	June 13	1970
98	Battleship Bargain Buying Used	*Practical Classics*	April	1990
102	Z Cars	*Classic & Sportscar*	Sept.	1986

BROOKLANDS BOOKS

ACKNOWLEDGEMENTS

As a companion to the Brooklands Book dealing with Ford of Britain's Mk1 & Mk2 Consul/Zephyr/Zodiac cars of the 1950s is this publication which covers the Mk3 & Mk4 models produced between 1962 and 1971.

Once again we have asked well-known Ford historian Michael Allen to write the introduction. Michael has supplied the cover photo for this volume, and again we have pleaseure in recommending his own major book "Consul Zephyr Zodiac Executive: Fords Mk1 to 4", published by Motor Racing Publications, as further reading for the Ford enthusiast.

To the proprietors of Autocar, Car and Car Conversions, Cars Illustrated, Car South Africa, Classic and Sports Car, Modern Motor, Motor, Practical Classics, Sporting Motorist and Wheels, we gratefully acknowledge their permission to reprint the road tests and articles which originally appeared in their respective magazines, and which are of considerable interest to today's enthusiasts of long-past motoring times.

R.M. Clarke

With new medium sized models effectively filling the gap between the small Anglia/ Prefect cars and the much larger Consul/Zephyr models, Ford were able to move their large-car range further upmarket when it appeared in redesigned Mk3 form early in 1962. The Consul name disappeared from the big four-cylinder car, with the latest version of that model given the new title of Zephyr 4. A similarly restyled Zephyr 6 ran alongside, whilst at the top of the range now came a Zodiac Mk3 which was somewhat further removed from the standard Zephyr than hitherto. Higher power outputs, and a new four-speed all-synchromesh gearbox resulted in appreciably greater top-end performance for the Mk3 cars, with the new Zodiac having the distinction of being Ford of Britain's first 100mph production car.

But no less important was style and luxury, and putting further emphasis on the latter qualities in particular was the sumptuous Zodiac Executive which came in 1965 as an additional top-of-the-range Mk3.

Bigger and bolder than ever was the predominent theme of the Zephyr Zodiac and Executive Mk4 models which took over during 1966, with their long-bonneted, short-tailed styling arousing considerable comment. Paradoxically, however, under that long and imposing front end were all-new and very compact V4- and V6-cylinder power units; whilst under the Mk4's tail was Ford's first independent rear suspension system, and there were disc brakes on all four wheels too.

None of these advances however lived up to expectations in their early days, with problems unfortunately proving sufficient enough to tarnish the excellent Zephyr/Zodiac reputation built up by the three preceding generations. But continuous development served to eventually eradicate most of the problems, and the Mk4 range matured into generally reliable cars, and with a firm following which allowed Ford to continue to take the largest share of the big-car market in Britain.

Michael Allen
Leeds
Yorkshire

An Entirely New Mk. III

FORD ZODIAC

The new Ford Zodiac . . .

. . . and the car it replaces.

100 m.p.h. ★ Six Seats ★ 5,000-mile Servicing ★ Four-speed all-synchro gearbox ★ All Curved Glass Windows ★ Luxury Interior

IN the days of the Model "T" Ford, customers could "have their cars in any colour provided it was black," to quote Henry Snr. Since those days the range of choice has widened greatly in Britain as well as in other countries. Now with the announcement of the latest 2½-litre Zodiac model, to be known as the Mk. III, Ford of Dagenham claim that they are exploring a market new to them.

The Zodiac has for some time been the most luxurious car in their range, but it has been nevertheless very similar to the Zephyr. The new version of this six-seater family saloon is a "prestige" car that is different both internally and externally. Furthermore it is the first Ford offered by the English company that can exceed 100 m.p.h. As a high performance car it is therefore fitting that its début in dealers' showrooms is to be followed tomorrow by its first competition, the East African Safari Rally. This timing is no coincidence for Fords set considerable store by this formidable event, in which they have consistently won the team award, although they are the first to admit that they have taken note of the make that has been the overall winner the last

few times. To this end the first prototype car was completed in late October, 1960, and since then development tests have been carried out here, on the Continent and in the United States.

The new Zodiac does, for all this, retain a substantial number of components basically similar to its predecessor and the overall layout of these components. Thus although the hull is totally different in appearance (it is the most changed part of the whole car) it can be regarded as a development of the Mk.II chassis. It is built around five bulkheads starting with the headlamps, then the engine and facia bulkhead, the cross member at the rear of the gearbox, the rear seat back and finally, the rear of the boot. The bulkhead at the rear seat back is now tied structurally to the rear parcel shelf, eliminating the necessity for the diagonal cross-bracing that was previously found at this point. Further strengthening at the rear has been achieved by spreading out the ends of the longitudinal rails that form part of the rear wheel arches where they join the centre section of the body. At the front the boxes that carry the top mounting points of the front suspension have also been reinforced so that the pressed steel tie

over . . . ▶

5

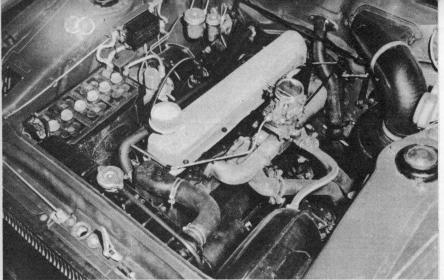

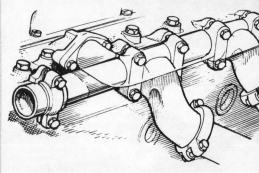

Up-rating the power unit (shown here with the air cleaner removed) has been achieved by the new size carburetter and the twin exhaust system, (above). There are no longer any tie-rods between the tops of the suspension struts and the bulkhead.

New Ford Zodiac Mk III

practice, a servo is incorporated in the system complete with vacuum reservoir. The life of the disc pads has been found to be comparatively so great that the width of the lining used at the rear has been increased by $\frac{1}{2}$ in. in order to even up the wear between front and rear.

With no vast difference in wind resistance between this car and the one it supersedes, there has of course been a certain amount of engine tuning in order to make it comfortably exceed three figures. The power unit is the same in overall layout, being an oversquare, o.h.v. pushrod, straight six of 2,553 c.c. capacity. It now delivers 109 b.h.p. nett instead of 85 b.h.p. Some $5\frac{1}{2}$ of these horses come from a new exhaust system. Since its inception this engine has had an exhaust manifold that con-

rods that were previously found running from them to the engine bulkhead are no longer necessary. All this has increased the rigidity of the shell from 5,800 lb. ft./degree to 7,000 lb. ft./degree.

Another chassis feature is the petrol tank, which instead of being underslung, is now sunk in the floor of the boot and bolted in place. This means that it also acts as a structural member, though as it lies outside the wheelbase it is not highly stressed. The doors of the Mk. III Zodiac differ from those on the previous car. Curved glass has been used for all windows, even the quarter lights, so the door and window frame can no longer be a single pressing. Thus a separate stainless steel frame is used for the windows. This arrangement gives more interior width for the occupants not only because of the curvature of the glass, but because its use allows the doors to be given a concave curve on the inside.

The suspension, by Macpherson struts at the front and semi-elliptic leaf springs at the rear, is the same in principle as before but detail improvements and alterations have been made. Completely new asymmetric leaf springs of lower periodicity than before are used with five leaves and an interleaving of butyl rubber between the four major leaves. The spring is held to the axle (which has the same casing as before) in rubber, with massive bushes to attach it to the chassis in the interests of silence.

The strut system of front suspension has been used by Fords for some years. To allow the body line to be lowered and to reduce "stiction" in the struts themselves, they are now mounted at a greater angle, their tops being inclined inwards, so that they lie nearer the best possible angle from the mechanical point of view. The internal working parts are mounted lower down in the base casting and this allows shorter struts to be used while providing the same amount of suspension movement. These changes allow the bonnet line to be lowered some 4 in. As before, the single lower radius arm is combined with an anti-roll bar which also acts as the front arm of the wishbone, so that the number of basic front suspension components is kept as small as possible.

Disc front brakes were introduced on the Ford large car range as an option in September of 1960 and they are naturally used on the latest Zodiac. They are paired with drums at the rear and in order to keep pedal pressures at a reasonably low figure, as is modern

The Ford Zodiac Mk. III retains the same basic layout and components as its predecessor although its lines are completely different. Details of interest which can be seen here are the gearbox mounting—rubber held on a cross member which is itself attached to the chassis by rubber—and the exhaust system which is, in contrast, held solidly to the underside of the car.

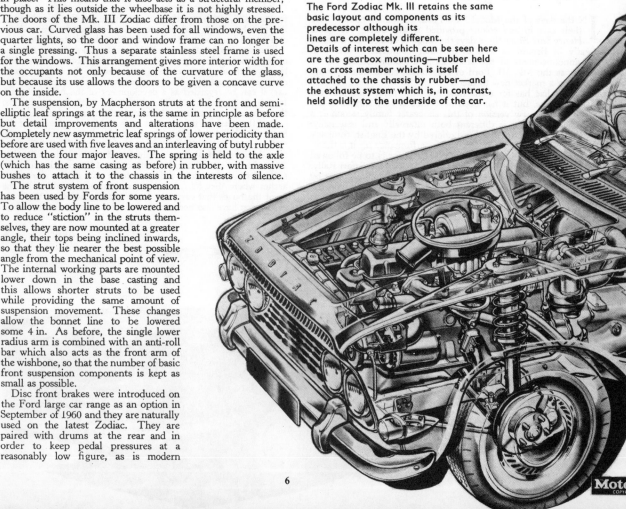

sisted of a single tube, pierced where it met the exhaust ports, bolted to the side of the cylinder head. At the rear this tube was blind while at the front it led away to the silencing arrangements. Now two separate tubes are used and exhaust gases are led away from the centre of each through twin silencers to the atmosphere. As before, a single Zenith downdraught carburetter is used but this is now of 42 mm. bore.

The cylinder head is fitted with larger valves and compression ratio has been raised from 7.8 to 8.3/1, although there is still a low compression option of 7/1. The hollow web cast crankshaft is carried on four main bearings and these and the big end bearings are now lead bronze. The connecting rods have also been strengthened, mainly by the fitting of larger big-end bolts and piston design and rings have been altered slightly. These are the main changes directly affecting performance and reliability but there are also many detail alterations and improvements. Among these the more notable ones are an improved material for the sump gasket, a new type of oil breather that prevents loss of lubricant at the higher speeds which the car can achieve, and a wax thermostat in place of the bellows type. Thermostats of this type, which are claimed to open more smoothly, have not been common here and the one fitted to the Zodiac is an American make, Dole, produced under licence in this country. Finally, a new paper element air cleaner is fitted to the carburetter; it is pan shaped in place of the previous cylindrical type and, along with the rocker cover is painted bright yellow, brightening the underbonnet scene.

Big changes have been made to the transmission and customers have a choice of three systems: four-speed all-synchromesh manual, the same but fitted with Borg-Warner overdrive, and fully automatic by Borg-Warner Model 35 box. With ratios of 1.0; 1.4; 2.2; and 3.2, the four-speed gearbox offers much higher speeds in the indirect gears than was the case with the previous three-speed box. The gearchange is on the steering column and the gear positions normal, i.e. first is towards the driver and up while top is away from the driver and down. The clutch on the manual box has certain features that help to make it even lighter than

before to operate. As in the Mk. II, it is hydraulically actuated, but the withdrawal arm now pivots on a knife edge and detail improvements have been made to the pressure plate. An overcentre helper spring is still found on the clutch pedal. The accelerator has been made more positive in operation by eliminating the long rod that was in torsion in the previous arrangement and substituting rods in tension.

Overdrive is optional and has the usual Borg-Warner feature of a kick-down which means that if the accelerator pedal is fully depressed when in overdrive an automatic change to direct drive is made. It will operate on any gear at speeds above 30 m.p.h. so that it is of practical use on 2nd, 3rd, and top. The other optional system, three-speed fully automatic, although familiar on other makes is new to Ford. The previous Zodiac was available with a different automatic box by Borg-Warner. The main engineering difference in the Model 35 is that there is torque conversion on top as well as on the lower gears. While from the driver's point of view it is now possible to exercise more control over gear changing.

With each successive model Ford have lately been providing better and better interior heaters. On the Zodiac this is a standard item, designed at Dagenham and completely new. It is rated at $5\frac{1}{4}$ kilowatts, about 2 kw. more than is normal in most cars of this size so it should be capable of keeping the occupants warm in all climates. Air mixing, instead of a metering water valve, is used to vary temperature and a useful feature in summer is that in its half-open position the outlet door directs cold air on to the passengers at face level. Steps have also been taken to ensure really efficient demisting and defrosting, so $2\frac{1}{2}$ in. diameter screen outlets (above which are deflectors) are fitted in place of the more familiar fishtail devices to direct hot air to the screen.

Quadruple headlamps are gradually gaining ground in this country and the Zodiac is the latest car to use them, sealed beam units being mounted within the alloy radiator grille. A lighting refinement is the parking light switch on the facia which extinguishes the nearside side and tail lights to reduce drain on the battery when the car is parked. As a safety measure this

over ● ● ● ▶

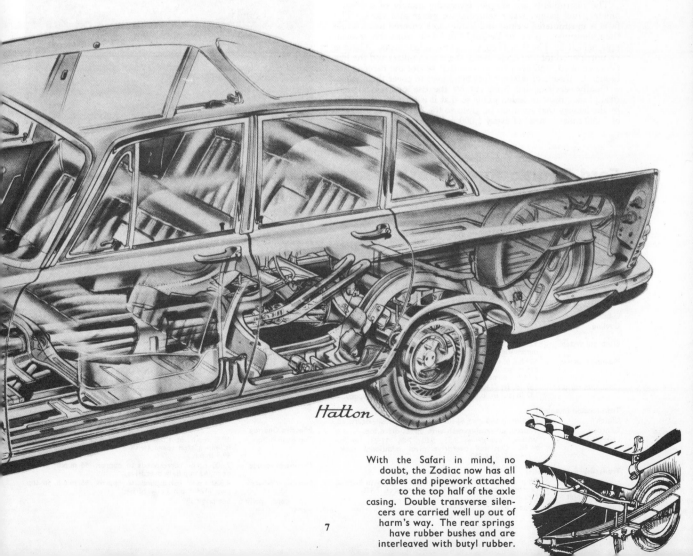

Hatton

With the Safari in mind, no doubt, the Zodiac now has all cables and pipework attached to the top half of the axle casing. Double transverse silencers are carried well up out of harm's way. The rear springs have rubber bushes and are interleaved with butyl rubber.

New Ford Zodiac Mk. III

These three pictures each show one of the three pieces of flat glass in the car—the rear view mirror, the clock and the speedometer. The open door reveals the curve in the window frame for the rear side window. Other unusual features are a dropdown glove box (above right) and the big demister outlets on each side of the facia-top loudspeaker.

switch also isolates the starter solenoid so that it is impossible to start the car in this condition.

The instruments are simple, consisting merely of a speedometer, fuel gauge, water temperature gauge and clock. The facia is in simulated walnut and leathercloth covered foam, while the upholstery is p.v.c. or Bedford Cord with crushed hide as an optional extra. The floor is covered in moulded carpet. There is no untrimmed interior body metal, the screen pillars and the like being covered, and even the screws that secure the capping are hidden by means of washers that bend over to cover their heads.

Finally servicing has been cut by the use of molybdenum disulphide grease in sealed joints so that it is now recommended by the factory that attention be given to the 12 points at intervals of 5,000 miles instead of every 1,000 miles as heretofore.

Ford Zodiac Specification

Engine

Cylinders	... ...	6 in line with crankshaft carried on 4 lead bronze bearings.
Bore and stroke	...	82.55 mm. × 79.5 mm. (3.25 in. × 3.13 in.).
Cubic capacity	...	2,553 c.c. (155.8 cu. in.).
Piston area	...	49.74 sq. in.
Compression ratio		8.3/1 (optional 7.0/1).
Valvegear	...	O.h.v. operated by chain driven side mounted camshaft.
Carburation	...	Single Zenith 42 W.I.A.-2 downdraught carburetter fed by camshaft operated diaphragm fuel pump, from 12-gallon tank.
Ignition	...	12-volt coil, centrifugal and vacuum timing control, 14 mm. Champion sparking plugs, type N5.
Lubrication	...	Full flow filter and 8-pint sump.
Cooling	... ...	Pressurized water cooling with pump, 4-blade fan and wax thermostat; 21-pint water capacity.
Electrical system	...	12-volt 57 amp. hr. battery (67/80 amp. hr. with automatic transmission) charged by 25 amp. generator.
Maximum power	...	109 b.h.p. nett (114 gross) at 4,800 r.p.m., equivalent to 115 lb./sq. in. b.m.e.p. at 2,500 ft./min. piston speed and 2.19 b.h.p. per sq. in. of piston area.
Maximum torque	...	137 lb. ft. (140.5 gross) at 2,400 r.p.m., equivalent to 133 lb./sq. in. b.m.e.p. at 1,250 ft./min. piston speed.

Transmission (manual)

Clutch	... ...	Ford/Borg and Beck 8½-in. s.d.p., hydraulically operated.
Gearbox	...	4-speed, all-synchromesh with direct drive top.
Overall ratios	...	Without overdrive: 3.55; 5.01; 7.86; 11.23; reverse 11.88. Optional overdrive gives additional ratios 2.734; 3.860; 6.052.

Transmission (automatic)

		Borg-Warner Model 35 torque converter with 3-speed gearbox; ratios 3.55; 5.147; 8.48; reverse, 7.419.
Propeller shaft	...	One piece, open.
Final drive	... ...	Hypoid bevel.

Chassis

Brakes	... ...	Girling, hydraulically operated disc/drum system, with vacuum servo and reservoir.
Brake dimensions	...	Front discs, 9.75 in. dia.; rear drums, 9 in. dia. × 2.25 in. wide.
Brake areas	...	98 sq. in. of lining (20.6 sq. in. front plus 77.6 sq. in. rear) working on 330 sq. in. rubbed area of discs and drums.
Front suspension	...	Macpherson independent by inclined, telescopic damper legs, lower wishbones, coil springs and torsion anti-roll bar.
Rear suspension	..:	Rigid axle, asymmetric semi-elliptic leaf springs with full length rubber interleaving and hydraulic lever arm shock absorbers.
Wheels and tyres	...	Bolt-on 5-stud disc wheels and tubeless nylon 6.40-13 in. tyres.
Steering	... ...	Recirculatory ball type.

Dimensions

Length	... ...	Overall 15 ft. 2 in.; wheelbase 8 ft. 11¼ in.
Width	...	Overall 5 ft. 9 in.; track 4 ft. 5 in. at front and 4 ft. 4 in. at rear.
Height (laden)	...	4 ft. 7½ in.; ground clearance 5¾ in.
Turning circle	...	35½ ft.
Kerb weight	...	25 cwt. (without fuel but with oil, water, tools, spare wheel, etc.).

Effective Gearing

Top gear ratio	...	19.9 m.p.h. at 1,000 r.p.m. and 38.1 m.p.h. at 1,000 ft./min. piston speed (with overdrive, 25.9 m.p.h. and 49.5 m.p.h.).
Maximum torque	...	2,400 r.p.m. corresponds to approx. 48 m.p.h. in top gear (62 m.p.h. in overdrive).
Maximum power	...	4,800 r.p.m. corresponds to approx. 95 m.p.h. in top gear (124 m.p.h. in overdrive).
Top gear pulling power		See page 399.

Ford Zephyr 4 MANUAL and AUTOMATIC 1,703 c.c.

SO far as the British market is concerned, the familiar Ford model name of Consul now becomes one mainly of the past. It is still used abroad in connection with the 1,340 c.c. Classics but the public at home already omits to use the full title of these cars. With the introduction of the new, big range of Fords, the Consul Mark II or 375 is replaced by the more logically named Zephyr 4, which is the cheaper Zephyr powered by the similar 1,703 c.c., four-cylinder engine. Unlike its predecessor, however, it is not shorter than the six-cylinder Zephyr but is identical in exterior dimensions. Minor differences in appearance have been introduced purposely to permit immediate model identification.

This new Zephyr 4 is a sensible, work-horse design; it is spacious, yet its price falls among those of medium-sized cars. Provided the driver is prepared to sit rather close to the steering wheel, it is to be regarded as an ample six-seater having plenty of luggage accommodation, but it is a pity that some 3in. more rear seat legroom has not been provided.

Owners of Mark II Consuls, on the whole, are a satisfied bunch; if pressed, they might mention the inadequacy of the three-speed gearbox and a certain lack of smoothness in engine and transmission. Ford have tried hard with the new Zephyr range—4 and 6—to meet desires and criticisms. Thus a four-speed, all-synchromesh gearbox has been pro-

vided and the engine and transmission have been made appreciably smoother and quieter. A quite good example of its kind, the column gearchange has a rather longer movement than one would wish. Purchasers are offered the option of a Borg-Warner overdrive (operative in all gears), which would seem to be superfluous on the Zephyr 4, or three-speed automatic transmission of the new Borg-Warner type at an extra cost of £110 0s 0d. This report covers both the manual transmission and the automatic cars, and full performance figures are listed for each variant. Both Zephyr 4 and 6 are also described in detail in the article preceding this test report.

Drivers familiar with the earlier Consul and Zephyr models will have no difficulty in detecting similarities in the new four-cylinder Zephyr, but only when the engine is being used to its full capacity does it become obstrusive—this feature being more apparent with the automatic transmission car than with the manual one.

With the manual box, the performance is quite a lot brisker now throughout the range of acceleration, and the standing quarter-mile figure is 21·4sec compared with 22·7 sec for the Consul Mk. II. This is also by virtue of the car's extra 9 b.h.p. net with a weight increase of only 55lb with the two cars laden as tested.

There is an increase in maximum speed, which rises from a mean of 76·3 m.p.h. for the Consul Mk. II to 84·0 m.p.h.,

PRICES							
Basic	...	...	...	...	...	£615	
Purchase tax	...	...	...	...	£231 12s	9d
			Total (in G.B.)	£846 12s	9d	
					£	s	d
Extras (total)							
Overdrive	...	...	...	...	58	8	9
Automatic transmission	...	...	110	0	0
Heater	...	...	...	...	20	12	6
Screenwasher	...	...	...	8	13	3
Hide upholstery	...	...	...	20	12	6

The orderly modern facia design has a padded top and a composite instrument presentation. The attractiveness of corrugated bright metal trim is a matter of taste

Make • FORD   Type • Zephyr 4

Manufacturers : Ford Motor Co. Ltd., Dagenham, Essex

Test Conditions
Weather............ Dry, with 5-15 m.p.h. wind
Temperature .... 49 deg. F. (9 deg. C.).
Barometer .... 26·6in. Hg.
Dry concrete and tarmac surfaces.

Weight
Kerb weight (with oil, water and half-full fuel tank)
22·8cwt (2,547lb–1,155kg)
Front-rear distribution, per cent: F, 52·8; R, 47·2
Laden as tested: ......25·8cwt (2,883lb–1,307kg)
Automatic: ....26·25cwt (2,940lb–1,333kg)

Turning Circles
Between kerbs .... L, 37ft 1in.; R, 36ft 8in.
Between walls ...... L, 38ft 10in.; R, 38ft 5in.
Turns of steering wheel lock to lock .... 4·25

Performance Data
Top gear m.p.h. per 1,000 r.p.m. .... 18·45
(Automatic 20·3)
Mean piston speed at max. power ...... 2,510 ft/min.
Engine revs. at mean max. speed .... 4,550 r.p.m.
B.h.p. per ton laden .... 52·8

MAXIMUM SPEEDS AND ACCELERATION (mean) TIMES

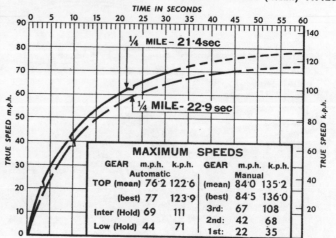

¼ MILE – 21·4sec
¼ MILE – 22·9 sec

MAXIMUM SPEEDS					
GEAR	m.p.h.	k.p.h.	GEAR	m.p.h.	k.p.h.
Automatic			**Manual**		
TOP (mean)	76·2	122·6	(mean)	84·0	135·2
(best)	77	123·9	(best)	84·5	136·0
Inter (Hold)	69	111	3rd:	67	108
Low (Hold)	44	71	2nd:	42	68
			1st:	22	35

6·6	9·9	15·3	23·3	44·5	Automatic	TIME IN SECONDS
5·3	8·5	13·4	19·6	32·1	Manual	
0	30	40	50	60	70	80	TRUE SPEED m.p.h.
	31	42	52	62	72	82	CAR SPEEDOMETER

FUEL AND OIL CONSUMPTION

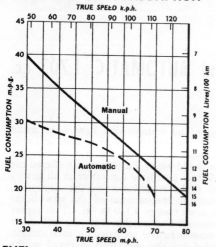

FUEL .... Premium Grade
(96 octane RM)

Test Distances
711 miles (Manual), 654 miles (Automatic)
Overall Consumption .... 23·8 m.p.g.
(11·9 lit/100km)
Automatic .... 23·1 m.p.g.
(12·3lit/100km)
Normal Range (both cars): 20–30 m.p.g.
(14—9·4lit/100km)
OIL: SAE 20W .... Consumption: None
measurable on either model

Speed range and time in seconds
Manual

m.p.h.	Top	Third	Second	First
10—30	—	8·3	5·1	—
20—40	13·2	7·7	5·5	—
30—50	14·8	8·4	—	—
40—60	17·2	10·8	—	—
50—70	21·2	—	—	—

Automatic

m.p.h.	Top	Inter	Low
10—30		7·0	5·4
20—40	10·3	8·8	6·1
30—50	14·4	11·4	—
40—60	24·4	13·8	—
50—70	34·8	—	—

BRAKES

BRAKES (from 30 m.p.h. in neutral)	Pedal load	Retardation	Equiv. distance
	25lb	0·36g	83ft
	50lb	0·75g	40ft
	70lb	0·96g	31ft
Hand brake		0·41g	74ft

CLUTCH   Pedal load and travel—38lb and 5·5in.

HILL CLIMBING AT STEADY SPEEDS

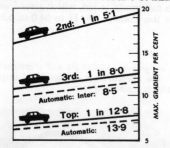

2nd: 1 in 5·1
3rd: 1 in 8·0
Automatic: Inter: 8·5
Top: 1 in 12·8
Automatic: 13·9

Manual

Gear	Top	3rd	2nd
PULL (lb per ton)	175	277	433
Speed Range (m.p.h.)	34–40	28–32	22–28

Automatic

Gear	Top	Inter
PULL (lb per ton)	160	263
Speed Range (m.p.h.)	30–35	25–28

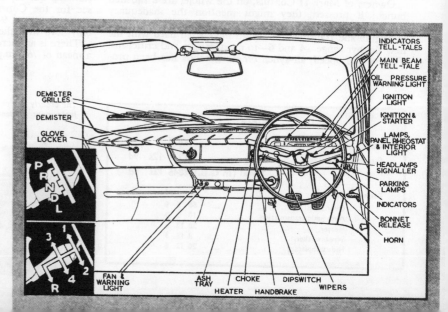

INDICATORS TELL-TALES
MAIN BEAM TELL-TALE
OIL PRESSURE WARNING LIGHT
IGNITION LIGHT
IGNITION & STARTER
LAMPS, PANEL RHEOSTAT & INTERIOR LIGHT
HEADLAMPS SIGNALLER
PARKING LAMPS
INDICATORS
BONNET RELEASE
HORN
DEMISTER GRILLES
DEMISTER
GLOVE LOCKER
FAN & WARNING LIGHT
ASH TRAY
HEATER
CHOKE
HANDBRAKE
DIPSWITCH
WIPERS

The interior is spacious and the seat cushions are wide. The front seat is shown two notches forward from its backstop, where many drivers would set it

but the Zephyr 4 will cruise without fuss at over 70 m.p.h. and, with its high 3·9-to-1 top gear ratio, it is particularly restful when cruising at about 60 m.p.h. This same high top gear does bring the need for an earlier downchange, both in slow traffic and for overtaking, but this is the natural outcome of the pleasant new four-speed box and sensibly-selected ratios. The Consul II accelerated from 30 to 50 m.p.h. in top gear in 13·4 seconds, while the Zephyr 4 takes 14·8 seconds but, for example, the Zephyr 4 manages 40 to 60 m.p.h. in third gear in 10·8 seconds and the Consul, which had to use second and top, took 17·3 seconds. The minimum comfortable top gear speed is now about 18 m.p.h.

With automatic transmission the picture is rather different and all the performances recorded are somewhat lower than those for the manual model. It takes 22·9 seconds to cover a quarter-mile from a standstill and the maximum speed is only just over 76 m.p.h. Overtaking usually needs careful timing and plenty of space. This version is 60lb heavier.

Since the automatic transmission is of the new Borg-Warner type with the torque convertor operative in all ratios, a brief reminder of its characteristics may be helpful. The selector lever can be moved to Low, Drive, Neutral, Reverse or Park, in that order on the quadrant from left to right, and as usual the engine can be started only when Neutral or Park are selected. Low, intermediate and high ratios are provided. In D automatic gear changes take place at predetermined points according to road speed and throttle opening. If the selector lever is moved from D to L when driving normally, intermediate is obtained at any speed. Intermediate having been engaged, and if the road speed is below about 35 m.p.h., operation of the kick-down switch will then bring in low and hold it.

To return to intermediate and to hold that ratio, the selector lever is moved back to D; as soon as intermediate re-engages in the normal manner at the change-up point, the lever is moved back to L. The maximum speed in intermediate is approximately 68 m.p.h. and the limit is one of power falling off, not of reaching valve bounce; the equivalent figure in low hold is 44 m.p.h. Automatic up-changes on full throttle are made at 38 and 60 m.p.h., using kick-down.

For those drivers who find virtues in automatic transmission but regret the inability to select a gear to suit an occasion, this box offers a compromise technique. As one approaches a corner to be taken fast, L is selected on the quadrant and this gives the equivalent of third gear engine braking with the manual box and ready pick-up. If an even lower gear is needed, this is obtained with a quick kick-down to give full low gear engine braking followed by acceleration. Coming out of a corner with maximum acceleration, whether in low or intermediate, D can be reselected to give automatic up-changes.

For normal driving the automatic changes are very smooth indeed and can scarcely be detected, up or down. An outstanding virtue of this transmission is that, once top has been engaged—or intermediate in the "hold" position —the next lower ratio can be obtained only by operation of the kick-down switch, unless the road speed falls to the pre-determined automatic drop-out point. Thus the annoyance of frequent automatic changes between ratios, or "hunting," is avoided.

The basic design of the suspension of the Zephyr 4 is similar to that of previous models. However, there are important detail changes, as described in the preceding article. The outcome is somewhat less firm springing and a softer ride. Roll is restrained, although when a full load is carried the back of the car will take on appreciable bank when cornering fast; this in turn has some effect on the cornering characteristics. Under heavy braking forces the nose is made to dip but the ride is normally free from pitching and well damped.

Good Road-holding

Adhesion in dry weather is very good indeed and it is difficult, with the power available, to make the back of the car move across unless the road surface is unusually rough. In wet conditions the adhesion is also good and definitely an improvement on that of the previous model.

Road noises and shocks are well insulated; only on one particular kind of road surface, dressed with small stones, is a mild droning heard inside the car.

With all the windows properly closed and fitting, comparatively little wind noise is heard by the occupants. On certain of the early production models we have tried, the relative silence has been upset by a slightly proud seal in the vicinity of the driver's side quarterlight. These have a front edge hinge which helps to prevent rain entering when they are opened and which also avoids wind roar when they are very slightly opened. A side window at front, back or both may be opened by as much as 2in. without causing draughts, buffeting or excessive noise. The car's excellent heating and ventilation system immediately works to greater capacity if a side window is opened to allow the air to flow through the interior.

Our test drivers were of the opinion that the steering wheel was larger than necessary, since the steering is quite light, and that were the ratio to be higher—say, 3½ instead of 4¼ turns from lock to lock—less arm-work would be needed. In other respects the steering is very acceptable, giving precise control of direction. These cars understeer mildly when cornering normally, but if plenty of power is used the characteristics become almost neutral, particularly when a full load is carried. In these conditions the roll already referred to has an initial oversteer influence. The Zephyr is not sensitive to side winds and holds a very straight course on a motorway. Self-centring action is

Note the Galaxie-type rear window and associated side panels, which clearly distinguish the Zephyrs from the Zodiac, "Automatic" appears below the Zephyr motif on the appropriate model

Ford Zephyr 4 . . .

only slight for small movements of the wheel from the straight-ahead position.

There is no doubt that the new disc front, drum rear brake system will be greatly appreciated. It has powerful, though not over-sensitive, servo assistance and moderate pressure on the pedal gives smooth and very powerful retardation. The pull-out handbrake is substantial, efficient and conveniently positioned. The rubbing areas of the rear drums have been increased to provide adjustment periods comparable with front disc pad life.

Even in the extreme conditions of standing start acceleration measurement and restarting on a 1-in-3 gradient, the clutch of the manual gearbox was smooth and effective. The travel is not unduly long and pressure is quite light. The automatic transmission car also starts without difficulty on 1-in-3, and on the same incline the handbrakes of both cars held firmly.

A new throttle linkage is provided which is much better than the rather abrupt and springy system on the previous cars; some drivers thought that the initial opening was still rather abrupt.

Although the Zephyr 4 engine now gives more power than that of its predecessor, fuel consumption figures are likely to work out almost exactly the same, and although, as would be expected, the automatic transmission car uses slightly more fuel, the difference is very small. Even "press-on" drivers should obtain in the region of 24 m.p.g. on journeys and those who drive gently should obtain 27 or 28 m.p.g.

Anything which needs topping up is conveniently placed in the engine compartment. The brake servo unit is just behind the battery

Since the total mileages covered during our tests of the two variants were somewhat less than usual, yet the full list of performance figures was obtained with each, the overall test averages give a rather pessimistic impression.

Drivers will approve of the bright and spacious interior, from which a good driving view is obtained, apart from the fact that the passenger side wing cannot be seen by the driver because of the height of the bonnet; the toggle opener for the latter is labelled "Hood" in the American way. Available equipment is thorough for a car of this class and is arranged in the modern manner, and while we prefer a hand lever for headlamp dipping (this does not apply to the automatic model in which the left foot is free to operate the foot switch), the additional flasher switch on the end of the direction indicator lever is appreciated.

An extra switch is provided which cuts out the near side lamps so that those on the off side can be used for parking. When this is operated, the panel lamps are switched off as a warning.

New Heater

A very effective layered system for heating and ventilation is listed as an extra in the case of the Zephyr 4. Two winged controls are twisted to obtain the desired temperature and to cut off or select demisting, defrosting or de-icing flow to the screen. At demist, cold air flows over the windscreen and ventilates the upper part of the car while either hot or cold air to choice is directed rearwards at seat level. The booster fan has an indicator light and delivers a large volume of air. The direction of flow is inclined to miss the driver's feet and ankles. In the padded scuttle top are two large grilles for the screen air. They lie flush and are of matching colour. Pale trims cause some unwelcome reflections in the screen in spite of the matt finish.

Interior detail finish is neat and synthetic trimming materials are used throughout. An open parcel shelf and, above it, a locker with key, are seen on the passenger side. No door pockets are provided on this model. Soft padded sun vizors are fitted, which can be swung across to give shade from the sides.

There is plenty of support area in the front bench seat; it is quite comfortable and there is sufficient rearward adjustment. For other than gentle driving, the absence of shaping to give lateral location leads the passengers to sway sideways on corners. Our test staff are agreed that the mounting of the seat is some 2in. too low. By using a cushion we found that the view over the scuttle and bonnet was at once improved, the angle between feet and pedals, —which meet the soles of the shoes edge-on—is slightly better and the driving attitude is more alert. Headroom and steering wheel clearance is ample to permit this small modification.

Three grown-ups can sit reasonably comfortably on the

back seat. It is not as easy as it might be for elderly people to get in and out, because the spaces between the central door pillar and the front corners of the seat are narrow. Armrests are provided on all four doors.

Single, low-mounted headlamps, on each side of the undivided grille, are a recognition point of the Zephyr 4; they give ample range and spread for the car's performance. The finish to the edges of the metalwork above them leaves much to be desired. The side lamps, applied somewhat vulnerably, are protected in part by substantial wrap-round bumper extremities, which stand proud of the wing edges by 2in. The main lamp switch is of the double pull-out type and, as found increasingly on modern cars of most nationalities, a twist of the same knob operates a rheostat for the instrument panel lamps; at the extremities of twist, the interior lamps are turned on or the panel lamps turned off. No reversing lamp is provided.

While it is pleasant to have an uninterrupted view of the instruments through the dished, two-spoke steering wheel, the flush horn button is now too difficult to hit in an emergency and the note produced is very humble. On the automatic model the illumination of the selector quadrant is too bright after dark.

A variable-speed electric windscreen wiper is fitted. Its blades clear a large area, leaving only a portion of the curved edges obscured. They did not park as low as they should

on the manual model tested, and after prolonged use ceased to be silent, producing a slapping noise. A screen washer is extra on this model. The wide, shallow interior rear-view mirror is very satisfactory.

Both the bonnet and the boot lid are self-supporting—an almost essential feature these days. Some manufacturers have wry fun hiding the release for the second, safety catch and giving it an illogical movement; not so Ford, who have placed it just where it should be. The bonnet opens wide and accessibility is quite good. The dipstick and its tube might well be extended and the diameter of the oil filler-breather on the rocker cover increased. When attending to contact breaker points, mechanics will find the distributor rather buried. Other than those for wheel changing, which are contained in a sack wedged between the spare wheel and the side of the car, there are no tools.

A welcome advance has been made in reducing servicing requirements. With the introduction of this new model, greasing of the 12 points is needed only at 5,000-mile intervals and when more experience is gained, it may be possible to increase this figure to 7,000 or even 10,000 miles.

With the introduction of their new Zephyr 4s Ford have again made substantial improvements over the models replaced; they offer greater refinement and several new features which owners will appreciate. Equally important, the price has been held at a very competitive level.

Specification

ENGINE
Cylinders	...	4 in line
Bore	...	82·55mm (3·25 in.)
Stroke	...	79·5mm (3·13in.)
Displacement	...	1,703 c.c. (103·9 cu. in.)
Valve gear	...	Overhead, pushrods and rockers
Compression ratio		8·3 to 1
Carburettor	...	Zenith 36VN
Fuel pump	...	AC mechanical
Oil filter	...	Full flow, external
Max. power	...	68 b.h.p. (net) at 4,800 r.p.m.
Max. torque	...	93·5 lb. ft. at 3,000 r.p.m.

TRANSMISSION
Clutch	...	Borg and Beck 8in. dia. single dry plate.
Gearbox	...	Four-speed, all synchromesh
Overall ratios	...	Top 3·90, 3rd 5·87, 2nd 9·17, 1st 17·21, reverse 18·20.
Automatic transmission	...	Borg-Warner model 35.
Overall ratios	...	Top 7·10-3·55; Inter 10·30-5·15; Low 16·96-8·49; Reverse 14·84-7·42.
Final drive	...	Hypoid bevel, 3·90 to (Automatic 3·55 to 1).

CHASSIS
Construction	...	Integral with steel body.

SUSPENSION
Front	...	Strut type, coil springs and wishbones, Armstrong telescopic dampers, anti-roll bar.
Rear	...	Live axle and semi-elliptic leaf springs, Armstrong lever arm dampers
Steering	...	Burman recirculating ball; wheel dia. 17in.

BRAKES
Type	...	Girling hydraulic; discs front, drums rear, with servo assistance
Dimensions	...	Discs 9·75in. dia. Drums 9·0in. dia., 1·75in. wide shoes
Swept area	...	F. 203 sq. in.; R. 99 sq. in. Total: 302 sq. in. (234 sq. in. per ton laden)

WHEELS
Type	...	Pressed steel disc, 5 studs, 4·5in. wide rim.
Tyres	...	Goodyear tubeless 6·40-13in.

EQUIPMENT
Battery	...	12-volt, 45-amp. hr.
Headlamps	...	50-40 watt bulbs.
Reversing lamp	...	None
Electric fuses	...	1
Screen wipers	...	2, variable speed, self-parking
Screen washer	...	Extra
Interior heater	...	Extra
Safety belts	...	No anchorages provided
Interior trim	...	P.v.c., optional cloth, hide extra
Floor covering	...	Rubber
Starting handle	...	None
Jack	...	Triangular screw type
Jacking points	...	2 each side under body sills
Other bodies	...	None

MAINTENANCE
Fuel tank	...	12 Imp. gallons (no reserve)
Cooling system	...	17 pints (including heater)
Engine sump	...	6 pints. Change oil every 5,000 miles; change filter element every 5,000 miles
Gearbox	...	2·5 pints SAE80. No oil change specified
Final drive	...	2·5 pints SAE90 Hypoid. No oil change specified.
Grease	...	12 points every 5,000 miles
Tyre pressures	...	F and R, 22 p.s.i. (normal driving) F and R, 26 p.s.i. (fast driving) F, and R, 28 p.s.i. (full load)

Scale : 0·3in. to 1ft.
Cushions uncompressed.

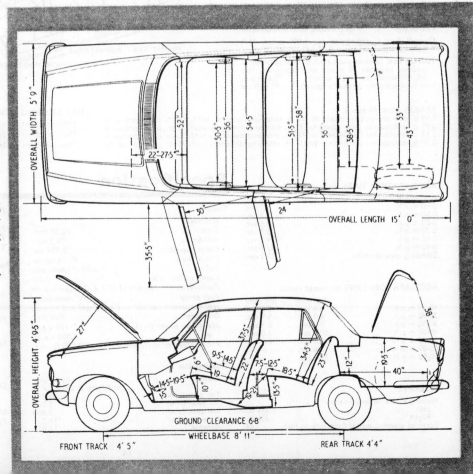

MAKE : Ford. TYPE : Zodiac Mk. III.

MAKER : Ford Motor Co. Ltd., Dagenham, Essex.

DATA

CONDITIONS: Weather: Cold and dry, wind 8-10 m.p.h. (Temperature 35°-44° F., Barometer 29.8 in. Hg.) Surface: Dry tarmacadam. Fuel: Premium grade pump petrol (approx. 97 Octane Rating by Research Method).

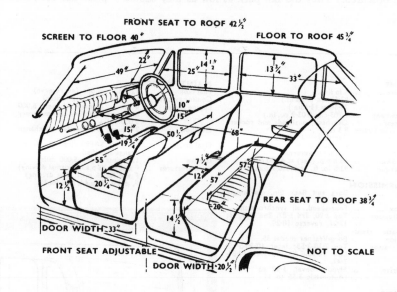

INSTRUMENTS

Speedometer at 30 m.p.h.	3% fast
Speedometer at 60 m.p.h.	2% fast
Speedometer at 90 m.p.h.	Accurate
Distance Recorder	1% fast

WEIGHT

Kerb weight (unladen, but with oil, coolant and fuel for approximately 50 miles)	25 cwt.
Front/rear distribution of kerb weight	54½/45½
Weight laden as tested	28¾ cwt.

MAXIMUM SPEEDS

Flying Mile

Mean of four opposite runs	100.7 m.p.h.
Best one-way time equals	102.3 m.p.h.

"Maximile" Speed (Timed quarter-mile after one mile accelerating from rest.)

Mean of opposite runs	96.5 m.p.h.
Best one-way time equals	98.9 m.p.h.

Speed in gears

Max. speed in 3rd gear	84 m.p.h.
Max. speed in 2nd gear	56 m.p.h.
Max. speed in 1st gear	39 m.p.h.

FUEL CONSUMPTION

37.0 m.p.g.	at constant 30 m.p.h. on level
32.0 m.p.g.	at constant 40 m.p.h. on level
28.5 m.p.g.	at constant 50 m.p.h. on level
25.5 m.p.g.	at constant 60 m.p.h. on level
22.5 m.p.g.	at constant 70 m.p.h. on level
19.0 m.p.g.	at constant 80 m.p.h. on level
15.0 m.p.g.	at constant 90 m.p.h. on level

Overall Fuel Consumption for 1,091 miles, 55.9 gallons, equals 19.5 m.p.g. (14.45 litres/100 km.).

Touring Fuel Consumption (m.p.g. at steady speed midway between 30 m.p.h. and maximum, less 5% allowance for acceleration) ... 22.6 m.p.g.

Fuel tank capacity (maker's figure) 12 gallons

BRAKES from 30 m.p.h.

0.99 g retardation (equivalent to 30½ ft. stopping distance) with 100 lb. pedal pressure.
0.91 g retardation (equivalent to 33 ft. stopping distance) with 75 lb. pedal pressure.
0.62 g retardation (equivalent to 48½ ft. stopping distance) with 50 lb. pedal pressure.
0.30 g retardation (equivalent to 100 ft. stopping distance) with 25 lb. pedal pressure.

HILL CLIMBING at sustained steady speeds

Max. gradient on top gear	1 in 8.9 (Tapley 255 lb./ton)
Max. gradient on 3rd gear	1 in 6.0 (Tapley 370 lb./ton)
Max. gradient on 2nd gear	1 in 3.8 (Tapley 570 lb./ton)

ACCELERATION TIMES from standstill

0-30 m.p.h.	4.0 sec.
0-40 m.p.h.	6.1 sec.
0-50 m.p.h.	9.2 sec.
0-60 m.p.h.	13.4 sec.
0-70 m.p.h.	18.2 sec.
0-80 m.p.h.	24.2 sec.
0-90 m.p.h.	37.9 sec.
Standing quarter-mile	19.2 sec.

ACCELERATION TIMES on upper ratios

	Top gear	3rd gear
10-30 m.p.h.	8.6 sec.	5.6 sec.
20-40 m.p.h.	8.8 sec.	5.9 sec.
30-50 m.p.h.	9.7 sec.	6.4 sec.
40-60 m.p.h.	10.9 sec.	7.0 sec.
50-70 m.p.h.	12.5 sec.	8.5 sec.
60-80 m.p.h.	13.6 sec.	—
70-90 m.p.h.	18.9 sec.	—

STEERING

Turning circle between kerbs:

Left	35½ ft.
Right	35½ ft.
Turns of steering wheel from lock to lock	4⅛

Specification

Engine

Cylinders	6
Bore	82.55 mm.
Stroke	79.5 mm.
Cubic capacity	2,553 c.c.
Piston area	49.74 sq. in.
Valves	Overhead (pushrods)
Compression ratio	8.3/1
Carburetter	Zenith 42 W.I.A.-2, downdraught
Fuel pump	AC mechanical
Ignition timing control	Centrifugal and vacuum
Oil filter	Full flow
Maximum power (net)	109 b.h.p.
at	4,800 r.p.m.
Piston speed at maximum b.h.p.	2,500 ft./min.

Transmission

Clutch	8½ in. dia. Ford/Borg & Beck s.d.p.
Top gear (s/m)	3.550
3rd gear (s/m)	5.013
2nd gear (s/m)	7.860
1st gear (s/m)	11.229
Reverse	11.878

Propeller shaft	Open, Hardy Spicer needle roller
Final drive	Hypoid bevel
Top gear m.p.h. at 1,000 r.p.m.	19.9
Top gear m.p.h. at 1,000 ft./min. piston speed	38.1

Chassis

Brakes .. Girling hydraulic with vacuum servo

Brake dimensions:
Front .. 9¾ in. dia. discs
Rear .. 9 in. dia. drums, 2¼ in. wide
Friction areas: 98 sq. in. of friction lining operating on 330 sq. in. swept disc and drum surface.

Suspension:
Front: Independent by Macpherson coil-spring damper strut and bottom wishbone incorporating anti-roll bar.
Rear: Live axle and semi-elliptic leaf springs.

Shock absorbers:
Front .. Armstrong telescopic
Rear .. Armstrong lever arm
Steering gear .. Ford/Burman recirculating ball
Tyres .. 6.40—13
four-ply nylon sports, tubed or tubeless

odiac Mk. III

WITH the new Zodiac Mk. III, a 100 m.p.h. saloon with sports car acceleration, the largest and most expensive British Ford moves into a new performance category although beneath a body/chassis structure of entirely new appearance the mechanical components are substantially similar to the well-tried units of the previous model.

The new car looks bigger and more imposing than its predecessor and yet, in fact, its size is largely an optical illusion; overall plan dimensions remain much the same as before and the height has decreased by some 3 in. giving much more elegant proportions and a lower centre of gravity which reflects very favourably in road behaviour. In external appearance the separate influences of current American, British and Continental fashions are blended harmoniously rather than strikingly; internal trim leans towards traditional British with no untrimmed body metal visible, pile carpets and a walnut-finished metal facia.

Performance & Price

THE six-cylinder o.h.v. engine retains a capacity of 2,553 c.c. but extensive internal changes have raised maximum power by 28%. A maximum torque increase of 3% matches a weight rise of 4% (to 25 cwt. unladen) so that with higher overall gearing the impressive acceleration, of which we shall speak later, owes a great deal to a new and very good four-speed gearbox. No other large saloon

available on the British market can offer speed and acceleration of the same order at a price as low as £1070.

A genuine two-way 100 m.p.h. was achieved by our very new test car which had done less than 1,500 miles when the figures were taken. A standing quarter mile took 19.2 sec. and 0-50 m.p.h. was recorded in 9.2 sec.; results which fall within a range normally exclusive to some of the better sports cars and to a few large-engined relatively expensive saloons.

In Brief

Price £778 plus purchase tax £292 15s 3d equals £1070 15s 3d.
Capacity .. .. 2,553 c.c.
Unladen kerb weight 25 cwt.
Acceleration:
  20-40 m.p.h. in top
    gear .. .. 8.8 sec.
  0-50 m.p.h. through
    gears .. .. 9.2 sec.
Maximum top-gear
  gradient .. .. 1 in 8.9
Maximum speed .. 100.7 m.p.h.
"Maximile" speed .. 96.5 m.p.h.
Touring fuel con-
  sumption .. .. 22.6 m.p.g.
Gearing: 19.9 m.p.h. in top gear at 1,000 r.p.m.

The increase in power output from the previous 85 to the present 109 b.h.p. (net) has been achieved partly by an increase in compression ratio from 7.8 to 8.5, at which the engine is still perfectly content with Premium grade fuel, but mainly by

Painted metal is now an accepted part of internal finish but the Zodiac has the much greater air of luxury that goes with a fully trimmed interior. Note the curved window frame of the nearside rear door; all the exterior glazing is curved. On the left of the facia is quite a large glove box which drops downwards on hinged links.

induction modifications which include a larger single choke carburetter, larger ports and valves and a twin exhaust system. Top gear acceleration figures show that power at high revs has not been bought at the expense of low speed torque and in spite of gearing which gives nearly 20 m.p.h./1000 r.p.m. an elapsed time of 8.6 sec. from 10 to 30 m.p.h. is the best of all the figures for 20 m.p.h. increments.

However, although on full throttle the Zodiac will pull away strongly and smoothly from below 10 m.p.h. in top gear, a light flywheel permits a rather jerky part throttle response at these speeds and makes it very easy to stall the engine if any attempt is made to trickle away from rest at low r.p.m. High gearing gives easy high-speed cruising with no intrusion of engine noise. Above 80 m.p.h. the only sound of which one is really conscious is wind noise and, although there are quieter cars from this point of view, the background level remains low enough for conversation to be easy and unstrained at maximum speed. Nylon speed tyres are a standard fitting so that fast cruising does not involve special tyre inflation.

Four Speeds

IN changing to a four-speed gearbox for the first time on one of their larger British cars, Fords have elected to fit synchromesh on all the forward gears, a particularly wise decision for a box which has well-chosen and fairly close ratios and lower gears which are intended for use rather than for emergency. Indeed, we found that the near 40 m.p.h. bottom gear was too high for a re-start on the 1 in 3 test hill, high revs producing fade from an otherwise very satisfactory clutch with light operation.

It is not easy to design a gearbox for a large and powerful engine with really effective synchromesh and still retain precision and lightness of control but Fords have succeeded. One can only criticize the Zodiac column gearshift on the grounds of rather a long travel which puts third gear at arm's stretch. Most drivers found, before they were familiar with the car, that it was very easy to think that third gear had been engaged when, in fact, the lever had not been moved sufficiently far.

All the gears are quiet, although cer-tainly not inaudible, and third is used extensively for motoring slowly in traffic, for overtaking on busy roads and for accelerating out of them very rapidly up to 70 m.p.h. with silky smoothness. On Devonshire hills, second gear is often needed for acceleration after a sharp corner. A double exhaust system which emits a deep and slightly sporting note outside the car is heard only remotely and unobtrusively inside.

Very Controllable

WITH 4½ turns from lock to lock, the Zodiac steering may be considered low-geared but freedom from play and a variable ratio mechanism giving higher gearing around the central position make this more obvious on sharp corners than on fast roads. When manœuvring it becomes a little heavy; at other times it is smooth, friction-free and accurate both on corners and on straight roads at speed. On wet roads or dry a noticeable understeer characteristic persists right to the well-balanced breakaway point; the back wheels can be made to slide first if a lot of power is

Independent front suspension is still by Macpherson struts but modifications to the layout have lowered their upper mountings and permitted a much lower bonnet line. The car is some 3 in. lower and longer than its predecessor.

used but the handling is only slightly throttle-sensitive and correction is very easy. Modern tyres do not squeal easily but it was not difficult to produce a loud scrubbing noise from the Zodiac front tyres on sharp corners.

Although photographs revealed the presence of considerable roll in extreme conditions, occupants felt that this Ford had more than average stability and a pleasing ability to change direction without disconcerting lurches. Although occasional bad bumps caused back axle hop and it was possible to generate wheelspin and tramp by full-throttle acceleration in second gear when cornering, the handling was characterized by lack of vice and by first-class controllability which imparted considerable confidence when hurrying over fast main roads.

Front-seat occupants enjoy a soft, well-controlled and generally comfortable ride; there is a certain amount of body shudder on sharp-edged bumps such as tar strips, and appreciable road noise is generated by certain surfaces. Those in the back are more conscious of the up and down movement that relatively soft damping allows and which is most noticeable with a full load.

The Interior

FROM the point of view of width the Zodiac has room inside for six people, but a driver no taller than 5 ft. 10 in. or so will normally have the bench front seat right back on its adjustment slides, and this leaves less than enough legroom for anyone of the same height to sit comfortably in the back. A better compromise might have been achieved by increasing passenger length at the expense of the very long boot which has some 22 cu. ft. of usable space.

Individual front seats adjustable for rake are offered as an extra but our test car had the standard bench seat with roll edges to the cushion and a folding centre arm rest; to compensate for a fairly low seating position the squabs slope back quite a lot and they have the strong profile curvature which characterises current Ford seats and which offers proper spinal support. Most people found them comfortable but a few would have preferred a more upright position. There is first-class visibility in all directions although the sloping bonnet affords little indication of the width of the car. The steering wheel is placed well away from the driver but has an awkward horn ring which is so pivoted that it is easiest to operate in the 6 and 12 o'clock position and most difficult around 3 and 9 o'clock where the hands normally rest.

The imitation walnut of the facia panel offends some people and not others. Speedometer, fuel gauge and thermometer are large and well placed but whereas the first of these is clear and easy to read, the other two are rather vague. Minor controls have been planned with care and thought and therefore lack the confusing symmetry of appearance and position on which some designers insist. The main light switch is well away from the others and headlamp flashing is conveniently arranged by a finger tip button in the end of the direction indicator lever. The foot dipper is less satisfactory in that it needs a downward movement which is natural only to a driver sitting very close to the wheel. To reduce the drain on the battery, a parking switch is provided which cuts out the nearside side and rear lamps and also isolates the starter switch as a deterrent against theft.

Windscreen washers and variable speed wipers are controlled by respectively pushing or twisting the same knob and the wiper blades, which are of the twin rubber type, deserve particular praise for their behaviour at cruising speeds in the nineties where they show no signs of lifting off the glass.

A pull-out handbrake under the facia was found convenient to use and powerful enough to hold the car on a 1 in 3 gradient. The brake pedal is also well placed and near to the floor so that the accelerator foot moves over to it naturally with a minimum of transition lag. Repeated use of these light progressive servo-assisted brakes (disc front) from high speeds failed to disclose any weaknesses.

A cavernous boot is ideal for those who do not believe in travelling light. The lid is spring-loaded open but if the car is standing on a steep upgradient it will not remain open wide enough for loading.

Coachwork and Equipment

Starting handle	*None*
Battery mounting	*Under bonnet*
Jack	*Triangular screw type*
Jacking points	*Two each side under door sills*
Standard tool kit	*Jack and wheelbrace*
Exterior lights	*4 headlamps, 2 side/flashers, 2 tail/stop lamps, 2 rear flashers, number-plate lamp.*
Number of electrical fuses	*One (plus one if radio fitted)*
Direction indicators	*Self-cancelling flashers*
Windscreen wipers	*Twin-blade, self-parking, variable-speed electric.*
Windscreen washers	*Manual pump type*
Sun visors	*Two, universally pivoted*
Instruments	*Speedometer (with total mileage recorder and decimal trip), fuel gauge, water thermometer, clock.*
Warning lights	*Generator, direction signals, oil pressure, main beam, heater fan.*
Locks:	
With ignition key	*Both front doors, glove locker and boot.*
With other keys	*None*
Glove lockers	*One in nearside of facia panel*
Map pockets	*One in each front door*
Parcel shelves	*One behind rear seat*
Ashtrays	*One front, one rear*
Cigar lighters	*One*
Interior lights	*Two courtesy lights in roof*
Interior heater	*Standard fitting fresh-air type*
Car radio	*Optional extra, manual or push-button types*
Extras available	*Radio and standard accessories*
Upholstery material	*Hide or cloth*
Floor covering	*Carpet on felt*
Exterior colours standardized	*12 single colours*
Alternative body styles	*None*

Maintenance

Sump	*6½ pints, S.A.E. 20W (plus 1½ pints in filter)*
Gearbox	*2½ pints, S.A.E. 80*
Rear axle	*2½ pints, S.A.E. 90*
Steering gear lubricant	*S.A.E. 90 EP oil*
Cooling-system capacity	*21 pints (2 drain taps)*
Chassis lubrication	*By grease gun every 5,000 miles to 12 points*
Ignition timing	*8° b.t.d.c.*
Contact-breaker gap	*.015 in.*
Sparking-plug type	*Champion N5*
Sparking-plug gap	*.030 in.*
Valve timing:	
Inlet opens 17° before t.d.c. and closes 51° a.b.d.c.	
Exhaust opens 49° before b.d.c. and closes 19° a.t.d.c.	
Tappet clearances (cold):	
Inlet	*.014 in.*
Exhaust	*.014 in.*
Front wheel toe-in	$\frac{1}{16}$ *to* $\frac{3}{16}$ *in.*
Camber angle	*1°-2°*
Castor angle	*0°-1°*
Steering swivel-pin inclination	*6° 17′ to 7° 17′*
Tyre pressures:	
Front	*24 lb.*
Rear	*24 lb.*
Brake fluid	*Girling*
Battery type and capacity	*12 v., 57 amp hr. (Optional heavy duty 80 amp hr. available)*

For the last few years Fords have been notable for heating systems of excellent power and controllability and the Zodiac is no exception although many people will prefer sliding controls, with easily visible settings, to rotary ones. A feature which should be particularly valuable in summer is a controllable deflector which allows a strong draught of cold air to be projected on the faces of the occupants. The booster fan is very quiet and a warning light has been incorporated in its switch.

It is a tribute not only to the engine but even more to the safety of the chassis that this powerful car was driven at full throttle a great deal during our test. The overall fuel consumption of 19½ m.p.g. is therefore reasonable although it would probably have been worse if secrecy considerations had not prohibited the usual substantial mileage in heavy rush-hour traffic. We see this new Ford as a car which will appeal particularly to the long-distance business motorist by virtue of the outstanding performance and impressive appearance at such a low price. It may have less attraction for the buyer who seeks maximum passenger space inside a car of compact overall dimensions.

The World Copyright of this article and illustrations is strictly reserved © Temple Press Limited, 1962

THE NEW

MARK 3 FORDS

High Performance, disc brakes, four-speed all-synchromesh gearboxes and outstanding value for money keynote of the new "big" range from Dagenham. Hundred miles per hour Zodiac with De Luxe specification and higher power-output.

The new and eagerly-awaited Ford "big" range, designated Zodiac, Zephyr Six, and Zephyr Four, are once again worthy upholders of the Ford tradition. They offer high performance, for six with economical fuel consumption, and low purchase and upkeep costs. The new cars supersede the Mark 2 range, and although engines almost identical in basic design to the earlier units are used for all three models (the four-cylinder 1,703 c.c. "Consul" engine now becomes the "Zephyr Four") they have been subject to many improvements and a substantial power increase.

Shape and styling of the Mark 3 models has been tagged "International" by Ford of Dagenham, and study of the lines will reveal traces of American, British and Continental derivation. The "Galaxie" roofline is very much in evidence, this clean-cut razor-edged pressing with large curved rear window providing a clean, crisp profile for all models.

Three-quarter rear view of the Zodiac reveals its extra side windows, and the generous size of its neat curved rear window. The rear window and the 22 cubic feet boot are common to all Mark 3 models.

The Zodiac has six side windows incorporated in the roof pressing, but the four and six-cylinder Zephyrs have four windows.

Design thinking behind the new cars has been to provide low-priced six-seaters with the option of four or six-cylinders in the Zephyr range, but to lift the Zodiac into the luxury/high-performance class with a different appearance and specification—and at a relatively low price.

The Mark 3 Zodiac has more windows, four headlights, a different grille, and a higher power-output than any other current British Ford. All models have 9.75 in. disc brakes on the front wheels (9-in. drums on the rear), the entire system being servo-assisted. As on the Mark 2 range all models have independent front suspension by the MacPherson coil spring "strut" system, with live axle and semi-elliptic leaf springs at the rear.

All three have a completely new four-speed all-synchromesh gearbox as standard, with

steering column control. The new box was designed and is manufactured at Dagenham but was rated so high by Detroit as to be adopted (with floor shift) by them for the Falcon Futura sports car. Alternative transmission on all models is the new Type 35 Borg-Warner automatic.

The power-units have identical bore and stroke dimensions to their corresponding predecessors but compression ratios have gone up to 8.5 : 1 (from 7.8), both inlet and exhaust valves have been enlarged, and ports have been reshaped. Camshafts remain as before, but power-outputs are increased to: Zephyr-Four, 73.5 gross b.h.p. at 4,800 r.p.m. (Consul Mk. 2 was 61 at 4,400); the Zephyr Six, 106 gross b.h.p. at 4,750 r.p.m. (Zephyr Mk. 2 was 90 at 4,400); and the Zodiac, 109 gross b.h.p. at 4,800 r.p.m. (Zodiac Mk. 2's output was identical to Zephyr.)

The new Zodiac's horse-power bonus over the Zephyr is due to a larger carburetter, and twin exhaust system. These components can be fitted to the Mark 3 Zephyr and will result in a similar power-output but the Zodiac's lead-bronze bearings are better suited to prolonged high-speed running. Another standard fitting on the Zodiac, aimed at ultra-high-performance, is a set of tubeless nylon speed tyres. Tubed tyres are optional. The Zodiac Mark 3 is Ford of Britain's first genuine 100 m.p.h. car, and on a recent test run on country roads, motorways, and on the Silverstone Circuit it was found to be a splendid performer with a high standard of comfort and roadholding.

On the M1 the car could be cruised quietly at an indicated 90 m.p.h., and the immense power and stamina of the brakes promoted confidence. The new four-speed column-control gearbox was light and pleasant to use, and visibility was excellent. On the Silverstone track every model was sampled, and the handling qualities were first-class. The weight distribution of 52/48 with the preponderance on the front wheels is near-ideal and high-speed curve-swinging could be indulged in with ease and accuracy. All three models displayed modest roll and would hold a predetermined line through a corner with no vices. There was slight understeer but the balance was so good and the steering so light that the characteristic was almost unnoticeable under normal fast driving conditions.

Although it was not possible to obtain timed maximum speeds for the new models there is little doubt that the Zodiac will exceed 100 m.p.h. as claimed, and that the Zephyr Six and Four will attain 80 and 98 m.p.h. respectively. On the road a Zephyr Six with Borg-Warner automatic easily reached

made overtaking and manual change-downs (if so desired) easy and certain. On the six-cylinder models too, the automatic transmission suited the engine characteristics very well and at no time suggested loss of driver control.

Trim, upholstery, and finish improves as the price range is ascended. The Zephyr Four has PVC cloth upholstery but hide is available as an extra. The Zephyr Six also has PVC upholstery as standard but with a folding armrest on the front bench seat. The Zodiac seats are in a new plastic cloth called Cirrus 500, a material of extraordinary softness with a texture and finish that is practically impossible to distinguish from real leather. It is claimed that it will keep its shape better than leather, can be quickly cleaned when soiled, and will not easily scratch. Crushed hide is also available for the Zodiac upholstery but this costs £25 extra. Both six-cylinder models have simulated wood graining on the facia, although the instrument layouts are different. The Zodiac has a large oddments box on the front passenger's side which drops down on hinges when the lockable button is depressed—the Zephyrs both have large open boxes. All models have combined headlight flasher-cum-trafficator switches, and electric variable-speed windscreen wipers.

The four doors (all of which are fitted with a new type of Wilmot-Breeden lock which is ultra-light in operation and shuts with a "coach-built" click) are trimmed up to the windows. This gives a pleasing effect and provides the maximum padded surface. All windows in the new Ford range are curved, the side window effect being to assist with the increased interior body width yet to allow a taper to the rooftop

Interior of the standard Zephyr Four has pleated PVC upholstery and rubber mats. The facia top is well padded and there is a large open oddments box on the passenger's side. Rotary heater/ demister controls are fitted. On the test cars the heaters were found to be most efficient, supplying a blast of hot air to the rear of the car as well as the front, even with the booster motor switched off. This car has the four-speed all-synchromesh gearbox with steering column control.

ABOVE. *Lush interior of the standard Zodiac has simulated wood grain facia, upholstery of Cirrus 500 (a new plastic that is difficult to distinguish from hide), and a neat instrument layout. The passenger's side is copiously padded, and the hinged oddments locker drops down when button is pressed. This model is fitted with the optional Borg-Warner Type 35 automatic transmission.*

LEFT. *A one-piece grille distinguishes the Zephyr Four. The six-seater body is identical to the six-cylinder models. Like the Zephyr Six it also has four main side windows.*

60 m.p.h. from a standing start in 15 seconds, all gear changes being smooth and quick.

Perhaps the best-handling car of the entire range was the Zephyr Four, the lighter power unit making for very precise steering, and an ability to corner extremely fast with negligible roll. The engine was quiet and smooth, and 70 m.p.h. could easily be exceeded in third gear. The automatic-equipped Zephyr Four seemed just as fast as the manual model, and the transmission was well suited to modern motoring requirements. Take-off was silky smooth, and the degree of "over-ride" with the easily selected "lock-up" lever position

where the increased width is neither necessary or desirable.

Great attention has been paid to sound frequencies and to noise insulation. The front bulkheads and dashboard areas are treated with a new application of blown fibre-glass, and bitumen pads are heat-applied to the floor. Combined with smooth-running mechanical features the new Fords compare very favourably with more expensive cars.

There will be Estate Car versions of all three models available in the near future, and to demonstrate their confidence in the new saloons, the Ford Motor Company entered Mark 3 models in Easter's African Safari Rally.

PRICES IN U.K.

Zodiac ......£1,070 15s. 3d. incl. P. Tax
Saloon   (Basic price £778)
Zephyr Six .. £929 2s. 9d. incl. P. Tax
Saloon   (Basic price £675)
Zephyr Four .. £846 12s. 9d. incl. P. Tax
Saloon   (Basic price £615)
Available extras include Borg-Warner **automatic transmission** (all models), **over-drive** (all models), **whitewall tyres** (all models), **hide upholstery** (all models), **individual reclining front seats** (all models), **heater and demister** (Zephyrs), **front folding centre armrest** (Zephyr Four), **rear folding centre armrest** (Zephyr Six).

TWO NEW ZEPHYRS

COMPLETING their new range of "large" cars, Ford of Dagenham have announced a Zephyr Four and Zephyr Six to come between the Consul Classic 315 and the Zodiac announced two weeks earlier. Externally, the new models are distinguished from the more luxurious Zodiac by a different roof line, two headlamps instead of four, and numerous detail changes. The Six uses the same engine as the Zodiac though in a lower-rated form, and the Four has the 1,703 c.c. four-cylinder engine used in the Consul 375 which it replaces. All three new models have a common wheelbase of 8 ft. 11 in., whereas the Consul's wheelbase was 2½ in. shorter than the previous Zephyr and Zodiac.

The variety that Ford now give in this range is an extension of their policy of offering many different cars from one basic model; although the customer has a mass-produced vehicle

it is still not quite the same as his neighbour's. Thus someone wanting a six-seater family saloon has the choice of a four-cylinder engine, or two 2,553 c.c. Sixes—the more powerful version in a luxury hull. Transmission is to choice: manual, manual with overdrive, or fully automatic. Thus there are nine variants to choose from.

Offering amenities and technical specifications basically similar to those of their predecessors, the Zephyrs provide in addition a completely new appearance, quieter running coupled with higher performance, and sundry improvements to details. They are almost unchanged dimensionally, save that they are slightly lower overall, although not at the expense of ground clearance. More elbow and hip room have been provided by using curved glass for all the side windows.

The Zephyrs use the same unit construction hull as is found

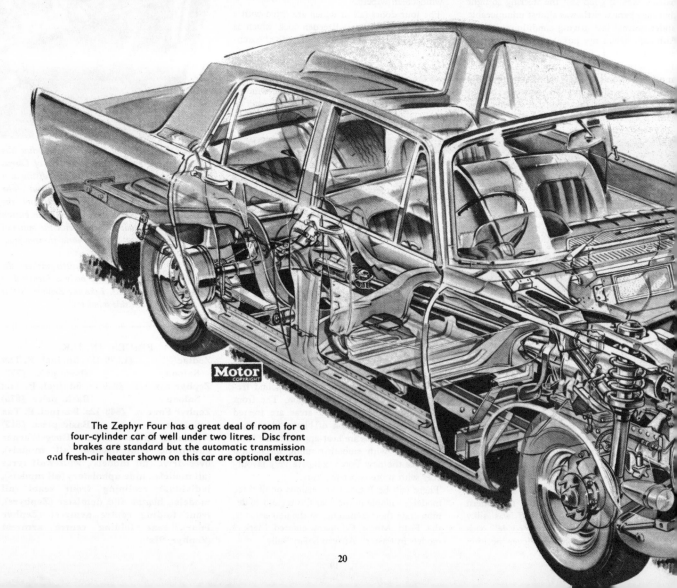

The Zephyr Four has a great deal of room for a four-cylinder car of well under two litres. Disc front brakes are standard but the automatic transmission and fresh-air heater shown on this car are optional extras.

The range completed. Besides different rear embellishment the radiator grilles of each model are distinctive. Note also that the curved glass of the side windows extends to the very back on the Zodiac.

The five stars on the back of the Zephyr Six act as a recognition feature for this model. As has been common Ford practice on this range, the fuel filler is concealed by the hinged rear number plate.

Ford Complete Their Large Car Range with 6- and 4-cylinder Family Cars

on the Zodiac. This is considerably stiffer than the one used for the Mk. II cars and has five bulkheads. Notable changes are the strengthening of the boxes carrying the front suspension units, to eliminate the necessity for tie-rods between the top of these and the engine bulkhead, tying the rear parcel shelf structurally to the bulkhead below it, and the spreading out of the rear wheel-housing rails where they meet the centre part of the floor. The petrol tank is now bolted into the floor of the boot instead of being underslung as it was before.

When Ford of Dagenham decided to use independent front suspension for their first Zephyr they opted for the Macpherson strut system, which they have favoured ever since. It has the merit of being simple as, apart from the telescopic strut unit, the only components necessary are a single track control arm on each side and an anti-roll bar, which has a dual role inasmuch as it also triangulates the track control arms, effectively forming a lower wishbone. In the latest cars the suspension legs lean further in at the top than previously and the internal working parts are mounted lower down in the strut, allowing its overall

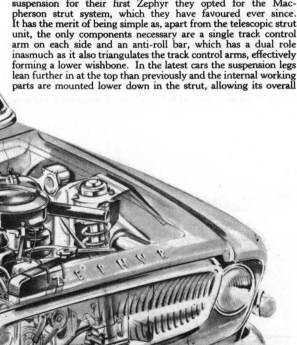

length to be reduced without affecting its effective operating length. Thus the bonnet line can be lowered since this is the determining factor.

The rear suspension, by semi-elliptic leaf springs, has also been developed, principally with a view to reducing road and suspension noise in the interior of the car. Large rubber bushes hold the springs to the hull and the axle is also held to the springs via rubber. The springs are themselves interleaved with butyl rubber. Steering is by recirculating ball, and the ratio at dead ahead is 18.6:1 increasing to 21:1 at full lock so that the 17-in. steering wheel remains light to turn when parking.

The disc/drum brake system with vacuum servo is the same as before except that 2¼ in. wide drums are now used on the Zephyr Six to even up the wear rate between front and rear. The Four retains 1¾ in. wide drums.

From the mechanical angle it is the engine department that distinguishes the Zephyrs from the Zodiac. The Six uses the same basic cast iron unit but its 4-bearing crankshaft has babbit-metal main bearings in place of lead bronze, though the latter is used for the big-end bearings. Connecting rods have been strengthened and a new taper-sided top compression ring is fitted to the modified pistons of all the engines. The cylinder head is the same as on the Zodiac and compression ratio has been raised from 7.8 to 8.3:1 though a low ratio is still an option. Larger valves have been fitted and different valve springs. The Six retains the exhaust system fitted to the Mk. II models, consisting of a single tube, pierced where it meets the exhaust ports, bolted straight on to the side of the cylinder head. The Zodiac has a twin system. The Six uses a new Zenith carburetter which again differs slightly from that used on the Zodiac. All engines have improved inlet manifolding. These alterations have raised the claimed net power output of the Zephyr Six from 85 b.h.p. at 4,400 to 98 b.h.p. at 4,750 r.p.m. (for comparison the further improved breathing found on the Zodiac gives a further 11 b.h.p.).

The Four shares the same bore and stroke measurements as the Six and can really be regarded as the same unit less two cylinders and one main bearing. It too has a different model carburetter and with the raised compression and other changes that have been made to it, as to the Six, its power output has gone up to

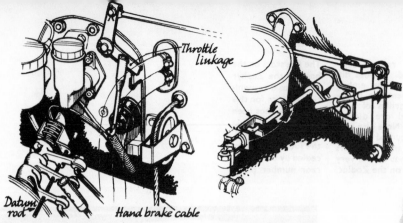

The throttle linkage has been improved on the new cars. The previous arrangement with a long rod in torsion has been replaced by a system of rods in tension, except for one short section where it joins the carburetter. Note also the datum rod used for setting up the gear-change linkage in correct adjustment quickly and accurately on assembly.

TWO NEW FORD ZEPHYRS

The rear spring leaves are interspaced with butyl rubber and the complete spring held to the axle via large rubber blocks.

68 b.h.p. net from the 59 b.h.p. it developed in the Consul 375. Torque has also been improved.

Optional transmission systems are available on both the Six and Four. The manual box has four speeds, all with syncromesh, in contrast to the previous three (the only three-speed manual gearbox found now in the Ford car range is on their cheapest model, the Popular). The new box may also be combined with Borg Warner overdrive for an extra £58 8s. 9d. on the total price. Alternatively for £110 the fully automatic Borg Warner Model 35 system is available. The Six uses a 3.55 final drive whichever transmission system is employed, but the lower powered Four uses a 3.9 ratio with the manual box, 4.1 when overdrive is used as well, and the 3.55 one only when the automatic transmission is chosen. Using this high ratio with automatic transmission should help economy, and because this particular gearbox "torque converts" on all three of its forward gears the performance of this slowest version of the Zephyr is still superior to that of the Mk. II Consul. A column-mounted control lever is used with all systems.

Following the trend that has been particularly noticeable in

North America towards longer periods between servicing, the Zephyrs both have sealed chassis lubrication systems that require attention every 5,000 miles instead of every 1,000 as before and in fact during development cars were run for considerably longer periods without attention.

The Zephyr Four offers a remarkably large body for its engine size. Ford have lately tended to provide large boots and the present one with just under 22 cu. ft. of space is no exception. The spare wheel is carried inside it, standing up at one side.

The Zephyrs have at last said goodbye to vacuum-operated screen wipers and now have variable-speed electric ones with inverted 'U' section blades which are claimed to remain on the screen at high speeds. They were introduced on the Classic. Another feature that was introduced on that car and is now found on the Zephyrs is a flasher for signalling with the sealed beam headlamps. New to this range is a special parking arrangement whereby the nearside side and tail lamps can be extinguished, leaving the offside only alight. In this state the starter solenoid is isolated to prevent the car being started up in this condition.

The optional heater has been completely redesigned and now

The large boot, with countersprung lid is a feature of the Zephyrs. The Six shown here differs internally from the Four in having a simulated wood facia but is otherwise very similar.

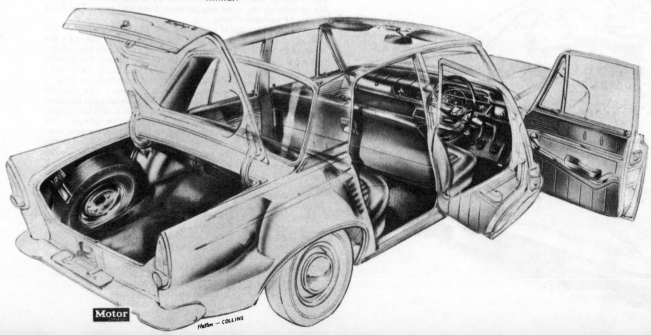

Motor

Hutton — COLLINS

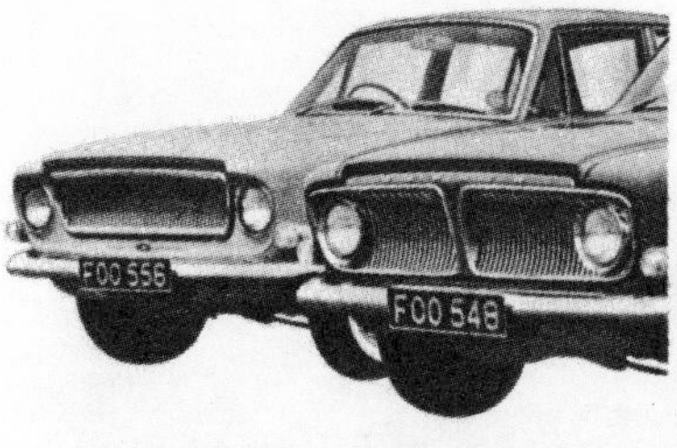

TWO NEW FORD ZEPHYRS

offers the refinement of air mixing and face-level cold air ventilation. It is rated at 5¼ kilowatts.

These new cars, complementary to the prestige Zodiac model now give those motorists who require an economy version of a large and impressive family saloon the chance to obtain one at an appropriate price.

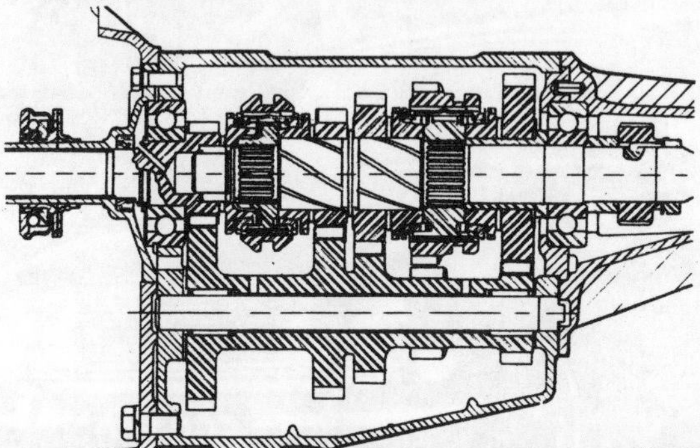

For the first time the large Fords have four speeds with syncromesh on all forward speeds.

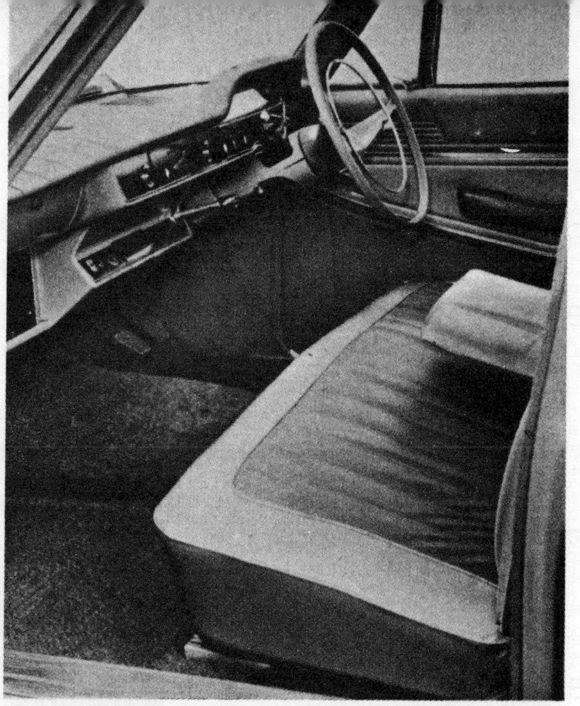

The front compartment of the new Zephyr (this is the Six) has been completely restyled. A "ribbon" speedometer is now used although instrumentation is still simple in the Ford tradition. Care has been taken to eliminate all untrimmed interior metal and the centre armrest is standard on the Six

Zephyr 6 Specification

ENGINE

Cylinders	6 in line with crankshaft carried in 4 white metal bearings.
Bore and stroke ...	82.55 mm. × 79.5 mm. (3.25 in. × 3.25 in.).
Cubic capacity ...	2,553 c.c. (155.8 cu. in.).
Piston area ...	49.74 sq. in.
Compression ratio ...	8.3/1 (7.0/1 optional).
Valvegear	Overhead valves operated by chain-driven side-mounted camshaft.
Carburation	Single Zenith 36 W.I.A.-2 downdraught carburetter, fed by camshaft-operated diaphragm fuel pump, from 12-gallon tank.
Ignition	12-volt coil, centrifugal and vacuum timing control, 14 mm. Champion sparking plugs, type N5.
Lubrication	Full flow filter and 8-pint sump.
Cooling	Pressurized water cooling with pump, 4-blade fan and wax thermostat; 19½-pint water capacity.
Electrical system ...	12-volt battery charged by 22-amp. generator.
Maximum power ...	98 b.h.p. nett (106 gross) at 4,750 r.p.m., equivalent to 105 lb./sq. in. b.m.e.p. at 2,480 ft./min. piston speed and 1.97 b.h.p. per sq. in. of piston area.
Maximum torque ...	134 lb. ft. net (139 gross) at 2,000 r.p.m., equivalent to 130 lb./sq. in. b.m.e.p. at 1,040 ft./min. piston speed.

TRANSMISSION

Clutch	Ford/Borg and Beck 8½ in. s.d.p., hydraulically operated.
Gearbox	4-speed, all-syncromesh with direct drive top.
Overall ratios ...	Without overdrive 3.55; 5.01; 7.86; 11.23; reverse 11.88. Optional overdrive gives additional ratios of 2.734; 3.860; 6.052.
TRANSMISSION (automatic)	Borg-Warner Model 35 torque converter with 3-speed gearbox; ratios 3.55; 5.147; 8.48; reverse 7.419.
Propeller shaft ...	One piece open.
Final drive	Hypoid bevel.

CHASSIS

Brakes... ...	Girling, hydraulically operated disc/drum system, with vacuum servo and reservoir.
Brake dimensions ...	Front discs, 9.75 in. dia.; rear drums, 9 in. dia. × 2.25 in. wide.
Brake areas	98 sq. in. of lining (20.6 sq. in. front plus 77.6 sq. in. rear) working on 330 sq. in. rubbed area of discs and drums.
Front suspension ...	Macpherson independent, by inclined telescopic damper legs, lower wishbones, coil springs and torsion anti-roll bar.
Rear suspension ...	Rigid axle, asymmetric semi-elliptic leaf springs, with full-length rubber interleaving and hydraulic lever arm shock absorbers.
Wheels and tyres ...	Bolt-on 5-stud wheels and 6.40—13 tubeless tyres.
Steering	Recirculatory ball type.

DIMENSIONS

Length	Overall 15 ft. 0¼ in.; wheelbase 8 ft. 11 in.
Width... ...	Overall 5 ft. 9 in.; track 4 ft. 5 in. at front and 4 ft. 4 in. at rear.
Height... ...	4 ft. 7½ in.; ground clearance 5¾ in.
Turning circle ...	35½ ft.
Kerb weight	24½ cwt. (without fuel but with oil, water, tools, spare wheel, etc.).

EFFECTIVE GEARING

Top gear ratio ...	19.9 m.p.h. at 1,000 r.p.m. and 38.1 m.p.h. at 1,000 ft./min. piston speed (with overdrive, 25.9 m.p.h. and 49.5 m.p.h.).
Maximum torque ...	2,000 r.p.m. corresponds to approx. 39.8 m.p.h. in top gear (51.7 m.p.h. in overdrive).
Maximum power ...	4,750 r.p.m. corresponds to approx. 94-95 m.p.h. in top gear (123 m.p.h. in overdrive).
Probable top gear pulling power.	250 lb./ton approx. (Computed by *The Motor* from manufacturer's figures for torque, gear ratio and kerb weight, with allowances for 3½ cwt. load, 10% losses and 60 lb./ton drag.)

Zephyr 4 Specification

As for Zephyr 6 except for:

ENGINE

Cylinders	4 in line with crankshaft carried in 3 white metal bearings.
Cubic capacity ...	1,703 c.c. (103.9 cu. in.).
Piston area ...	33.2 sq. in.
Carburation	Single Zenith 36 VN downdraught carburetter.
Lubrication	7½-pint sump.
Cooling	15½-pint water capacity.
Maximum power ...	68 b.h.p. net (73.5 gross) at 4,800 r.p.m. equivalent to 108 lb./sq. in. b.m.e.p. at 2,504 ft./min. piston speed and 2.05 b.h.p. per sq. in. of piston area.
Maximum torque ...	93.5 lb. ft. net (99 lb. ft. gross) at 2,000 r.p.m. equivalent to 136 lb./sq. in. b.m.e.p. at 1,040 ft./min. piston speed.

TRANSMISSION

Overall ratios ...	Without overdrive: 3.9; 5.87; 9.17; 17.21; reverse 18.2. With optional overdrive: 4.1 (o/d 3.16); 6.15 (o/d 4.74); 9.63 (o/d 7.42); 18.08; reverse 19.15. With optional automatic gearbox: ratios as Zephyr 6.

CHASSIS

Brake dimensions ...	Same diameter, 1¾ in. wide at rear.
Brake areas	81.1 sq. in. of lining (20.6 sq. in. front plus 60.5 sq. in. rear) working on 299 sq. in. rubbed area of discs and drums.

DIMENSIONS

Kerb weight	23 cwt.

EFFECTIVE GEARING

Top gear ratio ...	18.1 m.p.h. at 1,000 r.p.m. and 34.7 m.p.h. at 1,000 ft./min. piston speed (with overdrive, 22.3 m.p.h. and 42.8 m.p.h.).
Maximum torque ...	2,000 r.p.m. corresponds to approx. 36.2 m.p.h. in top gear (44.6 m.p.h. in overdrive).
Maximum power ...	4,800 r.p.m. corresponds to approx. 87 m.p.h. in top gear (107 m.p.h. in overdrive).
Probable top gear pulling power	190 lb./ton approx. (computed by *The Motor* from manufacturer's figures for torque, gear ratio and kerb weight, with allowances for 3½ cwt. load, 10% losses and 60 lb./ton drag).

Ford's Zodiac Mark 3 offers 100 m.p.h. luxury with disc brakes, "quad" headlights and three transmission options. Lavishly equipped, the fastest-ever British Ford has remarkably low price tag.

The "International Line". Ford's Zodiac Mark 3 has bold looks, and the "Galaxie" roof pressing incorporates six curved side windows. The concave grille and surrounds for the Lucas "quad" headlights are of non-tarnishing aluminium-alloy.

The large "Galaxie" rear window provides excellen visibility. Bumpers are well "wrapped around" to provid side protection, and the overiders are robust. Filler ca for the 12½-gallon fuel tank is under the hinged numbe plate. Wheeltrims are a standard fitting (as are nylo high-speed tyres) and are of polished light-alloy.

CARS ON TEST | FORD ZODIAC MK. 3

The Ford Motor Company has for many years set out to offer exceptional value for money, and there is no doubt that with the latest Mark 3 range of cars, it offers something for every pocket and fancy. Showpiece of the Mark 3 range is the swank Zodiac, first 100 m.p.h. car to come out of Dagenham, and this performance plus disc front brakes, luxury trim, "quad" headlights and many other features make this 2.6-litre six-seater saloon exceptional value at a U.K. basic price of £778. Purchase Tax adds nearly £293 to the price, but even at £1,070 15s. 3d. the Ford Zodiac Mark 3 is a very good buy.

In basic catalogue form the Zodiac comes with new four-speed column-change gearbox

with synchromesh on all forward ratios. At £58 8s. 9d. (including Purchase Tax) it can be supplied with Borg-Warner overdrive, and this will provide seven forward speeds (if you are keen!) or more normally, effortless high-speed cruising with relatively low fuel consumption. As supplied for test the Ford Zodiac was equipped with the Borg-Warner Type 35 automatic gearbox, a transmission which suits the sweet-running "six" very well. Driving the automatic Zodiac is child's play but the available amount of driver control can be exercised to make this anything but a dull way of driving. Perhaps the only desirable aspect of manual transmission that is missed by the enthusiastic driver is the overdrive.

Quick check:

PERFORMANCE...	1C
ROADHOLDING ...	9
GEARBOX.............	1C
COMFORT	9
FINISH..................	9
BRAKES	9
VISIBILITY.............	1C
ECONOMY...........	9
STARTING............	1C

All assessments commensurate with type o car and price tag. Max.: 10, each category.

AUTOMATIC Z–CAR

With the standard bench seat slid back to the limit of its adjustment (separate reclining front seats are available as optional extras) there is ample legroom for a six-footer, and general driving position is good—and would be even better with a non-dished steering wheel. The seat shape is excellent, the best ever fitted to a British Ford, with good thigh support and plenty of padding at the base of the driver's (or passenger's) spine. Upholstery in the test car was of "Cirrus 500", the new soft plastic that is very difficult to distinguish from leather. This remained soft and comfortable throughout the test but during cold weather when the powerful heater was being used there was a certain amount of "stickiness" evident. Hide upholstery is available as an optional extra.

With the front bench seat at the limit of its rearward adjustment, a position which gave comfort and control for a six-foot driver, there was little leg or kneeroom for the rear passengers. Width there was in plenty, the thick carpeting, armrests, and fully-trimmed door interiors all contributing to the feeling of expensive luxury.

From the performance aspect the Zodiac Mark 3 leaves little to be desired for a luxury six-seater of 2.6-litres. It will top 100 m.p.h.,

the option of power-assistance, they have standardized a "variable ratio" recirculatory ball steering box which provides, in effect, a lower steering ratio at the extremities of the lock than at straight-ahead and at the small degrees of lock encountered under normal main road driving conditions. The steering is light and pleasant to use under ordinary conditions, but the fact remains that lock to lock requires four full turns of the steering wheel, and this is a definite disadvantage to the fast driver who likes to make full use of the car's excellent cornering powers. For instance, to negotiate a round-about or tight turn fast, a manoeuvre of which the new Ford is eminently capable, requires wheel-winding of such intensity as to demand slower cornering. It is also extremely tiring for the driver.

Weight distribution on the new Zodiac is about 52-48 with the preponderance on the front wheels. This near-perfect arrangement shows up in the car's handling for it is an extremely well-balanced car with just enough understeer to assist with easy straightline running and effortless, fast cornering. Under "rally-type" cornering the understeer changes to predictable oversteer, the back finally breaking away with no vices.

The test Zodiac's disc-cum-drum brake layout provided impressive fade-free retardation but under maximum efficiency tests with the Bowmonk Dynometer recorded only .85 g (85 per cent). Since the test however a manual transmission Zephyr Six (virtually the same technical specification) has been subjected to braking tests with the same Dynometer, and on roads with good anti-skid surfaces 1 g (100 per cent efficiency) was easily recorded. From 30 m.p.h. this represents a stop in 30.2 feet.

Driver comfort has been very closely studied on the new Zodiac. Not only are the heating and demisting arrangements some of the most effective CARS ILLUSTRATED have tried, but the ventilation system is first-class. In warm weather cool air can be fed in through the windscreen demisting grilles and enjoyed at "face-level". In addition the front door quarter swivelling windows can be adjusted to circulate fresh air around the interior, and the opening quarter rear windows can be arranged to direct a stream of cool air right through the car. Another occupant-comfort aspect that has obviously been the subject of close study is that of noise. Although the exhaust note from the twin tail-pipes is quite "fruity" from outside the car, it can hardly

accelerate from 0-60 m.p.h. in 17.3 seconds (with automatic transmission), and cruise all day at 80 m.p.h. with a very low noise level. In spite of its overall length of 15 ft. 0½ in., and width of 5 ft. 9 in., the Zodiac's handling is good. There is little roll at all "normal" fast cornering speeds, and the ride is comfortable although there is a fair amount of pitching if high speeds are indulged in over poor-surfaced roads. Under these conditions the live rear axle will also tramp to an appreciable degree but control is easily maintained.

Fords have approached the problem of steering lightness from an unusual angle. Instead of loading the price of the Mark 3 range with

Despite the low-geared steering a good driver can cram the miles into the hour with the new Zodiac. The driving position is good, the seats comfortable, and the road visibility magnificent through the large curved glass area. During the test the car was driven (one-up) to Aintree and back, and for the first three hours of the northward journey it put 50 miles into each hour, even though a considerable mileage was covered on B-class roads, and amongst week-end traffic. The surging acceleration, quiet running, and powerful braking all produced confidence, and although the automatic gearbox was worked to the full, the fuel consumption worked out at 19 m.p.g. on premium spirit.

be heard from inside, unless the rear quarter windows are open, and even then it is only a pleasant burble.

It is pleasant to note the use of a trip as well as a season odometer on the 120 m.p.h. "ribbon" speedometer. This instrument has a neat and tidy appearance in the simulated wood dash but the diagonal "cut-off" of the horizontal speed indicator and the small dimensions of the numerals does not make for quick and easy reference. The fuel contents, and water temperature gauges which flank the speedometer have an ornate crystal ball look about them but are effective enough. Coloured lights supply warning for ignition, oil pressure, main headlight beam, and traffic indicators. The dash surround is crash-padded and there is a useful "drop-down" dash locker of large dimensions on the passenger side. There is a "cigar" lighter as standard equipment, and an electric clock. The traffic indicator switch projects from the right of the steering column and is a self-cancelling stalk switch with a useful headlamp flasher switch built-in to the tip. Although it is a "two-pedal" car the automatic Zodiac has three pedals for the driver to operate. There is an "organ-type" accelerator pedal, a large pendant brake pedal (for either foot) and a third "organ-type" pedal on the left of the floorboard which operates the foot dipswitch. It also serves as a very comfortable driver's footrest.

Driving the car with the Borg-Warner type 35 transmission was effortless and interesting. The fluid coupling took up the drive from a standstill with the silkiest of motions, and three upward gear-changes took place with commendable smoothness unless the speed was high and the throttle opening large. The Type 35 "has it" over the earlier Borg-Warner transmissions in that it is virtually a top gear unit. Once the car is in top gear (and this occurs early or late according to throttle opening) it stays there, all lowspeed power transmission being passed through the torque convertor. This obviates the annoying habit that earlier "automatics" had of changing down unnecessarily. If a lower gear and maximum acceleration is required it is only necessary to "kick-down" the throttle pedal and second or low gear (according to road speed) will engage and the car will leap forward.

The Type 35 transmission has a redesigned "quadrant" control. This has N (for neutral) in the centre and L (for Lock-up) to the extreme left. If the lever is pulled to the extreme left at any speed under 60 m.p.h., second gear will engage with full engine braking. With this excellent arrangement it means that the Zodiac (or any other Type 35-equipped car) can be driven as a completely automatic car (with the selector in D for drive position) or as a sports car, with a high measure of control over the three-speed /torque converter gearbox. For instance, a roundabout could be approached fast in the Zodiac, then the impressive power of the disc/drum brakes could be applied until the speed was down to 60 m.p.h., when the selector lever could be pulled into "L" whereupon second gear (and full engine-braking) would engage. Out of the roundabout the acceleration could be held up to about 70 m.p.h. with the selector lever in "L", then top could be re-engaged by pushing the lever into "D", or it could be returned to this position immediately after leaving the roundabout whereupon the car would automatically change itself into top at around 70 m.p.h. if the accelerator was fully depressed. For caravanning, or for descending really steep hills this quickly obtained second gear engine-braking is a first-class feature.

At night the Lucas "quad" headlights supplied road illumination in keeping with the car's performance, the dipped spread on two lamps

being extremely good. The Zodiac is fitted as standard with tubeless Nylon Speed tyres (tubes are optional) and the 6.40 by 13 Goodyears fitted to the test car were impressive both from the handling and silent running aspects. It was virtually impossible to make them squeal through fast corners and bends, the most they would emit being a "scrabble" as the tread pattern clawed for grip.

To sum up, it could be said that the Mark 3 Zodiac is the fastest, most luxurious, best-equipped, and finest car to emerge from the Dagenham factory. It offers comfort and high-performance for six and is certainly reasonably priced. Luggage space is enormous but it would have perhaps been better if the Ford designers had aimed for a little less boot space and a little more rear passenger leg room.

D.A.

SPECIFICATION

PERFORMANCE

0–30 m.p.h.... 5.5 sec.	30–40 m.p.h. (top gear)
0–40 m.p.h.... 7.8 sec.	10.0 sec.
0–50 m.p.h...11.5 sec.	40–60 m.p.h. (top gear)
0–60 m.p.h...17.3 sec.	Maximum speeds:
0–70 m.p.h...20.0 sec.	(automatic transmission)
0–80 m.p.h...32.0 sec.	Low, 45 m.p.h. Second,
	70 m.p.h. Top, 102 m.p.h

Car mileage at completion of test: 3,223.

ENGINE
Ford Mk 3 Zodiac six-cylinder-in-line, water-cooled. Overhead valves (pushrod). Bore: 82.55 mm. Stroke: 79.5 mm. Cubic capacity: 2,553 c.c. Compression ratio: 8.5 : 1 (7 : 1 optional for countries where high octane fuels are unobtainable). Power-output: 112 b.h.p. (nett at 5,000 r.p.m. Maximum torque: 140 lb. ft. at 2,800 r.p.m. Single Ford/Zenith 42WIA-2 downdraught carburetter. Lucas coil and distributor ignition (12-volt). AC mechanical fuel pump.

TRANSMISSION
On test car Borg-Warner Type 35 automatic gearbox with torque converter, fluid coupling and three forward speeds. Gear box ratios: Low, 2.39 : 1. Second, 1.45 : 1 Top, 1.00 : 1. Final-drive ratio, 3.5 : 1. Rear wheel drive through three-quarter floating, hypoid live axle.

SUSPENSION
Independent front by MacPherson struts incorporating coil springs and hydraulic dampers. Anti-roll torsion bar. Rear suspension by semi-elliptic leaf springs (with full-length rubber inserts), live axle and lever-type dampers. Recirculating ball steering box.

BRAKES
Servo-assisted Girling/Ford. 9½ in. discs on front wheels, 9 in. by 2¾ in. drums at rear. Steel bolt-on wheels with light-alloy wheeltrims.

BRAKING FIGURES
Using Bowmonk Dynometer. From 30 m.p.h., 85 per cent 35.6 feet (later test with Zephyr Six registed 100 per cent 30.2 feet).

DIMENSIONS
Wheelbase, 8 ft. 11 in. Track, front, 4 ft. 5 in., rear, 4 ft. 4 in. Length, 15 ft. 0½ in. Width, 5 ft. 9 in. Turning circle, 36 ft. 6 in. Kerb weight 25½ cwt. Ground clearance 6.8 in. Fuel capacity, 12½ gallons Imp.). Average fuel consumption (mostly fast country driving) 19.8 m.p.g Premium fuel. Tyres (on test car) Goodyear 6.40 by 13 Nylon Sports.

WATER PRESSURE TEST
Considerable leakage through both front quarter window locks, and through rubber seal of passenger's side quarter window.

BOOT CAPACITY
21.75 cu. ft.

PRICE
In U.K. As tested, with Borg-Warner Type 35 automatic transmission and white side-wall tyres: £1,198 8s. 6d. including Purchase Tax. (Basic price of automatic Zodiac £858.

Headlamps are set low, but parker/winkers look as though they could have been an after-thought. Lack of overriders is unfortunate.

IS THIS FORD'S BEST CAR?

WHEN Ford decides to change a model it, usually does so in a big way. The new Zephyr, examples of which are gradually appearing on our roads, is no exception.

Actually, the car was announced in the middle of the Falcon/Holden uproar and was, to some extent, glossed over by Ford for fear it would steal some of the Falcon's thunder.

Unlike the Falcon, which is almost entirely Australian made, the Zephyr is built up from panels imported from the UK, with items such as trim and rubber added locally. The Zephyr was also badly affected by the industrial dispute in which Ford was involved recently, so deliveries have been slow.

This new Zephyr looks almost totally unlike a Ford, either English, American or German. It is visibly bigger than the previous Zephyr and its bold lines bear no resemblance to those of the smooth Falcon.

Perhaps the most "Ford" feature in the styling is the Thunderbird-type roof line which is now common to the Falcon, Fairlane and big US Fords. Besides looking rather handsome it does provide good headroom for the back seat passengers and allows a full-width rear window.

There is ample glass area in the Zephyr. The screen is deep and curved but does not wrap around.

The least heralded but the most exciting of the new Ford range, the Zephyr, has the best specification and the smartest point to point performance of them all.

27

Mechanically the most interesting of the current Ford range in Australia, the Zephyr has plenty of performance from its 2.6-litre engine.

Zephyr engine is basically the same as previous model, but develops more than 100 bhp. Coupled to all-synchro four speed box, it gives excellent performance.

The pillars are reasonably thin, but I did detect some glass distortion in the test car. To achieve maximum interior width the glass of the side windows is curved. A small disadvantage of all this is that the rear vision mirror does not do justice to the back window.

For some reason Ford has decided to hinge the front ventilation panels from their leading edges. I cannot see any real advantage in doing so, but there must be some.

Frontal treatment is pleasing and not too fussy. The two headlamps are placed low down in the grille and the parker winkers occupy little nacelles on the width extremities. There is a gap of an inch or so between the top of the grille and beginning of the bonnet which may cause trouble in insect plaques in the bush.

The self parking windscreen wipers have parallel action but leave a nasty blind spot in the right hand corner of the screen, just where the driver does not want it. Admittedly the curvature of the glass makes it hard for the wipers to sweep the full screen, but I think a more satisfactory compromise could have been reached.

When the Zephyr is viewed in profile, it appears to sit up high at the tail. This is futher accentuated by the thick rear end styling. However, with a medium load the back sits down more neatly with no suggestion of abnormality.

Overhang has been minimised and there is good ground clearance.

There is a generous amount of unobstructed luggage space in the tail with the spare wheel stowed clear of the luggage. The lid is self supporting through a conventional system of torsion bars which, in the test car, had lost their tension and permitted the lid to come down again to the detriment of the people loading the compartment. The fuel filler cap is concealed behind the spring loaded rear number plate. The boot, by the way, is lined, but getting heavy cases over the lip can be awkward. No provision has been made for locating the tools; they remain loose.

The impression one gets from the outside of the car is that it has been thoughtfully designed, with careful avoidance of gimmick styling features which throw a car out of date so quickly. Ford has gone to a lot of expense making this new Zephyr so it has to have a long life to pay for tooling costs. It is an uncluttered car, devoid of fussiness and appealing enough in its simplicity.

About the only jarring thing I could find was the door handles, which did not look quite right.

Access to the cabin is good, even though the Zephyr is a low car. From the driver's seat my eyes were about level with the door handles on a Zephyr of the last series.

Head room back and front is sufficient even for people who rise more than six feet above the ground. In the back seat there is good knee room when the front seat is moved back to limit of its travel, where, I think, most drivers would have it most of the time.

In spite of the car's low build, the tailshaft tunnel has been kept reasonably low and does not really hinder passenger comfort.

Good-looking carpets cover the floors, but the rest of the trim is in washable plastic-based materials. The seats themselves are quite tastefully two-toned and there is a very well placed centre armrest in the front to supplement those on all four doors. There are conventional window winders, although the door handles have been done away with in favor of finger-tip pressure pads under the armrests.

Less satisfactory were the door locking buttons on the test car. They were so stiff that it was not

WHEELS ▸ FULL·ROAD TEST

wheels ROAD TEST

TECHNICAL DETAILS
OF THE
FORD ZEPHYR

SPECIFICATIONS

ENGINE:

Cylinders	six in line
Bore and stroke	82.55 by 79.5 mm
Cubic capacity	2553
Compression ratio	8.3 to 1
Valves	pushrod overhead
Carburettor	Zenith
Power at rpm	106 (gross) at 4750 rpm
Maximum torque	139 ft/lbs (gross) at 2000 rpm

TRANSMISSION:

Type	manual
First	11.23
Second	7.86
Third	5.01
Top	3.55
Rear axle	3.55

SUSPENSION:

Front	Macpherson independent
Rear	semi elliptic
Shockers	telescopic front, lever rear

STEERING:

Type	recirculatary ball
Turns, 1 to 1	4 1/3
Circle	35.5 ft

BRAKES:

Type	disc/drum

DIMENSIONS:

Wheelbase	8 ft 11 in
Track, front	4 ft 5 in
Track, rear	4 ft 4 in
Length	15 ft 0½ in
Width	5 ft 9 in
Height	4 ft 7½ in

TYRES:

Size	6.40 by 13

WEIGHT:

Dry	22½ cwt

PERFORMANCE

TOP SPEED:

Fastest run	98.7 mph
Average of all runs	96.1 mph

MAXIMUM SPEED IN GEARS:

First	38 mph
Second	57 mph
Third	80 mph
Top	98.7 mph

ACCELERATION:

Standing Quarter Mile:

Fastest run	19.7 secs
Average of all runs	19.8 secs
0 to 30 mph	4.0 secs
0 to 40 mph	6.6 secs
0 to 50 mph	10.0 secs
0 to 60 mph	14.9 secs
0 to 70 mph	20.8 secs
0 to 80 mph	NA secs
20 to 40 mph	8.5 secs
30 to 50 mph	10.0 secs
40 to 60 mph	10.6 secs

GO-TO-WHOA:

0-60-0 mph	17.8 secs

SPEEDO ERROR:

Indicated	Actual
30 mph	29.4 mph
40 mph	39.4 mph
50 mph	48.7 mph
60 mph	58.6 mph
70 mph	68.0 mph
80 mph	NA mph
90 mph	NA mph

FUEL CONSUMPTION:

Cruising speeds	24.1 mpg
Overall for test	19.9 mpg

Plain lines enhance the new Zephyr, rather than detract from it. Note the large rear window, good ground clearance and minimal overhang.

Mock-wood dashboard is jarring feature as is the placement of controls directly behind the steering wheel. Dash, is padded, but reflects in screen.

IS THIS FORD'S BEST CAR? continued

possible to unlock the driver's side door. However, this fault has apparently been cured on later production models.

Forward visibility is good. The driver can see the full width of the front of the car (which is not as wide from behind the wheel as it appears from the outside) and the tips of both rear mudguards are in easy view for parking. The dashboard is padded, but the interests of safety would be better served if the covering was matt, not gloss. As it is, it reflects quite badly in the windscreen at times, hampering vision.

The instruments themselves, well placed in front of the driver, are set in a not-too-realistic mock-wood panel—a throw-back to US cars of the 'thirties.

Like most Ford cars, the instruments consist of a speedo, water temperature and fuel contents gauges. Warning lights do the rest. The lights come into action by pulling a knob on the right hand side of the dash. This also controls the instrument lighting level and, when twisted to its limit, works the one interior light above the mirror.

A manual choke is fitted. Its knob is next to that of the screen wiper. Both are placed directly behind the steering wheel and can only be reached easily by people with two elbows in their left arm. The choke does not stay in the out position without manual assistance, which makes driving awkward for the first couple of miles each day. Positioning of minor controls such as these is something Ford designers would do well to examine again.

The pull-out handbrake is well placed for left handed use and because of its position on the lower part of the dash, visual verification as to its position is possible.

In England individual layback front seats are available as optional equipment on the Zephyr. These would be very nice when combined with a floor change for the really excellent four speed, all synchromesh gearbox. However, a floor change is not available. Not that the steering column shift is unsatisfactory—on the contrary it is light and positive, although rather long in movement—that wonderful box of cogs lends itself beautifully to a more sporty application.

It almost comes as a surprise to realise that the power plant is basically the same as the one that has been used in Zephyrs for years. The capacity—2.6 litres—remains the same, but there is 98 bhp available under foot. On the road it feels as though there is at least 3 litres up front. It is a very good engine and even with its newly found power is by no means overstressed. Super fuel causes no comment from the engine which, at all times, is smooth and flexible.

Although the engine will run smoothly at low speeds in high gear it does not really get with it until the speedo needle is hovering around the 35 mph mark. From there on there is ample acceleration. However, really staggering results can be obtained by using the gearbox. As the performance chart shows, high speeds can be obtained in the indirect gears which makes third ideal for overtaking on the highway or for use in twisty, hilly country. I found first, which has such powerful synchromesh that it can be engaged at almost any speed, ideal for hauling out of tight hairpins and getting cracking again after coming down to a dead-slow speed in traffic. Maybe some people think four speeds are too many for a car of this type, but it must be remembered that this is a fast touring car and not one designed specifically for softies to mope around town in.

Out on the open road the Zephyr will steam along at its steady 80 mph with still plenty in hand for overtaking. Servo assisted disc brakes have been used at the front only. These are remarkably effective and well able to bring the car to a grinding stop from high speed time after time without judder or fade. There is a tendency for the rear wheels to lock first at low speeds—a trait common to disc/drum combinations.

Ford, it would seem, has not overlooked roadholding. It matches the go and stop departments. The Zephyr sits down firmly on the road and feels taut and sure footed. Thrown around bitumen-surfaced corners really fast, the tail will break away first after initial understeer. I did detect some shake through the steering wheel during hard cornering which, I suspect, was coming from the inside front wheel.

On rough surfaces the car behaved well most of the time. I did encounter some hopping about of the tail, but never suspension bottoming. Although comfortable, the rough road abilities of the Zephyr could not be called completely smooth; the passengers are aware of surface changes but they never get jolted.

This new Zephyr is a worthy successor to the well established older model, but is a vastly different concept of car. Its appeal is wider and specifications enlightened as they must be for a car selling on the International market in 1962.

There are shortcomings, however. For instance, there is no heater/demister or even a windscreen washer. On the other hand the manual shift model sells for a modest £1369—around £300 less than most other cars of comparable specifications and performance.

This new Zephyr is a good car. I would even go as far as to say that it is the best in the current Ford range.   #

Ford Zephyr 6 Estate Car 2,553 c.c.

ESTATE car bodies for the large British Fords, until recently, have been rather obvious adaptations of standard saloons, adequate and praiseworthy but, distinctly, still conversions. With the current Zephyr 4 and 6 and the Zodiac III, E. D. Abbott Ltd. have been able to restyle the bodywork to make each estate car a Ford model in its own right, and the benefit is immediately apparent. There is an unbroken roofline, even though from forward of the centre door pillars the front is the same as the corresponding saloon. The designer's rather rakish treatment of the back half does not appear to have been hampered by any limitations of the standard saloon body shell.

Seafaring folk might well describe this estate car as a spanking big craft with a nice turn of speed. It is big, by our standards, but one soon forgets this as the ease of handling and the unusual smoothness and quietness become apparent.

We had rather longer than is usual with a Road Test vehicle to appreciate the Zephyr's qualities, for it took some members of our staff to Geneva and back, apart from the normal test mileage. For the 1,300 and more miles of this Continental journey, driven hard and well loaded, its fuel consumption was a very creditable 19·6 m.p.g., somewhat better than the 18·2 m.p.g. recorded during over 1,000 miles of normal test mileage in this country. Incidentally, the Zephyr 6 used no measurable quantity of oil at all in its runs across France and in Switzerland. London traffic caused the fuel consumption to rise to 16·6 m.p.g., whereas a very typical normal road journey through the English Midlands produced 24·9 m.p.g. By way of contrast, we noted that a steady 35 m.p.h. on the level in overdrive top gave the impressive figure of almost 40 m.p.g.

Premium fuel was used for taking our test figures, but the engine will also run very happily on a 50-50 mixture of premium and regular petrol without pinking.

This 2,553 c.c. six-cylinder Ford engine gives the impression of being a glutton for work, if not for fuel, and is particularly smooth and quiet throughout its range. It started readily, hot or cold, except when the carburettor fuel level produced jet starvation on a 1-in-3 test hill.

Since a Zephyr estate car was last tested (2 August 1957) the net engine power has been increased from 85 b.h.p. at

PRICES	£	s	d
Estate car	922	0	0
Purchase tax	192	12	11
Total (in G.B.)	1,114	12	11
Extras (including P.T.)			
Overdrive	51	7	1
Heater	18	2	6
Screenwasher	1	15	0
Safety belts (each)	5	0	0
Radio (push button)	26	17	0

Make · FORD   Type · Zephyr Six Estate Car

Manufacturers: Ford Motor Co. Ltd., Dagenham, Essex

Test Conditions

Weather, mainly dry, occasional showers, with 12-15 m.p.h. wind
Temperature ... 45 deg. F. (7 deg. C.). Barometer 29·8in. Hg.
Dry and wet concrete and tarmac surfaces.

Weight

Kerb weight (with oil, water and half-full fuel tank) 25·8cwt (2,893lb-1,312kg).
Front-rear distribution, per cent F, 53; R. 47.
Laden as tested .... 28·8cwt (3,229lb-1,465kg.)

Turning Circles

Between kerbs .... L. 37ft 0in.; R. 36ft 7·5in.
Between walls .... L. 38ft 11in.; R. 38ft 6·5in.
Turns of steering wheel lock to lock.............. 4·5

Performance Data

Overdrive top gear m.p.h. per 1,000 r.p.m. 26·2
Top gear m.p.h. per 1,000 r.p.m.................. 20·3
Mean piston speed at max. power 2,470ft/min
Engine revs. at mean max. speed ...... 4,470 r.p.m.
B.h.p. per ton laden 69

FUEL AND OIL CONSUMPTION

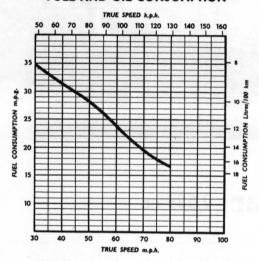

FUEL.................................Premium Grade (97 octane RM)
Test Distance ....2,407 miles
Overall Consumption ....18·9 m.p.g. (15·0 lit/100 km.)
Normal Range ....16-28 m.p.g. (17·7-10·1 lit/100 km.)
OIL: SAE 20 ... Consumption 10,000 m.p.g.

MAXIMUM SPEEDS AND ACCELERATION (mean) TIMES

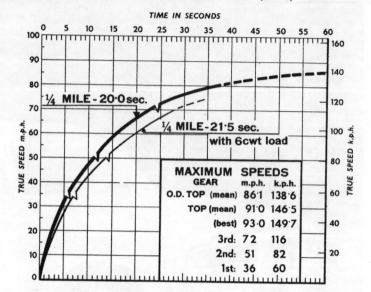

¼ MILE - 20·0 sec.
¼ MILE - 21·5 sec. with 6cwt load

MAXIMUM SPEEDS		
GEAR	m.p.h.	k.p.h.
O.D. TOP (mean)	86·1	138·6
TOP (mean)	91·0	146·5
(best)	93·0	149·7
3rd:	72	116
2nd:	51	82
1st:	36	60

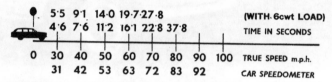

							(WITH 6cwt LOAD)
5·5	9·1	14·0	19·7	27·8			
4·6	7·6	11·2	16·1	22·8	37·8		TIME IN SECONDS

0	30	40	50	60	70	80	90	100	TRUE SPEED m.p.h.
	31	42	53	63	72	83	92		CAR SPEEDOMETER

Speed range and time in seconds

m.p.h.	Top	3rd	2nd	1st
10—30	—	7·0 (8·8)	4·4 (5·2)	3·4 (3·5)
20—40	10·7 (12·4)	7·0 (8·4)	4·7 (5·8)	—
30—50	11·0 (13·3)	7·1 (9·1)	6·1 (7·6)	—
40—60	12·7 (15·6)	8·3 (11·4)	—	—
50—70	15·5 (18·8)	11·1 (13·5)	—	—
60—80	39·9	—	—	—

(figures in brackets with 6cwt load)

BRAKES	Pedal load	Retardation	Equiv. distance
(from 30 m.p.h. in neutral)	25lb	0·26g	116ft
	50lb	0·63g	48ft
	75lb	0·95g	32ft
	80lb	0·99g	30·6ft
	Handbrake	0·24g	126ft

CLUTCH   Pedal load and travel—50lb and 5·5in.

HILL CLIMBING AT STEADY SPEEDS

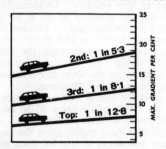

2nd: 1 in 5·3
3rd: 1 in 8·1
Top: 1 in 12·8

GEAR PULL	Top	3rd	2nd
(lb per ton)	175	275	410
Speed range (m.p.h.)	40-46	35-43	30-35

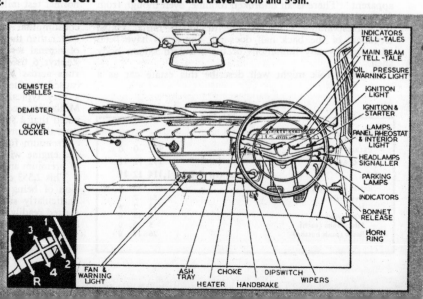

4,400 r.p.m. to 98 at 4,750 r.p.m., and the mean maximum speed is now a very useful 91 m.p.h., 8 m.p.h. more than before. However, the last model lacked what is surely the most important Ford advance for years, the four-speed all-synchromesh gearbox now fitted, so that there are no equivalent intermediate gear ratios which can be compared for acceleration times.

For a standing quarter-mile, the present estate car takes 20·0sec, the former 20·9sec. From rest it reaches 50 m.p.h. in 11·2sec and 80 m.p.h. in 37·8sec, whereas the corresponding times before were 12·6 and 40·2sec respectively. These are appreciable, if not outstanding, gains which result in the livelier road performance demanded by modern conditions. Both cars weighed roughly the same, the new one being the heavier by only 65lb.

Concerning the gearbox, it was unfortunate that on the Geneva journey the pilot bearing in the first motion shaft failed. This caused noise and roughness in the indirect gears, compelling the drivers to use direct and overdrive top much more than they would have normally. However, this was an additional test of the flexibility and good slogging power of the engine. When the bearing fault had been rectified back at the works, the gearbox became a very quiet one, with well-spaced ratios giving practical maximum speeds of 36, 51 and 72 m.p.h. for first, second and third.

Borg-Warner overdrive was fitted as an extra to our test car and operated on second, third and top—even on bottom if you wanted to have a bit of fun. With the good spacing of the direct ratios we decided that the most practical value of the overdrive was with top gear on motorways and the long straight roads of France. It is engaged or locked out by a push-pull control below the facia, in conjunction with the usual Borg-Warner kick-down mechanism operated by the accelerator pedal.

On all four gears the synchromesh operation was beyond reproach. The steering column gearchange mechanism was quite good, but there was just that trace of whippiness in the lever and the slight lag in response that make many drivers prefer a floor change for its directness. Like the engine, the transmission had no vibration periods. There is quite a long travel on the clutch pedal before anything happens, and the small amount of working motion can result in some jerky take-offs unless care is taken and the pedal is fully depressed. The clutch itself proved well up to all demands made on it, including several attempts to start on a 1-in-3 gradient. This proved just too much for the Zephyr, although it gets away happily on 1-in-4.

Consistent Under Varying Loads

Most estate cars behave quite differently between running light and fully loaded. Not so the Zephyr, which very nearly ignores such minor irritations as a 6cwt load of concrete blocks in the back, or a full load of passengers and luggage. With the 6cwt load it took only 1·5sec more (21·5sec) for a standing quarter-mile, at the end of which it was doing 64 m.p.h. (unladen 68 m.p.h.).

In normal trim its ride qualities are impressive, and it sails along on good or indifferent road surfaces without exhibiting any vices. Little road noise is transmitted to the interior and even on quite sharp corners the amount of heeling over is small. Perhaps because of Ford experience in the East African Safari, the suspension shows up particularly well on a simulated "washboard," or corrugated surface. At 40 m.p.h. on this the car feels better than most others we have put to this severe test, the ride smoothing out to a remarkable degree. It is less happy at the same speed on *pavé*, bouncing around quite a lot, while at 50 m.p.h. the car becomes difficult to keep under control. All these characteristics remain unchanged with a 6cwt load, except that on reasonably good surfaces the general comfort of the ride is enhanced. With this load there was a slight amount of rear-end swing, but nothing like so much as with most other estate cars.

Rather low-geared, the steering is light and positive. The car understeers, but not obtrusively, and is directionally stable. On a motorway in a fresh breeze it holds its

Opening well clear of the heads of all but the very tall is this big tailgate. The guard rail at the front of the load space is also a lifting handle for the folding squab

course well without constant and tiring need for steering corrections, and the large body is not particularly affected by gusty side winds. There is no unusual tendency for the tail to slide on wet roads, and deliberately induced skids can be controlled very easily.

With gentle applications at low speeds the brakes, disc at the front, drums at the rear, seem at first to lack "bite." Only a small increase in pedal load brings in full servo action smoothly and the brakes then become excellent. As will be seen from our table, an 80lb load on the pedal is enough to give maximum braking. Loads above this simply increase the stopping distance by locking the rear wheels. At maximum braking there is no wheel locking, judder or sideways movement of the car. In fact, the system is highly satisfactory.

The handbrake lever is of the pull-out T-handle type below the facia to the left. It is quite a long reach to get

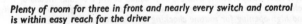

Plenty of room for three in front and nearly every switch and control is within easy reach for the driver

This view shows the lines of the Zephyr estate car to advantage

Ford Zephyr 6 Estate Car . . .

at it, and although it would hold the car, up or down, on a 1-in-4 hill, it would only just hold it facing down 1-in-3, not up.

A comfortable driving position and room for two passengers distinguish the front bench seat, and there is a wide, folding central armrest, useful for locating a single passenger. The p.v.c. upholstery material is non-slip and the squab gives good support at the vital lower part of the back, preventing slouching. The driver sits high, and the vast surrounding areas of glass give him, and all passengers, a commanding all-round view. Pedal angles are quite good, the organ-pedal type accelerator being well positioned, but the dipswitch is rather deeply embedded in the floor covering and not always easy to use quickly.

Door release catches are unobtrusive, below the front

ends of the four armrests, and these catches have been modified in shape recently for easier operation. The window winders are also well placed for easy use, but the heater switch, which has a warning light, is a long way from the driver and would be better at the opposite end of the central panel carrying this, a cigarette lighter and an ashtray. The heater itself delivers a good volume of air and has two large control knobs on the facia. Unfortunately, a lot of the air seems to miss the driver's feet, and only warms him above the ankles. The demister grilles also seem to disperse the hot air rather widely instead of concentrating it right on the windscreen.

The back seat squab is too upright for comfort over long distances. This is probably connected with the hinging arrangements for folding the back flat to increase the size of the luggage platform. All doors give good clearance for getting into or out of the seats, and interior air circulation can be varied widely by using the front-door quarter lights

Left: Rear compartment with the seat squab down, a second means of access to the luggage space. There is a lot of room on the floor behind the front seat for baggage wanted in a hurry. Right: Like the tailgate, the self-supporting bonnet gives a wide and high opening for routine checking and maintenance

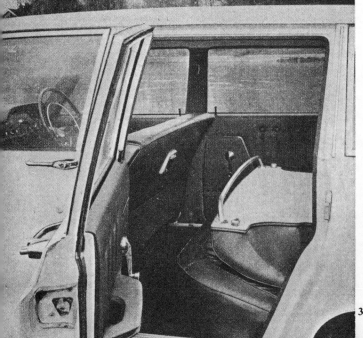

or the large forward-hinged windows behind the rear doors.

Safety features include a plastic surround to the interior mirror, padded edges to the facia and the shelf below it on the left, a dished steering wheel and soft sun vizors. A make-up mirror is well embedded in the padding of the passenger's vizor. There is no shelf for oddments below the facia on the driver's side, but there is a slim map pocket in each front door.

A cowled horizontal-strip speedometer, with mileage recorder but no separate trip register, is visible through the large steering wheel, and its panel incorporates a fuel gauge, water temperature gauge and indicator lights. The screen wipers are effective at all car speeds, and the control knob varies the speed of wiping. It also operates the washer, but this knob is rather out of the way behind the steering wheel and gear lever. With its locking glove box on the left, the facia is plain but neat and functional.

A headlamp flasher knob on the end of the turn indicator lever is for finger-tip use from the steering wheel, and the headlamps give plenty of light for fast driving. One ingenious Ford device is a switch at the extreme right of the facia, for parking purposes. This leaves only one front and one rear lamp lit (offside in Britain) and at the same time isolates the ignition and starter. Thus the car cannot be started with only these two lamps operating.

When the rear seat squab is folded forward there is still clearance between its end and the back of the front seat. This enables loads to be reached more easily through the back doors. The tailgate, which has a window as wide as that of the Zephyr saloon, is of fibreglass. It gives a high and wide opening, and is supported by vertical stainless steel struts linked to torsion bars below the floor, which is covered with a tough p.v.c. material, easy to clean.

A stainless steel bar is mounted behind the rear seat squab, for use as a handle for moving it and as a guard rail for stopping bulky luggage from sliding forward under sudden braking. The floor space, with the seat back flat, is 5ft 10in. long and 4ft 9.5in. wide, but unlike that of the more recent estate car in the Ford family, the Cortina, this floor is very high above ground. Available carrying space is said to be 61 cu. ft. with the floor flat and 29 cu. ft. with the back seat in use.

How much of this space is safely and conveniently usable depends on the owner and what he wants to carry. Normal holiday luggage for six people would probably disperse itself just as well, and more securely, in the 21 cu. ft. boot of the standard saloon, but a pig or two would probably complain. Spare wheel and tools are below the rear floor in a separate compartment.

Fords were pioneers of reduced maintenance, and although there are still 12 points needing a grease-gun, this is required only at 5,000-mile intervals. Engine oil changes are recommended at the same mileage, while the gearbox and final drive simply call for the occasional check and topping-up.

For those who want a fast, big, tough estate car that will take everything in its long stride, the Zephyr 6 should have a very strong appeal. In a dual role of workhorse and town carriage it can have few rivals at the price.

Specification

ENGINE

Cylinders	...	6 in-line
Bore	...	82·55mm (3·25in.)
Stroke	...	79·50mm (3·13in.)
Displacement	...	2,553 c.c. (155·8 cu. in.)
Valve gear	...	Overhead, pushrods and rockers
Compression ratio	...	8·3-to-1, option 7·0 to 1
Carburettor	...	Zenith 36 WIA-2 downdraught
Fuel pump	...	AC Delco mechanical diaphragm
Oil filter	...	AC Delco or Purolator-Tecalemit full flow
Max. power	...	98 b.h.p. (net) at 4,750 r.p.m.
Max. torque	...	134 lb. ft. at 2,000 r.p.m.

TRANSMISSION

Clutch	...	Ford-Borg and Beck single dry plate 8·5in. dia.
Gearbox	...	Four-speed all-synchromesh, with Borg-Warner overdrive; column gear change
Overall ratios	...	OD Top 2·75, Top 3·55, OD 3rd 3·89, 3rd 5·0, OD 2nd 6·1, 2nd 7·85, 1st 11·21, Reverse 11·86
Final drive	...	Hypoid bevel 3·55 to 1

CHASSIS

Construction	...	Integral with welded steel body

SUSPENSION

Front	...	MacPherson independent coil spring and Armstrong telescopic damper units; anti-roll bar
Rear	...	Live-axle with half-elliptic springs, Armstrong lever-arm dampers
Steering	...	Burman recirculating ball Wheel dia., 17·0in.

BRAKES

Type	...	Girling hydraulic, with Bendix vacuum mechanical servo. Disc F., drum rear
Dimensions	...	Discs 9·75in. dia. Drums 9·0in. dia. 2·25in. wide shoes
Swept area	...	F. 203 sq. in.; R. 127 sq in. Total: 330 sq. in. (235 sq. in. per ton laden)

WHEELS

Type	...	Pressed steel disc, 4-stud. 4·5in. wide rim
Tyres	...	Goodyear tubeless, 6·70–13in.

EQUIPMENT

Battery	...	12-volt 57-amp. hr.
Headlamps	...	Lucas sealed beam 50-40-watt
Reversing lamp	...	None
Electric fuses	...	1
Screen wipers	...	2, variable-speed self-parking
Screen washer	...	Extra
Interior heater	...	Extra
Safety belts	...	Extra, Irving lap and diagonal
Interior trim	...	P.v.c.
Floor covering	...	Moulded rubber
Starting handle	...	No provision
Jack	...	Screw type
Jacking points	...	2 each side
Other bodies	...	Four-door saloon

MAINTENANCE

Fuel tank	...	12·5 Imp. gallons (no reserve)
Cooling system	...	21 pints (including heater)
Engine sump	...	6·5 pints SAE20 or 20W. Change oil and filter element every 5,000 miles
Gearbox and over-drive	...	4 pints SAE80. Change oil after first 5,000 miles only
Final drive	...	2·5 pints SAE90. No provision for oil change
Grease	...	12 points every 5,000 miles
Tyre pressures	...	24 p.s.i. F and R (normal driving); 30 p.s.i. F and R (with 6cwt load)

Scale: 0·3in. to 1ft.

Cushions uncompressed.

OVERALL LENGTH 15′ 0″
OVERALL WIDTH 5′ 9″
OVERALL HEIGHT 4′ 10·5″
GROUND CLEARANCE 6·8
FRONT TRACK 4′ 5″   WHEELBASE 8′ 11″   REAR TRACK 4′ 4″

Kelsey and Trevor Blokdyk at the controls, and should be a rising force in the 1965 series.

During this test it was necessary to conserve the clutch, which at that stage was virtually standard and therefore prone to slipping on take-off. So these acceleration times (which compare favourably with a car like the 3·4 Jag) are by no means the best this enraged Zodiac is capable of.

The test was also kept to the minimum as it would be

F O R D ZODIAC MK. 3
(with Superformance stage 5 racing conversion)

THE arrival of a completely-new saloon in national production car racing is always something of an event. There have been odd Zephyrs raced in club events, and the lively and tough 2·5-litre engine has been used in one or two racing specials and G.T. prototypes in South Africa over the past decade.

But now, for the first time, we have a full-blooded and serious Zodiac conversion running in the national championship series and in such major events as the Nine-Hour Race.

The Zephyr/Zodiac small-six unit is not exactly a peach for conversion because of its awkward porting, but Raymond Mays licked this one some time back with his cast-aluminium 6-port head.

Using this as a basis, Basil van Rooyen of Superformance went to work on a standard, brand-new Zodiac

QUICKER-THAN-SOMEWHAT

to make this luxury saloon do things which will surprise most owners of what is a dignified road car.

Details are given elsewhere in this report, so we need only summarize and say that Basil has raised the Zodiac's b.h.p. to a claimed 222 at 6,200 (quite a jump from the standard 114 at 4,800) to produce sparkling acceleration and a top speed of about 117 m.p.h.

Capacity is not affected, except that the engine is bored to the permissible oversize and 85·1 mm. pistons are used in place of the standard 82·55 mm., raising capacity to just over 2·7 litres.

Compression ratio has gone up to 10·5 to 1, triple twin-choke Webers are used, together with Superite tuned-length twin exhausts straight-through.

Basil and his Superformance team also breathed on the Raymond Mays head with their own brand of magic, and dropped and stiffened the suspension for the circuit.

We should remark that this car is equivalent to what Superformance lists as its Stage 5 tune, though it has not yet had the full works. It was still using standard exhaust valve sizes, at the time of this test run, though this was scheduled for a change for the Nine-Hour.

It is a car still under development and only raced experimentally at this stage. Its full potential, Basil believes, is yet to come. It has shown itself to be fastest in its class (Class W in the saloon series) with Bob

pointless to risk R3,600 worth of highly-specialized car more than was strictly necessary to get basic figures, using the calibrated rev-counter (which is accurate).

With its standard gearbox, 3·9 rear axle and using Dunlop R6 tyres, the Zodiac was geared for 17·8 m.p.h. per thousand r.p.m. in direct top (23·0 m.p.h. in overdrive) and showed ripping acceleration right through.

In its 0·777 to 1, overdrive, for instance — which is only occasionally used towards the end of the longer straights — the car picks up speed fairly strongly. On balance, though, direct drive is slightly undergeared and overdrive overgeared, and the car has a 120-plus speed potential.

Up to the time of this test its racing career, still experimental, had been dogged by gremlins, but it certainly shows great promise.

Its first outing was in the Border 100 in July, where it was third fastest car in practice, but threw a rod at high revs. At Lourenço Marques on July 26, Bob Kelsey was lying second overall when the sump plug fell out. In the Rand Winter Trophy at Kyalami on August 1 it was running behind the Lotus-Cortina twins when a side shaft broke.

At Maritzburg on August 23, it came fifth overall behind the Lotus twins, the Cortina G.T. and Adler's Taunus. Then at Killarney on September 19 it showed itself to be much faster than the Taunus, and was running fourth behind the Lotus pair and the Marriner Studebaker when Trevor Blokdyk landed it in the sand at the trackside and had to be pushed out.

But it has been getting better all the time, and should have a bright future, gremlins notwithstanding.

Early experiences have decided Basil to keep a normal working limit of 6,000 r.p.m. (about 76 m.p.h. in third, 107 m.p.h. in top) though we were able to use 7,000 in short bursts during this test.

Roadholding is good, with stability at speed.

In all this is a polished conversion, though at its overall cost of something like R1,200 it is not the sort of thing that the ordinary man will ask for over the counter. Nevertheless, Basil has used the car on the road, and in 85 m.p.h. cruising on normal premium fuel he claims about 22 m.p.g.

On the track this drops to the region of 12 m.p.g.,

which is about the same as the standard car at full bore, but at much higher speed.

As a last feature of the test, we put the sound level indicator to work, and the Zodiac nearly took it off the clock. We registered 106·5 dB at the ton.

Even shouts at 12 in. range became meaningless blurs of sound under those conditions, and communication is impossible except by signs. Not to blame the Zodiac for this, though: every racing saloon with straight-throughs under the front seats has similar side-effects.

One last point of interest: Superformance market a Stage 3 version of this Zodiac modification (for Zephyrs as well), for about R250 plus fitting.

This consists of two twin-choke Webers, a Van Rooyen road camshaft, modified head and Superite manifolds to yield 145 net b.h.p. and give an estimated maximum speed of 110, while retaining such smoothness that the car will idle at 400 r.p.m.

It all depends on how far one wants to go!   ●

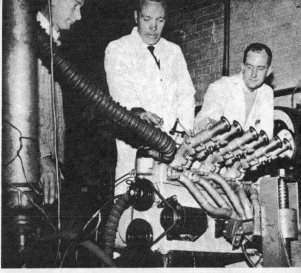

(From left to right) **Bob Kelsey, Brian Wheble (test bed manager), and Peter Kelsey (Bob's brother, who works at Voms), preparing to run the potent Superformance Zodiac engine on Voms' test bed in Johannesburg.** *(Picture: Barry Curtis).*

ZODIAC MK. 3 (Superformance conversion)

SPECIFICATION

MAKE AND MODEL: 1964 Zodiac with overdrive, modified for racing by Superformance, still under development.
TRANSMISSION: Standard 4-speed with overdrive, column shift.
GEAR RATIOS: 1st: 3·163 Top: Direct
  2nd: 2·214 O/D: 0·777
  3rd: 1·414
FINAL DRIVE RATIO: 3·9 to 1.

MODIFICATION DETAILS

ENGINE CAPACITY: 2,708 c.c.
BORE AND STROKE: 85·1 x 79·5 mm. (slight bore oversize).
COMPRESSION RATIO: 10·5 to 1.
CYLINDER HEAD: Aluminium 6-port Raymond Mays, modified by Superformance.
CARBURETTORS: Three twin-choke 42 mm. Webers.
CAMSHAFT: Van Rooyen track camshaft, with 10·6 mm. lift.
EXHAUST MANIFOLDS: Tuned-length twin manifolds by Superite.
EXHAUST: Straight-through twin exhausts.
FLYWHEEL: Lightened, balanced, and stepped to improve clutch pressure.
CRANKSHAFT: Standard, dynamically-balanced.
TYRES: Dunlop R6 racing.
SUSPENSION: Lowered about 2 in. front and rear, Koni shock absorbers at rear.
INTERIOR: Front bucket racing seats by Superformance, wood-rim steering wheel.

PERFORMANCE

(Figures based on corrected rev-counter readings.)
ACCELERATION THROUGH GEARS:

M.P.H.	Sec.	M.P.H.	Sec.
0—30	2·9	0—70	10·5
0—40	4·2	0—80	13·9
0—50	5·8	0—90	20·1
0—60	7·6	0—100	28·0

STANDING-START QUARTER-MILE: 14·95 sec.
GEARED SPEEDS AT 6,200 R.P.M.:
  1st: 35·0 3rd: 78·5 O/D Top: 142·6
  2nd: 50·0 Top: 110·4
MAXIMUM SPEED IN TOP: 116·4 m.p.h.
MAXIMUM SPEED IN O/D TOP: 116·8 m.p.h.
ROAD FUEL CONSUMPTION: 22 m.p.g. at about 85 m.p.h.
RACING FUEL CONSUMPTION: About 12 m.p.g.
MINIMUM INTERIOR NOISE LEVEL: 106·5 decibels at 100 m.p.h.
CAR SUPPLIED BY: Superformance, 68, Booysens Road, Reuven, Johannesburg.

MODIFICATION EFFECTS

ENGINE OUTPUT: Raised to about 222 b.h.p. at 6,000 r.p.m. at coast.
TORQUE: Not measured.
TOTAL COST OF MODIFICATIONS: About R1,200.

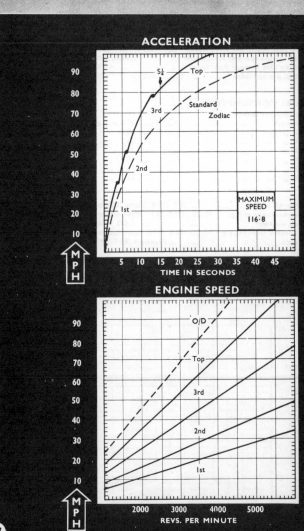

Autocar Road Test 2022

MAKE: **Ford**

TYPE: **Executive Zodiac 2,555 c.c.**

Speed range, gear ratios and time in seconds

m.p.h.	Top (3·55-7·10)	Inter (5·16-10·32)	Low (8·48-16·96)
10—30	—	6·5	4·2
20—40	8·5	6·6	4·7
30—50	10·3	7·1	—
40—60	12·1	8·3	—
50—70	13·9	10·9	—
60—80	18·2		

TEST CONDITIONS

Weather ... ... Showery with 10-15 m.p.h. wind
Temperature ... ...7 deg C. (44 deg. F.)
Barometer, 29·00in. Hg. Mainly dry concrete and tarmac
surfaces

WEIGHT

Kerb weight (with oil, water and half-full fuel tank)
25·2cwt (2,833lb-1,286kg)
Front-rear distribution, per cent ... 52·4F., 47·6R
Laden as tested ... ... 28·2cwt (3,159lb-1,438kg)

TURNING CIRCLES

Between kerbs ... ... L, 38ft. 0in.; R, 36ft. 10in.
Between walls ... ... L, 40ft. 2in.; R, 39ft. 0in.
Steering wheel turns lock to lock ... ... 4·6

PERFORMANCE DATA

Top gear m.p.h. per 1,000 r.p.m. ... ... 20·3
Mean piston speed at max. power ... 2,500ft./min.
Engine revs at mean max. speed 4,630
B.h.p. per ton laden ... ... 77·2

FUEL CONSUMPTION

At constant Speeds
30 m.p.h. ... ... 33·0 m.p.g.
40 ,, ... 30·0 ,,
50 ,, ... 26·3 ,,
60 ,, ... 21·6 ,,
70 ,, ... 18·2 ,,
80 ,, ... 15·2 ,,
90 ,, ... 12·3 ,,

Overall m.p.g. ... ... 17·7 (15·9 litres/100km)
Normal range m.p.g. 15-20 (18·8-14·1 litres/100km)
Test distance ... ... 1,453 miles
Estimated (DIN) m.p.g. 16·6 (17·0 litres/100km)
Grade ... ... Premium (95-97RM)

OIL CONSUMPTION

SAE 20W/20 ... ... 3,700 m.p.g.

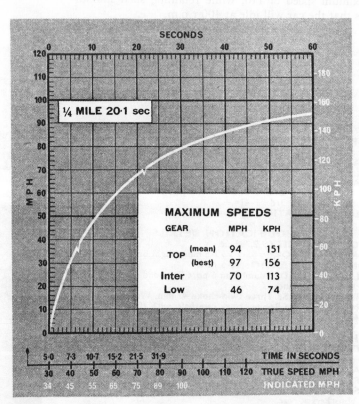

¼ MILE 20·1 sec

MAXIMUM SPEEDS

GEAR		MPH	KPH
TOP	(mean)	94	151
	(best)	97	156
Inter		70	113
Low		46	74

TIME IN SECONDS
5·0 7·3 10·7 15·2 21·5 31·9
30 40 50 60 70 80 90 100 110 120 TRUE SPEED MPH
34 45 55 65 75 89 100 INDICATED MPH

BRAKES

	Pedal load	Retardation	Equiv. distance
(from 30 m.p.h.	25 lb	0·22g	137ft
in neutral)	50lb	0·55g	55ft
	75lb	0·97g	31·0ft
	Handbrake	0·35g	86ft

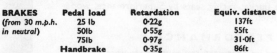

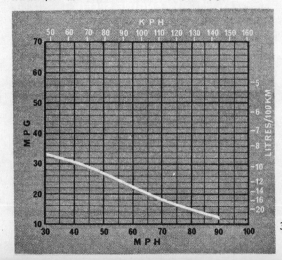

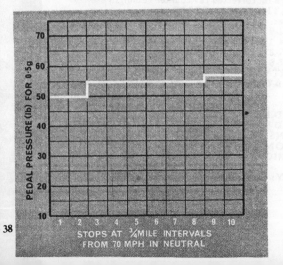

STOPS AT ¾MILE INTERVALS
FROM 70 MPH IN NEUTRAL

Ford Executive Zodiac 2,555 c.c.

AT A GLANCE: Performance and comfort below expectations; Powerful and stable braking; Suspension satisfactory in the U.K., less so on continental roads; Smooth and quiet engine; Good detail finish and full equipment.

Autocar Road Test

NUMBER 2022

MANUFACTURER:
Ford Motor Co. Ltd., Warley, Brentwood, Essex

PRICES

Basic	£1,099	1s	1d
Purchase Tax	£216	0s	9d
Total (in G.B.)	£1,315	1s	10d

PERFORMANCE SUMMARY

Mean maximum speed... ...	94 m.p.h.
Standing start ¼-mile ...	20·1 sec
0-60 m.p.h.	15·2 sec
30-70 m.p.h. in intermediate ...	18·0 sec

FUEL CONSUMPTION

Overall fuel consumption ...	17·7 m.p.g.
Miles per tankful	212

CERTAINLY not demonstrative by nature, the British sometimes display surprising quirks of exhibitionism and individuality when it comes to personal possessions. Whether the Ford market research department were relying on this to account for the success of their latest "new" model, the Executive Zodiac with its extra fittings, or simply the status-conscious young businessman eager to make his mark, is not known. Whatever the reasons, the car has caught on, and already examples can be seen quite often on the streets. With no noticeable styling changes since the range was introduced over three years ago, the Zodiac now covers a broader potential market.

Among the items Ford consider essential to the executive are radio, seat belts, fog and spot lamps, separate reclining front seats and automatic

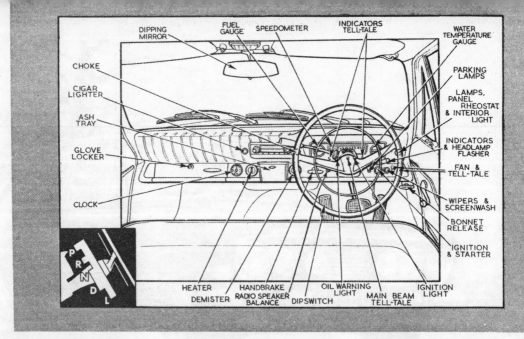

Diagram labels: DIPPING MIRROR, FUEL GAUGE, SPEEDOMETER, INDICATORS TELL-TALE, WATER TEMPERATURE GAUGE, CHOKE, CIGAR LIGHTER, ASH TRAY, GLOVE LOCKER, CLOCK, PARKING LAMPS, LAMPS, PANEL RHEOSTAT & INTERIOR LIGHT, INDICATORS & HEADLAMP FLASHER, FAN & TELL-TALE, WIPERS & SCREENWASH, BONNET RELEASE, IGNITION & STARTER, HEATER DEMISTER, HANDBRAKE RADIO SPEAKER BALANCE, DIPSWITCH, OIL WARNING LIGHT, MAIN BEAM TELL-TALE, IGNITION LIGHT

transmission. To convey an impression of aristocratic sobriety, the inside is trimmed in a mixture of black leather, p.v.c. and carpet (even in the boot), and special paints are available like the acrylic gold of our test car. Even after two Alpine crossings through snow and slush, and parking for several nights under trees inhabited by birds, a quick wash was sufficient to restore the gleaming gloss.

Mechanically the car is a Zodiac with the 2½-litre six developing a claimed 109 b.h.p. net at 4,800 r.p.m. (11 more than the Zephyr 6). A recent change to all Zodiacs has been to replace the dual-outlet exhaust system with a single, large-bore one, which leaves a vacant niche under the tail of the car, as on the Zephyr 4 and 6. We say "claimed" advisedly, because by comparison with the automatic Zephyr 6 tested a year ago not all this power seems to be realized.

Performance

Despite the encouragement of a speedometer that is a full 10 m.p.h. fast at the top end, the mean maximum of our test car was only 94 m.p.h.—just 0·7 better than the Zephyr. Acceleration times, too, show little difference, the step-off being a bit smarter and saving just over a second from rest to 60 m.p.h. (Executive Zodiac 15·2; Zephyr 6 16·5sec). From 30 to 70 m.p.h. in top gear took 24·2sec on our Zodiac, compared with 24·6sec on the Zephyr.

The automatic changepoint from low to intermediate takes place at 36 m.p.h. and we found that, although the engine would run happily up another 10 m.p.h. when held in low, these extra revs made no difference to the acceleration times. Holding intermediate gave a corresponding lift to its speed range, from the automatic limit of 60 to about 70 m.p.h., and here it cut the times by about a second if one delayed the change into top.

On the open road one tends to use this over-ride quite a lot, partly to avoid the surge of a kick-down change at full throttle, but chiefly to engage intermediate above the maximum kick-down speed of 49 m.p.h. From 50 to 70 takes 3sec less in intermediate, so overtaking is appreciably quicker and one has the added security of full engine braking when tucking back into a line of traffic.

Transmission

In towns, of course, it is best to leave the selector in its "D" slot and let the transmission do the work instead. Normally there is only very slight creep (one could just hold the car static on the flat without the brake lamps lighting), but the idling speed of our engine was set rather slow; a little too slow, perhaps, because after a cold start the choke knob had to be left about half an inch out for two or three miles to avoid the embarrassment of the engine dying in the middle of a junction just as one moved off; restarts take a little longer with an automatic because one must first move the selector to neutral (or Park), operate the starter, then move the lever back to D.

Upward gear changes of this Borg-Warner type 35 box were not as smooth as other examples we have tried. At full throttle from intermediate to top the car seemed to take a great gulp which set passengers' heads nodding, although with a bit of practice one could do better lower down the speed range by letting up the accelerator for an almost imperceptible engagement. Engaging intermediate to supplement the braking was somewhat delayed. Downward changes from top to intermediate on the over-run—for instance, at the approach to a roundabout—had to be anticipated by about 3sec, as there was this delay between the message and the action. This lag represents about 100yds at 60 m.p.h.

For such a large car without power steering the effort is light, and even when parking one does not have to heave at the wheel. The low gearing is not a handicap either, and with its compact turning circle of 37ft between kerbs, the Zodiac is an easy car to manœuvre through city streets. The sides bulge slightly, but one sits high enough to see the near side edge of the bonnet, and the standard wing mirrors act as "sights." Reversing presents no problems either, with the high rear wings giving a good guide to the tail overhang. Twin reversing lamps are built into the bumper.

Steering and Cornering

At speed the steering loses some of its directional precision and the car sometimes surprises the driver by darting slightly one way or the other. Joints and ridges in the road surface deflect the tyres off course quite noticeably.

Cornering is aided by the stabilizing influence of slight understeer, although in the wet this becomes more neutral as the tail swings slightly. With a fluid torque converter in the transmission, power cannot be applied so abruptly as with a manual gear train, so tail slides from this source are far less frequent. The biggest discouragement to fast cornering is the way the car lurches over on to its front suspension as a bend is entered, causing loose articles to roll about and passengers to clutch for something firm. This non-executive treatment is out of character with the car, and it feels happiest trickling round much more sedately in top.

However, when really pushed to the limit there is far more adhesion than one might expect, and the car always remains stable. Braking from high speeds gives every feeling of confidence as the large front discs pull the car up with commendably light pedal loads. Maximum braking efficiency required only 75lb on the pedal, anything more causing wheellock. The handbrake, too, was powerful—unusually so for its type—holding the car securely and easily on a 1-in-3 test hill. Getting away again

Left: Interior trim is all in black, with dark wood panels below the facia capping. The armrest between the front seats has a lift-up lid, with a useful tray in front. Right: There are three armrests and three ashtrays in the back, but the gap for getting feet in and out is narrow

Ford Executive Zodiac...

on a damp surface caused wheelspin, and the transmission could be felt changing up and down with the variations in grip, but the car pulled away smoothly.

On English roads the suspension of the Zodiac gives a reasonably favourable impression. It has a big car feel with a comfortable ride most of the time, although rough patches of roadworks and bumpy tracks set the suspension thumping around noisily. A lot of these disturbances are accentuated rather than deadened by seats which are too firmly sprung. Taking the car abroad on French roads proved somewhat revealing, all the passengers complaining of the choppy ride. In the front the seat springs could be felt quivering beneath—one driver even finding this numbed his posterior! And with these movements one's shoulders fret against the backrest. In the rear compartment it was a good deal better, although the curvature of the backrest padding does not support the shoulders much unless one slumps down.

The back seat is not really up to executive travel, for legroom is cramped even when those in the front aren't being greedy with the adjustment. Moreover, the gap between front and back seats makes it difficult to climb out without the feet getting jammed, or tied up with the seat-belt loops. In other aspects back-seat passengers are well catered for. There are three ashtrays, a swinging assist-strap each side above the door (white plastic which soon showed grubby finger marks), armrests and an extra radio speaker on the rear shelf.

Driving Position

Most of our drivers found the steering wheel too close to the chest, and with no clutch to press to the floor even a 5ft 8in. tester would have liked to get farther from the pedals. Through the steering wheel the driver sees a ribbon-type speedometer flanked each side by spherical dials for the fuel gauge and engine thermometer. The figures on the speedometer are pale, and there are times when bright sunlight catches the glass and makes them illegible. At night the instrument lighting turns them into a clear white-on-black.

The rest of the dashboard layout is new and individual to the Zodiac. Dark wood veneer panels are set beneath matt black capping with

HPU 886B

The boot floor is lined with black carpet, which also covers the spare wheel on the left. Over-riders have rubber pads, and there are twin reversing lamps built into the bumper

Zodiacs have opening rear quarterlights as well as swivelling ones in the front doors. Twin wing mirrors are standard, and the single exhaust system is new

switches well scattered in accessible positions. Most controls are down on the right, with the main lighting switch sensibly remote. This is the excellent universal type which does everything, including dimming the panel lamps and turning on the interior light. The wiper switch is pressed to work the washers, and twisting it varies the wiping speed from 52 to 66 strokes a minute. Unfortunately most of the dirt is left on the edge by the right-hand screen pillar where it can mask the driver's view. Above 80 m.p.h. in a cross-wind the wiper blades lift off the glass.

To left and right of the large central ashtray (big enough for executive cigar ash, incidentally) are the circular controls for the latest heater. This has a hot-matrix air-mixing system which can be adjusted instantly for temperature, and the air to the floor and screen can be regulated inde-pendently. Although the heater knob was a little stiff and insensitive, it was not difficult to arrange for a good wafting flow of warm air right through to the back footwells, yet at the same time to keep the temperature at face level refreshingly cool. Seldom was the single-speed booster fan needed, so long as the car was moving; it is not noisy, but not really quiet enough to justify the red warning lamp alongside its switch.

Noise Level

With front and rear swivelling quarterlights it is easy to promote a through-flow of air, but even with everything shut tight there is a lot of wind roar above about 75 m.p.h. Most of this seems to come from around the front door edges and it makes conversation difficult during a long day's motoring.

In each of its three gears the trans-mission worked quietly, and there was never any signs of mechanical noises intruding on the interior. The engine ran up to its maximum revs with the characteristic smoothness of a straight six and we thought the new exhaust system muffled more decibels than the older one Only when cold, and perhaps lightly coated with rust after a damp night, did the brakes issue a subdued groan when being dragged by transmission creep on a fast warm-up idle.

During our continental tour we re-turned 17·7 m.p.g. while cruising most of the time in the 80s. Back home on normal domestic duties, the same car managed nearly 20 m.p.g. in stop-start conditions of gentle running. Family owners therefore should find no difficulty in getting this figure, but on a quick business trip by motor-ways to the north would most likely drop some 4 m.p.g. With a 12-gal tank the safe range between fill-ups is well under 200 miles.

	80	90	100	110
Ford Executive Zodiac				
M-Benz 190 Aut				
Vanden Plas Princess R				
Rover 3-Litre Auto.				
Daimler 2½ V8				
MAXIMUM SPEED (mean) M.P.H.				

	10	20
Ford Executive Zodiac		
Mercedes-Benz 190 Auto.		
Vanden Plas Princess R		
Rover 3-Litre Auto.		
Daimler 2½ V8		
STANDING-START ¼-MILE (secs.)		

HOW THE FORD EXECUTIVE ZODIAC COMPARES:

	0	10	20
Ford Executive Zodiac			
Mercedes-Benz 190 Auto.			
Vanden Plas Princess R			
Rover 3-Litre Auto.			
Daimler 2½ V8			
0-60 M.P.H. SECONDS			

	10	20
Ford Executive Zodiac		
Mercedes-Benz 190 Auto.		
Vanden Plas Princess R		
Rover 3-Litre Auto.		
Daimler 2½ V8		
M.P.G. Overall and Estimated (DIN)		

Although this is one Ford on which the boot can be opened without using the key every time, the filler cap for the fuel tank must be locked before the key will come out. The boot is lined with thick carpet, and the spare wheel, clamped upright on one side, has a tailored cover in the same material to avoid damage to luggage. Behind this is a space for extra tools or odds and ends such as a can of spare fuel, and stitched to its cover is a pocket for the standard tool kit. A lamp (which did not work) was fitted in the boot of the test car.

A basic manual Zodiac costs £1,028, apparently £287 less than the Executive model. However, a few minutes with a Ford price list adding up the catalogued extras to make the Executive specification, just about produces a balance sheet. This, therefore, is what the model is, a Zodiac with all the extras. Judged as a Zodiac it is the best, since it offers many of the creature comforts which make motoring more pleasant. As a model in its own right one had been led to expect more performance and comfort, but nonetheless it provides bulk and roominess with a prestige image somewhat above the ordinary run of the mill.

SPECIFICATION : FORD EXECUTIVE ZODIAC FRONT ENGINE REAR-WHEEL DRIVE

ENGINE

Cylinders	...	6 in-line
Cooling system	...	Water; pump, fan and thermostat
Bore	...	82·6mm (3·25in.)
Stroke	...	79·5mm (3·13in.)
Displacement	...	2,555 c.c. (155·9 cu. in.)
Valve gear	...	Overhead, pushrods and rockers
Compression ratio	...	8·3-to-1; Optional 7·0-to-1
Carburettor	...	Zenith 42 W1A2
Fuel pump	...	AC mechanical
Oil filter	...	Full-flow, various makes
Max. power	...	109 b.h.p. (net) at 4,800 r.p.m.
Max. torque	...	137 lb. ft. (net) at 2,400 r.p.m.

TRANSMISSION

Gearbox	...	Borg-Warner, 3-speed with torque convertor
Gear ratios	...	Top 2·0-1·0; Inter 2·90-1·45; Low 4·78-2·39; Reverse 4·18-2·09
Final drive	...	Hypoid bevel, 3·55 to 1

CHASSIS AND BODY
Integral steel body and chassis

SUSPENSION

Front	...	Independent, coil springs, lower wishbones, MacPherson struts, Armstrong telescopic dampers, anti-roll bar
Rear	...	Live axle, half-elliptic leaf springs, Armstrong lever-arm dampers
Steering	...	Ford-Burman recirculating ball Wheel dia. 17in.

BRAKES

Make and type	...	Ford-Girling disc front, drum rear
Servo	...	Bendix vacuum-mechanical
Dimensions	...	F, 9·75in. dia; R, 9·0in. dia, 2·25in. wide shoes
Swept area	...	F, 218 sq. in.; R, 127 sq. in.; Total 345 sq. in. (245 sq. in.) per ton laden

WHEELS

Type	...	Pressed steel disc, 5 studs; 4·5in. wide rim
Tyres	...	Firestone Sports 130 tubeless, 6·40-13 in.

EQUIPMENT

Battery	...	12-volt 57-amp.-hr.
Generator	...	Lucas C42-30 amp.
Headlamps	...	Lucas dual system 50-37·5-watt
Reversing lamps		2
Electric fuses	...	2
Screen wipers	...	Variable speed, self-parking
Screen washer	...	Standard, manual plunger
Interior heater	...	Standard, air blending type
Safety belts	...	Standard, front, Irvin
Interior trim	...	Leather seats, p.v.c. headlining
Floor covering	...	Carpet
Starting handle	...	No provision
Jack	...	Screw pillar type
Jacking points	...	4 under door sills
Other bodies	...	None

MAINTENANCE

Fuel tank	...	12 Imp. gallons (no reserve), (54·6 litres)
Cooling system	...	18·75 pints (including heater) (10·6 litres)
Engine sump	...	9·75 pints (5·5 litres) SAE20W/20 Change oil every 5,000 miles; Change filter element every 5,000 miles
Gearbox	...	15 pints ATF type M-2C-33 A/D. No oil change
Final drive	...	2·5 pints SAE 90. No oil change
Grease	...	No grease points
Tyre pressures	...	F, 24; R, 24 p.s.i. (normal driving); F, 30; R, 30 p.s.i. (fast driving)

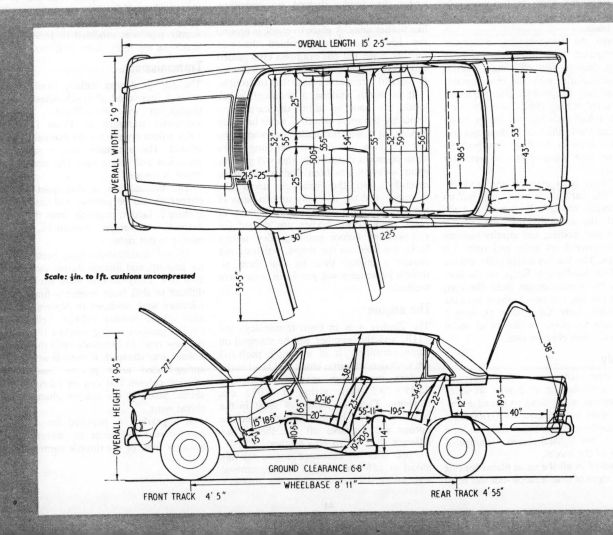

OVERALL LENGTH 15' 2·5"

OVERALL WIDTH 5' 9"

Scale: ⅛in. to 1ft. cushions uncompressed

OVERALL HEIGHT 4' 9·5"

GROUND CLEARANCE 6·8"

WHEELBASE 8' 11"

FRONT TRACK 4' 5"

REAR TRACK 4' 55"

Zephyr 4

THE Zephyr 4 inherited a role almost invented by its predecessor the Consul for a big, roomy five-seater powered by an economical four-cylinder engine and ideal in the role of taxi, commercial traveller's hack, or for the family man who wants space allied to low running costs.

Although the newcomer has a slimmer look compared with the more bulbous Consul it does in fact offer more interior space, particularly with the modifications introduced only five months after the model was marketed in May 1962. These covered a one and a half inch increase in the width of the rear track allied to a three-quarters of an inch drop in the floor pan, both designed to give more room to rear-seat passengers.

There have been many minor modifications in the car's three years' life, but no really major change. It shares a body shell with the more expensive six-cylinder Zephyr 6 and Zodiac, and identity features are a one-piece front grille and only two headlamps. The Six has a split grille and the Zodiac four headlamps. Script on the boot identifies the three cousins from the rear, but from the side the two Zephyrs have the same profile, only the Zodiac showing a quarter-light in place of the blind metal panel on the two cheaper cars.

The body

By a coincidence we were able to examine a whole fleet of Zephyr 4s which representatives were using to attend a conference. Most had covered 40-50,000 miles in 18 months to two years' life, so were certainly not hand-picked pampered examples of the model.

We looked in all the usual places for rust or other signs of deterioration, but this body seems to be particularly resistant to wear and tear and lacking specific weak points which give trouble. A check inside the boots and on what Ford call the rocker panels—the panels running the length of the car under the doors—showed no corrosion, nor was there any around the attachments like flasher units. A place to check is around the filler cap hidden behind the rear number plate, but our examples even passed this check. Look also under the doors to see if blocked drain-holes have led to trouble.

It is worth making a thorough check inside the boot by lifting the carpet and removing the spare wheel. If water has been leaking in it will run under the wheel into the well there, and if the rubber bung shows signs of recent disturbance this will give the game away: it has been drained. Examine carefully also the valances under the bumpers, and the normally unseen parts of the door-jambs to see that there is plenty of paint there. Ford bodies are dipped for rust-proofing before painting. Zero-torque locks are used on the doors, which do not require a mighty slam to shut them, although passengers will persist in brute-force methods.

The engine

The Zephyr 4 is in Ford terminology the 211E, and this number will be stamped on engine castings. It is a simple push-rod o.h.v. design with iron block and head in the modern over-square manner, dimensions 82.55 × 79.5 mm, giving a 1,073 c.c. capacity. There is plenty of meat in the block, as shown by the fact that over-size pistons are available off the shelf in six different sizes up to plus 60 thou.

Ford offer an exchange engine for this model at £58 10s. plus, of course, removal and fitting labour charges. We drove a hard-worked car with 42,000 on the clock which gave no smoke signals, and the owner of another with a similar mileage said he was using about one pint of oil per 350 miles, which is as good as some new cars.

Engine life of 70/80,000 miles is not unusual. Most of the engines we examined were oily and dirty on the outside, but much of this appeared to have come from careless topping-up. Possible leak-points are the valve-chest cover sideplates and the rocker-box gasket. Valve-gear is not normally noisy, and if it is suspect lack of oil. The supply pipe was modified in June 1964 to make the assembly more foolproof.

Transmission

The Zephyr 4 was initially available with either a four-speed all-synchromesh column change or with Borg-Warner Type 35 automatic transmission. From December 1963 a floor change for the manual box was offered. The automatic box is smooth in operation and has a long life, and a slight whine is normal.

The manual box is also quiet and the change should be positive and easy to use. If there is judder, probably from the clutch, suspect worn engine mountings, a small matter to put right.

Several modifications have been made to the gearbox and linkage during the production run. Early models were prone to be difficult to shift from reverse to first and the selectors were modified in November 1962 after vehicle number 162434. Yellow paint on the gearbox casing marked the first of the new type. In February 1963 the selector linkage was changed. If there is wear on the spring-loaded arms at the base of the steering column this can be taken up with shims. Slack in the column change would reveal wear.

If a gearbox is removed for any work care should be taken to disconnect all linkages first, or the throttle control can be

bent. Check by pressing the pedal to the floor and observing if the throttle butterfly is fully open. Another point to watch is the clutch assist spring adjustment. This coil spring which assists in clutch withdrawal is often mistaken for a return spring. If it is wrongly adjusted the clutch will be either floppy in action or too stiff.

Maintenance

After January 1964 this model went over to sealed-for-life joints in the steering and drive shaft, and when old parts are worn the new type can be fitted. Before that there were grease nipples, and a point to watch is that if the ball-joint gaiters are worn or damaged dirt or water may enter the joints and cause stiffness or noise.

There have been many minor changes, as already stated, in the three-year life of the Zephyr 4, and some could be made to older cars if it is found that they have not already been incorporated. In June 1964 the right front coil spring was lengthened by three-quarters of an inch to improve tyre wear, and it should be possible to obtain and fit a replacement spring.

In November '64 a new grille was fitted to the heater to improve front-seat warmth, and this too is available and can replace the old type. Two problems can arise in connection with carburation, both easily put right. One is that the fast-idle rod which is also the choke linkage can foul the air cleaner and give rise to a rich mixture with its attendant troubles; the remedy is to cut $\frac{3}{16}$ of an inch off the rod. The other is that the accelerator pump control rod may foul the air cleaner sealing ring and prevent the throttle opening fully; the answer is to cut a piece out of the rubber seal to make clearance.

General

Our feeling after examining a number of well-worn Fours is that there is no dreaded trap into which a potential buyer of a used one can fall. The one we drove performed as well as a new car except that the speedometer swung between an indicated 80-100

The neat, clear facia has an easily read speedometer and logically-placed controls.

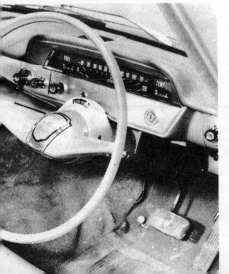

Plenty of room to work on the engine thanks to the wide body.

m.p.h. at maximum speed, indicating the need for a new cable or some lubrication. But this is a minor irritation, and there were no noises, rattles, thumps, or anything untoward.

The changes made in the model not already noted help in dating. A new type of brake servo came in 1962 from vehicle number 174272, and this involved a change in the body shell bulkhead. An improved rear main bearing seal has been fitted for a long time; after engine number 177648 a hole drilled in the main drive gear bearing retainer drained off oil which might otherwise find its way on to the clutch; suspension knock on very rough roads was overcome by cutting an inch off the rebound stop tubes in the Macpherson units.

The front seat was modified to go back one inch farther and to give a slight rake adjustment in the backrest in April 1963. At the same time, in April 1963, the front brake hoses were armoured for safety in case of fouling on suspension parts. The gearbox main drive gear oil seal was changed after vehicle number 023605 from simple rubber to a steel backed rubber, but is interchangeable.

In August 1963 the plastic door-handles were changed to metal due to being too flexible; fouling the armrest may also stop them working properly. In October of the same year the flasher bulbs were changed to a long-life type, increasing wattage from

21 to 24, and unless the flasher unit is exchanged too—48 instead of 42 watts—the rate of flashing will depart from standard if new-type bulbs are fitted as replacement, but will still be within the legal range of 60/120 per minute.

The accelerator pedal was modified in October 1963 because of breakages in the rubber lug joining the pedal to the control rod. A tip here: never pull the carpet back over the pedal, but undo the bolts holding the pedal to the floor first. At the same time an idler arm was fitted to the steering incorporating a damper to give more feel. A parts kit is available. Shock-absorbers on later cars have stiffer settings on the rear, and the oil-breather on the overdrive (where fitted) has been changed to prevent fitting the wrong way round with consequent loss of oil. Final change: in the clutch action to reduce pedal effort and promote smooth action. **M**

Brief specification

Engine: Four-cylinder, 1,703 c.c.
Gearbox: Four-speed manual or Borg Warner type 35 automatic.
Dimensions: *Length:* 15 ft. 0½ in. *Width:* 5 ft. 9 in. *Weight:* 26 cwt.

Performance

Maximum speed: 81 m.p.h.
Acceleration: 0–50 through gears, 14.7 sec.; 20–40 in kick-down, 5.9 sec.
Fuel consumption: 27.2 m.p.g.
Braking from 30 m.p.h.: 32 ft.

Identity parade

Introduced in **May 1962**, and 99,234 made by **September 1**. All models known as Series III.

Previous Spot checks

Vauxhall Victor I	March 14 **1964**	Wolseley 1500 and Riley 1.5	October 17	
Ford Consul Mk. II	March 21	Vauxhall Victor FB	November 7	
Austin A30/35	March 28	Citroen DS/ID/DW and Safari	November 21	
Standard 8/10	April 4	Volvo B16 and B18	December 5	
Renault Dauphine	April 11	Fiat 600 and 600D	December 19	
Morris Minor	April 18	Hillman Husky	January 9 **1965**	
MG TD/TF	April 25	Saab	January 23	
Hillman Minx Series III	May 2	The Big Healeys	February 6	
B.M.C. 1½-litre "Farinas"	May 9	Ford Anglia 105E/123E	February 13	
Standard Vanguard III	May 16	Simca 1000	February 27	
Ford 100E	May 23	Renault 4L	March 27	
Triumph TR/TR3	May 30	XK Jaguars	April 3	
Austin A40	June 6	Ford Capri and Classic	April 17	
Jaguar 2.4/3.4	June 13	Triumph Spitfire	May 1	
Vauxhall Velox/Cresta	June 20	Armstrong-Siddeley Sapphires	May 15	
Skoda Octavia	June 27	Ford E93 variants	May 29	
Triumph Herald	July 11	Peugeot 403	June 12	
B.M.C. Sixes	July 25	B.M.C. 1100s	June 26	
B.M.C. Minis	August 8	Hillman Imp	July 10	
VW 1200	August 15	Rover 3-litre	July 24	
Sprite I and II	September 5	Vauxhall Velox and Cresta PB	August 7	
Rover P4	September 19	Sunbeam Rapiers	August 21	
Ford Cortinas	October 3	Fiat 500	September 4	

The two faces which distinguish Ford's two 2½-litre six-cylinder saloons; on the left, the Zephyr with bifurcated grille; on the right the Zodiac with four headlights.

The Ford Zephyr Six and Zodiac Mk III

FEW large cars have proved more popular in Britain, to say nothing of export fields, than Ford of Dagenham's two variations on a single sturdy theme, the Mk. III Zephyr Six and Zodiac, introduced in April 1962. Using the same body shell with variations in the radiator grille, windows, trimming and equipment, and the same suspension units, over 180,000 examples have so far been produced. Both use the same 82.55 x 79.5 mm. 2,553 c.c. six-cylinder pushrod o.h.v. engine, the Zephyr unit giving 106 b.h.p. (gross) at 4,750 r.p.m. and the Zodiac 114 b.h.p. Both are spacious, perform well, reliably and economically, and have worldwide servicing facilities. Demand for second-hand examples is naturally brisk, and an over-three-year-old Zephyr of average mileage still sells at around £500.

The design is conventional, well-proved and uncomplicated, following logically on that of the Zephyr Mk. II but offering more room, greater smoothness, modern styling and the four-speed all-synchromesh gearbox for which Mk. II owners have yearned for so long. The Mk. IIIs have undergone only minor changes during their production span, such as widening of the rear track by 1½ in. to improve rear seat room, improved trimming and equipment, so that the secondhand purchaser has nothing to fear regarding replacement parts.

The engines

These are straightforward in-line pushrod o.h.v. units with an excellent reliability record. The Ford Motor Co. estimate the average life at around 60,000 miles before overhaul becomes necessary, but many Mk. IIIs used by the police have attained the 100,000-mile mark while one taxi-driver covered 150,000 miles on one engine—accentuating the benefits of constant use of a car, as against short-mileage commuting with engines all too often cold, when wear is at its greatest. When reboring becomes necessary, 0.0025, 0.005, 0.015, 0.030, 0.045 and 0.060 in. oversize pistons are available, while main bearing shells for reground crankshafts are obtainable in 0.002, 0.010, 0.020, 0.030 and 0.040 in. undersizes. Complete engine exchange units cost £75 both for the Zephyr and Zodiac (automatic transmission models: £77).

The engines are normally oil free, but leaks can result from badly fitted or defective rocker box or filter gaskets. "Cold tap"—i.e. piston slap when cold—can be expected from 30,000 mile-plus engines; if slap remains when the engine is warm attention may be required. Listen, too, for valve clatter. It may mean wear, or simply the effects of unskilled do-it-yourselfers. Undue vibration in extended mileage engines may result from

"tired" engine mountings; check them for rubber deterioration. Excluding normal wear and tear, abnormal oil consumption may be due to defective rubber valve seals, which tended to become brittle on early cars after about 50,000 miles, letting oil past the valve stems into the engine. A change in rubber specification made early in 1964 cured this.

Transmission

Like the Zephyr Four (Spot Check, September 18, 1965, issue) the sixes have four-speed, all-synchromesh gearboxes and a single dry plate clutch. Any clutch judder apparent could mean the aforementioned engine mountings, an unfeeling previous owner, perhaps, or leakage of oil from the forward gearbox oil seal on to the clutch plate. The transmission and final drive are normally quiet and the gearchange smooth and positive; if it isn't, adjustment of the gear rods may put it right. Up to January 1964 the clutch pedal had an assist spring which sometimes impeded full pedal return; a new design of pedal dispensed both with the spring and the trouble. Early models had steering column gearchange only, but an optional floor change was introduced in October, 1963.

Steering

The recirculatory ball system of steering used by Ford is notably long lasting, and any wear is more likely to be traceable to the track rod ends. On 1962-63 models these required servicing, but in early 1964, "Lube for life" permanently-lubricated joints were introduced. Some early examples developed front wheel "shimmy", first remedied by careful wheel balancing, but later by employing a damper instead of an idler arm in the steering. Another early fault was undue wear of the offside front tyre, due largely to driver-only use of the car and cured after June 1964 by fitting an offside front suspension spring ¾ in. longer than its nearside partner.

The Ford Zephyr Six and Zodiac Mk III

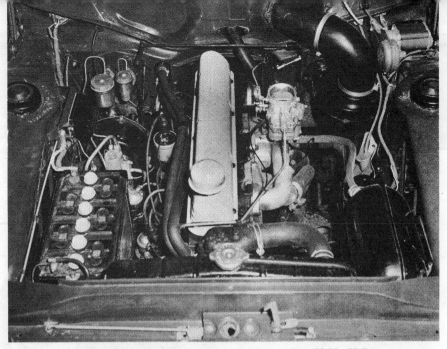

Power for both the Zephyr and the Zodiac comes from this lively, reliable 82.55 × 79.5 mm., 2553 c.c. six-cylinder unit, giving 106 b.h.p. (gross) in the former and 114 b.h.p. in the latter.

The brakes

Disc front and drum rear brakes are standard on the Mk. IIIs. They are servo-assisted, initially by a hydraulic unit, changed later in 1962 to a mechanical unit giving more "feel", more progressive action and easier servicing. The front discs should be checked for scoring; replacements cost £2 16s. each. Check hydraulic hose lines for chafing, possibly from incorrect fitting whereby the hose contacts a suspension member. On early cars the front brake pads tended to rattle against the discs, remedied by a damper spring fitted behind the pad, a set costing 8s.

The bodywork

The all-steel integral body shells of the Zephyr and Zodiac are virtually identical, though the Zodiac has a triangular rear quarter-light and four-headlight system, and the radiator grilles differ. To combat rust, bodies are given a zinc-rich primer coating, then a slipper dip for the lower 18-24 in., followed by the normal paint preparation coats. An acrylic-based finish was introduced in mid-1964.

Nearly four years' production has not brought to light any points of abnormal corrosion, but potential buyers should check around the wing edges and body flanks where stones, grit, salt, etc., may have been thrown up with deleterious effects. A rattling may merely indicate the need for adjustment of the doors, or for tightening (by bending) of the balancing rods in the luggage boot.

Equipment

The cars are wired 12 volt. Both models have twin, variable-speed self-parking wipers, but Zodiac instrumentation is more lavish. Both rely on a green indicator light for oil pressure warning. A feature which often puzzles those unfamiliar with the Mk. III is the parking light isolator switch to the right of the steering column. This security device operates the offside front and rear parking lights, but cuts out the ignition and near side lights at the same time.

Estate car versions of both types were introduced in October, 1962; these differ in the rear suspension rate, increased by six-leaf instead of five-leaf springs, and in slightly increased kerb weight.

Spares

All spares are obtainable from Ford dealers. Besides engines, other components available under the exchange scheme include the automatic gearbox (£35), brake pads and shoes, clutch discs and pressure plates, connecting rods, distributors, petrol pumps, radiators and bumpers. A complete loose-leaf Workshop Manual at 65s. and instruction books are available from Ford main dealers, and useful handbooks have also been issued by outside publishers.

Brief Specification

Engine: Six-cylinder, 82.55 × 79.5 mm. bore and stroke, 2,553 c.c.; Zephyr output, 106 b.h.p. (gross) at 4,750 r.p.m. Zodiac, 114 b.h.p. at 4,750 r.p.m.

Transmission: 4-speed all-synchromesh gearbox. Borg and Beck 8½ in. single dry plate clutch. Hypoid bevel final drive. Borg-Warner automatic transmission, Model 35, optional. Column or floor gearchange optional (from October, 1962).

Suspension. *Front:* Macpherson strut type independent by coil springs and wishbones; Armstrong hydraulic telescopic dampers, anti-roll bar. *Rear:* Semi-elliptic leaf springs and live axle; Armstrong lever arm dampers.

Brakes: Girling hydraulic; disc front, drum rear.

Dimensions. *Length:* Zephyr; 15 ft. ¾ in.; Zodiac 15 ft. 2¾ on. *Width:* 5 ft. 9¼ in. *Kerb weight;* 2,620 lb.

Performance

Zephyr Six

Maximum speed: 91.0 m.p.h.
Acceleration: 0-50 m.p.h.: 11.1 sec. **20-40 m.p.h. in top gear:** 11.1 sec.
Fuel consumption: touring 21.6 m.p.g.; overall, 18.6 m.p.g.
Brakes from 30 m.p.h.: 31 ft.

Zodiac

Maximum speed: 100.7 m.p.h.
Acceleration: 0-50 m.p.h.: 9.2 sec. **20-40 m.p.h. in top gear:** 8.8 sec.
Fuel consumption: touring 22.6 m.p.g.; overall, 19.5 m.p.g.
Brakes from 30 m.p.h.: 30.5 ft.

Identity Parade

Zephyr Six and Zodiac

February 1962: Production commenced (Zephyr, vehicle No. 54B048196 on; Zodiac, 64B037276 on. (Introduced, April 1962).

October 1962: Wider rear track, more rear seat room by changes to rear bulkhead.

October 1962: Estate car introduced.

August 1963: Improvements to facia, trim and fittings on Zephyr.

September 1963: Improvements as above to Zodiac, plus new reverse lamps built into rear bumper, modified over-riders with rubber inserts, deep pile carpet.

October 1963: Floor gear change optional.

October 1964: Interior paintwork matching trim (cloth trim optional) on Zephyr from 5D282216; Zodiac from 6D282270.

January 1965: Executive Zodiac introduced.

Previous Spot checks

Vauxhall Victor 1	March 14 **1964**	
Ford Consul Mk. II	March 21	
Austin A30/35	March 28	
Standard 8/10	April 4	
Renault Dauphine	April 11	
Morris Minor	April 18	
MG TD/TF	April 25	
Hillman Minx Series III	May 2	
B.M.C. 1½-litre "Farinas"	May 9	
Standard Vanguard III	May 16	
Ford 100E	May 23	
Triumph TR2/TR3	May 30	
Austin A40	June 6	
Jaguar 2.4/3.4	June 13	
Vauxhall Velox/Cresta	June 20	
Skoda Octavia	June 27	
Triumph Herald	July 11	
B.M.C. Sixes	July 25	
B.M.C. Minis	August 8	
VW 1200	August 15	
Sprite I and II	September 5	
Rover P4	September 19	
Ford Cortina	October 3	
Wolseley 1500 and Riley 1.5	October 17	
Vauxhall Victor FB	November 7	
Citroen DS/ID/DW and Safari	November 21	
Volvo B16 and B18	December 5	
Fiat 600 and 600D	December 19	
Hillman Husky	January 9 **1965**	
Saab	January 23	
The Big Healeys	February 6	
Ford Anglia 105E/123E	February 13	
Simca 1000	February 27	
Renault 4L	March 27	
XK Jaguars	April 3	
Ford Capri and Classic	April 17	
Triumph Spitfire	May 1	
Armstrong Siddeley Sapphires	May 15	
Ford E93 variants	May 29	
Peugeot 403	June 12	
B.M.C. 1100s	June 26	
Hillman Imp	July 10	
Rover 3-litre	July 24	
Vauxhall and Cresta PB	August 7	
Sunbeam Rapiers	August 21	
Fiat 500	September 4	
Ford Zephyr 4	September 18	
Vauxhall Viva	October 2	
Ford Corsair	October 16	
Singer Gazelle	October 30	
NSU Prinz 4	December 4	
Reliant Regal three-wheeler	December 18	
Lotus Elite	January 1 **1966**	
Jaguar Mk. X	January 15	
Renault 8 and 1100	January 29	
Triumph 2000	February 26	
Humber Hawk and Super Snipe	March 12	

 **ZEPHYR/ZODIAC** MK. 3

*
Owners have little specific criticism of the popular "Z cars", and strong loyalty is apparent . . .

THE Ford "Z Cars" have been popular in South Africa since they were introduced here more than a decade-and-a-half ago. About 10 years ago, in fact, the Zephyr was South Africa's best-selling car, and the two Z cars have remained consistent sellers — usually at the top of their class — ever since.

The Mk. 2 models featured in one of the first CAR Owner Reports six years ago, and now it is the turn of the Mk. 3 versions, introduced here in 1962 and ranging up to 1965 models.

The type of use varies enormously: there are owners who report doing only 600 miles a month, and equally many doing 3,000 miles or more monthly in business use. The average for all cars works out to 1,211 miles a month, which is about typical of the average car under South African conditions.

Fuel consumption works out to 21.0 m.p.g. about town for the Zephyr 6, and 24.5 on the open road. Curiously enough, the Zodiac returns slightly poorer figures — 20.3 and 24.0 respectively — perhaps because more use is made by these owners of performance. In either case, fuel consumption is one of the criticised features of the cars.

There was no discernible difference in owner opinions on Zephyr and Zodiac, so we have grouped them together in the report proper.

The most popular feature is performance, cited by exactly half of owners, and an only slightly smaller vote goes to interior comfort. Other main favourable features are the front disc brakes, four-speed gearbox, the car's reliability, its appearance and the size of the boot.

No single feature gets any outstanding proportion of comment, indicating a car with all-round qualities, and perhaps lacking in colourful character.

A smaller proportion of good-feature votes goes to quiet running, good value and luxury features (usually from Zodiac owners), ranging down to spaciousness, handling qualities, roadholding and cruising ability.

The disliked features are few, and the fact that the list is headed by "door and window rattles" — a complaint by one owner in four — may cause some blushes. The need for frequent front wheel balancing —

SOME PRAISE . . .

"Even at 70-plus the engine is quiet . . . "

"A truly wonderful car."

"Parts are inexpensive."

"Finest value for money anyone can buy."

"Gives pride of ownership." (Zodiac Sports).

"Powerful, comfortable ride."

"An excellent car, of outstanding performance, yet basically simple and free of gadgets."

"Ideal for combined town-country work.'

"Most comfortable car I have driven — gives me endless pleasure."

"Very pleasant car — best-looking in its class."

"Excellent value for R2,000." (Several owners).

"A lot of car for the money."

"Excellent on poor gravel roads." (A lighthouse keeper.)

"Never lets you down."

"Tows a caravan well."

SOME CRITICISMS . . .

"One's legs drop off after an hour's drive."

"Assembly poor — one headlamp globe was missing when I got it!"

"Reliable, but body cannot stand up to Bechuanaland roads."

"Bodywork leaves much to be desired."

"Top gear slightly weak." (Zephyr.)

"Very dissatisfied with front suspension — too soft for corrugated roads."

"Three attempts at dust-proofing, without success."

"Fairly expensive to maintain."

"Trunk lid too soft — hand pressure makes dents."

"Second gear too low." -

"Boot shape is awkward." (Several owners.)

"Customer has to practically re-assemble the car." (Several complained of assembly and finish faults.)

"My second Zodiac. The first had column shift, which was hopeless. I thought the Sports floor shift would be better, but it is just as bad."

WHY A ZEPHYR?

"Value for money — excellent equipment." (Zodiac Sports.)

"I liked the Zephyr's looks, and people who owned them seemed satisfied."

"Styling and interior finish."

"Top of its class in sales, indicating good value."

"No spares or service difficulties."

"I just loved that four-speed Gearbox!"

(Editor's Note: This section, giving reasons for buying the car, is new, based on the new-look Owner Report form introduced in November. It was not included in the earlier questionnaire form. As more of the new forms come in, it will be expanded.)

something apparently quite common in cars with the McPherson strut system and 13-in. wheels — causes owner irritation. Minor criticism — by fewer than one owner in five — goes to fuel economy, softness of the front suspension and the quality of the body seal. One owner in 10 also criticises the column gearshift.

Well over half of owners report having no trouble at all with their Zephyrs and Zodiacs, and the trouble encountered is primarily minor — gearbox linkage, silencer failure and oil leaks being the only items to get significant mention. Mechanically, the car emerges with a fairly clean bill, particularly on major items.

Dustproofing is roundly criticised, and fewer than half of owners report satisfaction here. Weatherproofing is much better, endorsed by four owners out of five.

Nearly three-quarters report using Ford dealer service, and the general standard of service is given as "good — tending to average". The fair number of "excellent" ratings is shared by Pretoria, Johannesburg, Cape Town, King William's Town, Humansdorp, Grahamstown and Kroonstad.

Other cars in the six-cylinder class head the field among cars considered at time of buying Z cars, led by the equivalent Vauxhall models and the Valiant. Nearly a quarter of Zephyr/Zodiac owners considered no other car, usually having owned Z cars before.

Next time, say 55 per cent of owners, they will specify "same again". Another 15 per cent list other Ford models, ranging from Cortina GT to Fairlane V8.

One owner in seven is undecided, and the only two serious rivals emerging are the Valiant (11 per cent) and Jaguar models (10 per cent).

Generally, Zephyr/Zodiac owners seem very proud of their cars, in spite of a fair proportion of minor irritations.

A Pretoria owner says: "I've now had 23 Fords, the last three being Zodiac Mk. 3's. They have looked after me so well, and service is so good, that I will only buy another Ford."

From Kuruman comes this ingenuous comment: "I am of the opinion that the Zephyr 6 is the Mercedes for the poor man."

As one of our staff commented: "It depends whether you mean poor like a farmer — or poor like a journalist!"   ●

MOST-LIKED FEATURES

Performance	50%
Interior Comfort	46%
Disk Front Brakes	31%
4-speed gearbox	29%
Reliability	25%
Appearance	21%
Large boot	21%
Silent running	19%
Value for money	17%
Luxury features	17%
Roadholding	15%
Interior space	13%
Handling ease	11%
Cruising ability	10%

DISLIKED FEATURES

Door rattles	25%
Wheel imbalance	19%
Body seal	17%
Soft suspension	17%
Fuel consumption	17%
Column gearshift	10%

TROUBLESOME FEATURES

Gear linkages	11%
Silencers	11%
Oil leaks	10%

MAKE AND MODEL

Make	Ford Zephyr/Zodiac
Model	Mark 3

MILEAGES:

Total	1,079,055
Average monthly	1,211

ZEPHYR M.P.G.:

About town	21·0
On long trips	24·5

ZODIAC M.P.G.:

About town	20·3
On long trips	24·0

BODY SEAL:

Weatherproof	78%
Dustproof	48%

DEALER SERVICE:

Use Ford service	70%
Quality	good to average

WHY NOT DEALER SERVICE:

Poor quality	11%
Geographical reasons	10%
Own service	8%

OTHER CARS CONSIDERED

Vauxhall 3-litre	32%
No other	23%
Chrysler Valiant	21%
Other Fords	15%
Chevy 2	15%
Peugeot	13%
Volvo	13%
Mercedes-Benz	10%
Opel	11%
Vauxhall Victor	10%

REASONS FOR CHOICE:

Appearance	30%
Good value	20%
Extra equipment	20%
Good reputation	10%
Towing ability	10%
Popularity	10%
Spares/service facilities	10%

NEXT CHOICE:

Same again	55%
Other Ford	15%
Undecided	15%
Chrysler Valiant	11%
Jaguar	10%

ZODIAC
TO SOFIA

A 3,700-MILE TROUBLE-FREE WEEK

by STUART BLADON

IT makes a wonderful change from routine motoring to take the right car to the Continent on a job that calls for driving fast and far, swallowing up the miles for hour after hour. This is exactly the pattern which comes with reporting that splendid annual marathon, the Liège-Sofia rally.

Memories of the week's hard driving which resulted blur into an endless sequence, especially of the night hours—the speedometer hovering around the 90 m.p.h. mark as the minutes and hours flit by; the trip mileometer clocking up its fantastic total for the 24 hours' run, until you forget when it was last reset and suddenly the impressive row of

nines becoming ones again as it goes over the thousand; the beams of the four headlamp system reaching out along straight and monotonously flat miles of concrete; and the continual roar of the tyres.

Then there is the lull of the driver's change over. By torchlight, another two jerricans of green Yugoslav petrol go swilling into the tank, and blankets, pillow and a reclining seat give the off-duty driver a chance to relax. On the move again, the noise and the restless movements of the car at first defeat attempts to sleep, but in the end the tiredness of hours on the trot wins through. Another hush, as the car pauses in its rush through the night and draws up beside

Below: So often Austria and northern Yugoslavia greet one with pelting rain which obliterates the scenery; but when it is fine, as it was on this trip, the views of mountain peaks reaching up into a perfect blue sky can be magnificent. This view was taken on the descent of the Wurzen Pass into Yugoslavia. Above: Clouds of dust blow up from the wheels on one of the dirt tracks of the interior, but the number of such unmade roads on main routes is diminishing every year

the road, brings sudden wakefulness from the hour's sleep which you never knew you had.

With its long sortie into Yugoslavia, this is a wonderful rally, and one quite different from most of the other Internationals. Only the Coronation Safari is comparable, with its combination of bad roads and fantastically high speeds which would never be possible in any but countries with very limited traffic. The time schedule goes so far adrift, and surviving competitors are so few, that in the final stages in Yugoslavia you can stop and wait for half an hour to photograph competitors and finally give up in despair think-

ZODIAC TO SOFIA

ing that no more are to come. Yet half the field of survivors can still be on their way. This year, although running about four hours late, the Sprinzel Cortina finished, but even the most patient observers (including John Sprinzel's fiancée) had given up waiting by the time it arrived.

For the pressmen, the approach is very different from that of competitors, because it just does not do to use the car to modify the Serbian scenery or to break the suspension and abandon it for service crews to recover at leisure. Yet to cover the rally thoroughly it is necessary to go over almost the same mileage in much the same time. The answer is that we take the bad going at nothing like the speed of the rally cars, and pull off the road to see them pass as each one catches up. Lost time is recovered by the two-way day-and-night flog on *autoputs* and *autobahnen* instead of some of the long sections of bad roads covered by the route. A reporting team can only sample a rally; if car and crew were able to keep up with its progress *and* stop to take notes and photographs, then they would be wasting their time reporting it—they should be competing, and winning it.

This year we chose a Ford Zodiac with overdrive as our high-speed mobile quarters for the long thrash to Sofia and back, and it came very, very near to the ideal of reliability without fuss. Often there is no time to spare for maintenance, and even stops to put petrol in are made grudgingly, knowing that some hoped-for photograph probably will be missed as a result. So it was a great joy to have a car that kept going with no more attention than frequent removal of the mass of unfortunate insects from their windscreen graveyard at each refuelling halt. From time to time we made a cursory check of tyre pressures and the

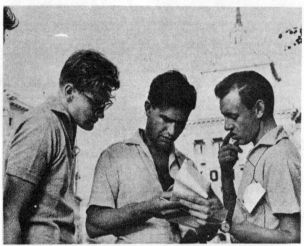

Still leading the rally at Sofia, and destined to win, Rauno Aaltonen (right) and co-driver Tony Ambrose (left) study a list showing the rally order at the previous control

Dense traffic is not shaken off until the Yugoslav border, and was at its worst on the two-lane German autobahnen

In the vast interior wilderness of Yugoslavia, the cart drawn by horse or ox is still an important form of transport. Where minor tracks cross the autoput these carts are a hazard for which the driver must always be on the look-out

oil level, but none dropped measurably throughout the trip. Even on return to Britain, the engine still did not need even half a pint of oil added to the sump. For hours on end, it had been held at or near full throttle, and there was frequent use of kickdown into direct top for overtaking on fast roads, yet fuel consumption was consistently better than 20 m.p.g., and the overall figure for 3,718 miles was an unexpectedly good 21·5 m.p.g.

The only spot of trouble occurred, unfortunately, when time could least be spared to rectify it, but when we found what was wrong we had to forgive the car. It was on the long trek in gorgeous sunshine from Belgrade back to northern Yugoslavia; the engine undoubtedly was holding back at high speeds, and the symptoms pointed to fuel starvation, suggesting a fuel blockage or petrol pump failure. In these conditions it is asking for trouble to continue, since if it is fuel starvation, the combination of weak mixture and high speeds and temperatures can easily burn a hole in a piston crown.

Stitch in Time

Reluctantly we stopped, and were busy checking fuel lines when it was noticed that the rubber of the heater pipe was soft at the point where it lay alongside the high tension lead from coil to distributor. The high tension current had been arcing through the insulation and into the water in the heater pipe. The fact that the heater was not on, of course, in that fierce Yugoslav sunshine, made no difference; it still contained water and provided an easy way home to earth. Separating the pipes gave a quick and easy cure. In time, of course, the pipe would have burst, and we would have had a boil-up as well.

As well as meeting the needs for plenty of space and high cruising speed ability, the Zodiac proved very comfortable and restful to drive or to travel in as passenger for long spells. However, the individual reclining seats —a Ford listed "extra"—had collapsed to such extent that a cushion was necessary to give the driver reasonable forward visibility over the steering wheel.

The steering itself proved unusually accurate for a big family car, and gave precise control at high speeds, with lightness on lock, appreciated when tackling passes like the 1-in-4 Wurzen Pass from Austria into Yugoslavia. The servo-assisted disc brakes could be made to fade if worked really hard on prolonged mountain descents, but they were excellent in more normal use. They coped especially well with occasional severe stops from high speed when there were such excitements as the sudden appearance of a horse and cart rushing across the *autoput*, obviously on the principle: "Never mind about whether it's clear or not, the quicker we get across, the less time they have to hit us."

Supplementing its mechanical efficiency, the car's rigidity over bad roads, and pleasantly soft ride without excess sponginess, were also invaluable. These allowed a lot of rough rally sections to be taken pretty quickly, even if not quite at the same pace as the take-it-or-break-it progress of the rally cars. The unevenness of the Belgrade-Zagreb *autoput*, which is badly broken up or deformed most of the way, was absorbed well, though with some float and front end plunge at times. Also, even on the very bad and rough section from Nis to the Bulgarian border, the car never grounded once. It is a great help to have high ground clearance and sturdily fastened exhausts for such conditions.

On the return trip we left Yugoslavia in the afternoon, seeing the depleted convoy of 20-odd rally cars filter in ones and twos through Ajdovscina on their way to Udine in Italy. Then during the night we headed north-west on a direct route, though one which crossed the frontiers of Austria and Italy many times. At the top of the little-known pass over Mount Cavallo, with its rough, winding track all to ourselves, we found a blaze of lights, and frontier guards keeping their all-night vigil for the occasional traveller. A road accident had blocked the way to the great Europa bridge at Innsbruck, so we went underneath it, awestruck by its colossal size, even more imposing in the dark. Eventually we joined the *autobahn* west of Munich, thronged with traffic even at 5 a.m.

After a vigorous wash to clear the dirt and grime of "seven days' hard" from the car, the Zodiac was handed back in even better trim than when taken over, as we had found time at one of the controls to liberate a bulb from the Triumph service team, to put the right-hand indicator back into action. Yet in that single week in August, the Zodiac more than doubled the mileage which it had amassed in its previous service for nearly a year as a Ford export demonstrator. Twice in the week, the car exceeded 1,000 miles in 24 hours. It also came from Belgrade to Liége (1,300 miles) in 28 hours, including stops.

OWC 410D

Unveiled in Tunisia

FORD'S NEW V6 ZEPHYR and ZODIAC

JUST lately we've been seeing a lot of good news emerging from the Ford Motor Co., starting with the Anglia about seven years ago which got the go-faster brigade whooping with wild delight over the snappy little oversquare engine. This was followed by the Cortina, which set a pretty high standard for roadholding and, in G.T. form, of performance too, while last year the Corsair was given a V4 engine which, if not quite what we'd hoped for in terms of performance, at least carried on the recent tradition of new thinking at Ford of Britain.

This new range left the big bangers somewhat out in the cold, with in-line-six engines and strictly trad cart springs at the rear, along with styling which didn't exactly get the onlooker moon-eyed with admiration. The Mark 4 Zephyr and Zodiac put all that right, however, with new V6 power units and a very good i.r.s. which means that at long last Henry's boys have got well and truly with it in terms of rear suspension.

Ford's way of showing these new cars to the press was to take twenty or so of them to Tunisia, in North Africa, and then fly out sixty-odd motoring scribes to thrash them around seven hundred miles of desert and North African town at immensely high average speeds until, presumably, something fell off. So far as the cars were concerned, nothing dropped off, and the only real casualty was your faithful editor, who managed to make his mark on the North African motoring scene by returning with one foot well and truly lashed up in plaster of Paris. Well, plaster of Tunis, really.

But of this, as they say, more anon. Meanwhile, back at Luton airport the assembled mob was led by Ford's publicity men Walter Hayes and Sid Wheelhouse, even unto a Britannia-sized camel which duly magic-carpeted us off the European map and out to Tunis, where Harry Calton, the third member of the Ford trio responsible for seeing that the thing went off all right, bribed the immigration authorities to let us in and all was well. All, in fact, was well for the next four days—when Fords organise something it gets organised, and even editorial ankles can't shake 'em.

We had seen the new cars before in the course of a slap-up nosh at the London Hilton (where else, after all?). As you can see from the pretty pictures, the new models share the same body style in general terms, apart from the number of headlights and so forth, and the whole thing looks dead sporty and rather Mustang in overall appearance. It tends to sit rather high off the ground at the front, the blunt end

is truncated to give an effect of everything important being concentrated towards the rear, along with an impressive bonnet of the sort we used to admire vintage Bentleys for. We didn't exactly get out our Arabic tape measures, but a handy little list that Fords gave us indicates that the Zephyr is three-quarters of an inch longer, for some reason, than the Zephyr V6, and is about half-a-hundredweight heavier. In all other dimensions they are the same. The Zephyr comes in two engine sizes—the 2-litre V4 (out of the Corsair G.T.) and a 118.5 b.h.p. 2½-litre V6, with a Zenith carb to let it breathe through, and a four-speed all-synchromesh gearbox with either floor or column change—you can also have an automatic gremlin-box if you fancy the idea. Top whack is not far short of the ton, they say, and certainly we managed to get it romping along at well over ninety for hundreds of miles. It's pretty lively, too, Ford's talking about a 0—60 time of 13 seconds, which is up to the standard of a rapid Cortina G.T.

Top of the shop in the new big Ford range is the Zodiac, old four-eyes just like its predecessor and similar to the Zephyr except that it has a 3-litre motor developing 144 b.h.p., which gives it a top whack of over the ton and a 0—60 time of 11½ seconds or so. Inside its a bit more de-luxe, and you get a full set of instruments including a rev-counter, oil pressure and water temperature gauges, an ammeter, a clock and a speedometer with a trip and total mileage counters. They've all got fifteen gallon fuel tanks, and they reckon you ought to get a bit over twenty to the gallon out of the Zodiac; they've all got the magnificent Aeroflow ventilation, too. But the other big news is the independent rear end, of which more anon. So far as the engines are concerned, the V6s are all over-square, and they are all of 60 degree V layout. The 2½-litre version has a bore and stroke of 93.6 mm. x 60.3 mm., giving a total capacity of 2,495 c.c., and runs on a compression ratio of 9.1 to 1. The Zodiac job has the same bore but is given a longer stroke, at 72.4 mm., and this gives a total capacity of 2,994 c.c. with a compression ratio of 8.9 to 1. Maximum power on both engines is developed at 4,750 r.p.m. and maximum torque, at 3,000 r.p.m., is 145 lb./ft. for the 2½-litre and 192 lb./ft. for the big banger. Like the V4 range, the crossflow cast iron heads are of the "Heron" type, with bowls in the piston crowns, and the conventional rocker shaft is replaced by individual stud mountings for each rocker: the crankshaft runs in four main bearings. Inlet and exhaust ports are separate, and both the Zenith carb on the 2½-litre job and the 40 DFA Weber twin-choke instrument fitted on the

3-litre have automatic chokes. The Zephyrs have generators to supply loads of current but the Zodiac proudly boasts a Lucas alternator.

Now then, back to the suspension. At the front, there are MacPherson struts with off-set coil springs and an inter-connecting stabiliser bar which allows a slight degree of fore-and-aft deflection. Sounds complicated, but it works well enough. At the back is the all-new, all-singing, all-dancing independence, though, where there are semi-trailing arms with coil springs and telescopic dampers: the suspension arm is shackle-mounted to allow correct wheel articulation without sliding friction.

Steering? Re-circulating balls (their expression) and power assistance is available on the V6 models. Brakes? Discs all round, with servo assistance, and 9.6 in. discs at the front and 9.9 in. at the rear. The cars sit on 6.70 x 13 in. tyres which in turn go on 4½ J rims, and the spare wheel is mounted in front of the engine, which demands a low-slung radiator.

How does it all work on the road? Ford's must have been pretty confident of their new product, for not many people drive harder than motoring journalists and there can't be many tougher test routes than the one they gave us—close on seven hundred miles in temperatures around seventy degrees F., on roads which varied from straight smooth tarmac to un-made tracks across the desert. Drifting sand, water splashes, strong winds and, no doubt, somewhat indifferent petrol, despite its high cost. The Fords came through with flying colours. Sixty-odd journalists seldom agree on anything, but no one doubted that this was a pretty impressive motor car. Just about the only criticism was the steering, which to be honest is vague, dead, and too low-geared and about five turns lock-to-lock.

The engines are pure gold, running as smoothly as turbines (a much over-worked phrase, but when all's said and done the only one that comes to mind) and runs up to five-five in the gears with no effort at all. It is also damn near noise-less, even at close to maximum revs., and on the Zodiac five thousand revs.—over the ton—comes up quite easily. We cruised some of the cars for over 100 miles without the speedo needle dropping below ninety, and yet despite the ambient temperature—that of a hot summer day over here— oil pressure and water temperature remained steady and with the needles in the right places. A reassuring thought. The suspension works a real treat. On one car we bottomed once, travelling three-up, and that was when we hit a drain at around the ton. Apart from that, high-speed motoring, even on indifferent roads, is completely free from pitching, there is only a moderate degree of roll on corners and when you reach the point of no return the back breaks away first, with plenty of warning. And when it goes, it is easily corrected—it would be even easier if the steering was higher-geared, but I suppose we HAVE to remember that auntie might want to go shopping. Never mind, eh.

The bench seat you find in the front of the standard Zephyr 6 could stand improvement, of course—nobody expects very much from bench seats. But the reclining bucket seats you get on the standard Zodiac, or as optional equipment on the Zephyr, leave very little to be desired.

As you might have guessed, we came back from sun, sand and camels mightily impressed with these new Fords. Apart from being very well-engineered, they are extremely sporting carriages, and we reckon it won't be long before they become as popular wear for the enthusiast as the Cortina—and that's saying something. All we want now is an independent rear end as good as this is on the rest of the Ford range and they will have a pretty unbeatable list of models with which to tackle the opposition. And beat it, if we're any judge—at the price you can't do much better.

Flexible five-seater

"Acceleration an outstanding feature . . . ride and handling a little disappointing . . . generally roomy . . . all seats rated comfortable for long journeys"

AT a time when European luxury cars are tending to shrink in size, Ford have uncompromisingly enlarged the Zodiac in every way—it is longer, wider, higher and more powerful than its predecessor. To its considerable credit the gain in passenger space and luggage room greatly outmatches this increase in external dimensions, the weight has risen by only a little over a hundredweight and the more powerful 3-litre engine endows the car with acceleration which is striking by any standards as well as with a maximum speed comfortably over 100 m.p.h. And all this with no appreciable increase in fuel consumption.

The car was in our hands over a month ago and without its identifying badges and insignia we were entertained by the speculation which we overheard. Unhesitatingly people recognized the styling as American and curiously enough, in spite of the Mustang front, most of them went on to place it as a General Motors design. Whether such a typically transatlantic appearance will appeal to the British public we are not qualified to say; in certain directions we feel that styling has been given unjustified precedence over engineering demands but certainly the end product is impressive and represents remarkable value for money.

Under the skin there are some advanced engineering features—

a V-6 engine, disc brakes all round and, above all, independent rear suspension of a design which is ingenious yet simple and sturdy. Under extreme conditions of driving and in bad weather the results, in terms of ride and handling, are a great improvement on the previous Zodiac but not quite as good as we had expected; this, we feel, is not the fault of the fundamental design, but shows that there is room for further development in weight distribution and in matching the front suspension characteristics to those of the rear.

There are a number of other points which still need some attention—most of them just details like the throttle linkage. For the 10 years or so for which we can expect to see this model in production it is likely to develop into a car which is hard to beat for motorists with unusually large families.

Performance and economy

Acceleration is certainly an outstanding feature of this new Zodiac. The engine is tractable and flexible and low speed torque is such that it can be driven nearly all the time in top gear if the driver is so minded. Pulling power increases to a peak in the middle speed range—about 50 m.p.h. in top gear—giving the ability to climb hills of the 1 in 7 variety without zhanging down and without loss of speed. On the other hand, if you want to use the gearbox fully to extract the last ounce of performance, then the

PRICE £1,010 plus £218 4s. 0d. equals £1,228 4s. 0d.

Continued on the next page

Ford Zodiac Mk. IV
continued

standing start figures show that the only sports cars which can hope to stay with you on a straight road are those with as much or more urge than, for example, a Triumph TR4. A restart on the 1 in 3 test hill was accomplished with singular ease.

Unfortunately, the basic tractability of the engine was spoiled, at least on our car, by a throttle control which made it impossible to drive smoothly at low speeds. So far as we could see this stickiness was caused by a nylon ball-joint in the linkage which tightened under initial pedal pressure and then freed itself with a jerk; moving it to a new position provided a cure which was only temporary.

Maximum speed is comfortably over the 100 m.p.h. mark. On a flat, straight road we would expect to improve a little on the figure we recorded on a rather cramped banked track but since the engine is then running well over the peak of its power curve, the potential improvement is probably no more than one or two m.p.h. More important is the ability to reach cruising speeds in the eighties or even nineties very quickly indeed and to hold them with an engine quietness and smoothness which makes this speed very deceptive.

When accelerating hard in the gears, the power unit is less unobtrusive; it always remains smooth, although not as silky as the best straight sixes, but the engine note becomes rather looser and harsher as the speed rises over 4,000 r.p.m. Power tails off at the top end and there is little point in going over 5,000 r.p.m. and none at all in entering the red sector on the rev counter which extends from 5,500 r.p.m. to 6,000 r.p.m.

The automatic choke works perfectly both for cold starting and for warming up, which is apparently very quick. We couldn't check this from the temperature gauge because it failed very early in the test, but the heater comes into action extremely rapidly. Hot starting often demands a considerable throttle opening.

Overall fuel consumption (18.4 m.p.g.) was very similar to that of the last Zodiac Mk. III we tested and the steady speed figures were also close over most of the range—a little worse below 50 m.p.h. but better from 70 m.p.h. upwards. Considering the increased size and weight of the Mk. IV, its larger engine and greater performance, this is a satisfactory result. Our 2,200 miles of testing could really be split into two parts; for about 1,500 miles the car was driven extremely hard (but with little mileage in London traffic) and averaged 17 m.p.g.; the remaining 700 miles included a long tour to the north of England at more moderate speeds giving 21 m.p.g., a reasonably close approach to our estimated touring consumption of 21.6 m.p.g.; with a 15-gallon tank, the refuelling range will be in the region of 250–300 miles for most drivers. Oil was consumed at the rate of about one pint to 500 miles.

Transmission

Our test car had a four-speed all-synchromesh gearbox without overdrive and with a floor gear lever—there are several other transmission options as mentioned in the description. The intermediate gears are generally quiet except on the overrun at low speed in first and second and the gearchange, although it has a long travel, is a good one for a large car. At first the synchromesh felt rather obstructive for fast changes but it became smoother as the miles mounted; although it seemed almost unbeatable on the three lower gears, top gear synchromesh was obviously faulty, making fast changes impossible without protest.

The lever is spring-loaded laterally to the right and some drivers would have preferred a weaker spring or none at all—others hardly noticed it. There was also some difference of opinion about the ratios which are rather widely spaced—third gear offers extremely rapid acceleration for overtaking up to the present legal speed limit

Performance

Conditions

Weather: Dry, cool, light wind 10-15 m.p.h.
Temperature: 42°—46°F. Barometer 29.7 in. Hg.
Surface: Dry tarmacadam.
Fuel: Premium grade (97 octane R.M.).

Maximum speeds

	m.p.h.
Mean lap speed banked circuit	102.5
Best one-way $\frac{1}{4}$-mile	103.5
3rd gear	77.0
2nd gear at 5,500 r.p.m.	49.0
1st gear	34.0

"Maximile" speed: (Timed quarter-mile after 1 mile accelerating from rest.)

Mean	97.8
Best	100.0

Acceleration times

m.p.h.	sec.
0-30	3.5
0-40	5.6
0-50	7.5
0-60	11.0
0-70	14.2
0-80	20.1
0-90	28.1
Standing quarter-mile	17.9

m.p.h.	Top sec.	3rd sec.
10-30	—	5.2
20-40	8.0	4.8
30-50	7.1	4.5
40-60	7.0	5.4
50-70	7.7	6.5
60-80	8.7	—
70-90	12.9	—

Hill climbing

At steady speed		lb./ton
Top	1 in 6.9	(Tapley 320)
3rd	1 in 4.5	(Tapley 490)
2nd	1 in 3.1	(Tapley 700)

Speedometer

Indicated	10 20 30 40 50 60 70 80 90 100
True	10½ 21 31 41 50 58½ 67 75½ 85 94
Distance recorder	accurate

Steering

	ft.
Turning circle between kerbs	
Left	33¾
Right	35½
Turns of steering wheel from lock to lock	5

Steering wheel deflection for 50 ft. diameter circle = 1.65 turns

Fuel consumption

Touring (consumption midway between 30 m.p.h. and maximum less 5% allowance for acceleration) ... 21.6 m.p.g.

Overall	18.4 m.p.g.
	= 15.35 litres/100 km.
Total test distance	2,185 miles
Tank capacity (maker's figure)	15 gal.

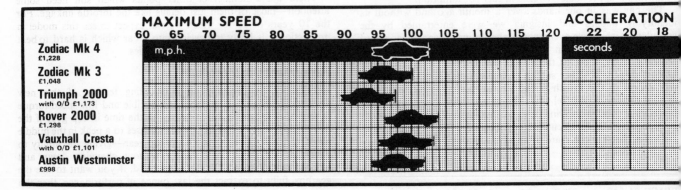

	MAXIMUM SPEED	ACCELERATION
	60 65 70 75 80 85 90 95 100 105 110 115 120	22 20 18
Zodiac Mk 4 £1,228	m.p.h.	seconds
Zodiac Mk 3 £1,048		
Triumph 2000 with O/D £1,173		
Rover 2000 £1,298		
Vauxhall Cresta with O/D £1,101		
Austin Westminster £998		

of 70 m.p.h. but second is low and very close to first, giving the general effect of a three-speed box with an extra emergency bottom gear. This is excellent for reluctant gear changers, less satisfactory for those who enjoy stirring the lever. Some experience of the new Zephyr with a steering-column change makes us believe that anyone who does not need a bench seat will be a great deal happier with the lever on the floor.

Although the use of a diaphragm clutch with hydrostatic adjustment has reduced pedal effort to only about 30 lb., its operation was curiously lacking in feel; together with the poor throttle, to which we have already alluded, this made both initial take-off and gear-changing into jerky processes unless the driver concentrated very hard.

Handling and brakes

Since this is the first British Ford to have independent rear suspension, we approached it with particular interest. Let us say right away that in comparison with the previous Zodiac the extra cost of this arrangement is justified in every way in terms of road-holding, handling and ride—but by comparison with the best all-independent saloons from some other manufacturers we found it a little disappointing.

To deal with the creditable side first, the steering is directionally very stable and the driver never has to pay conscious attention to it except occasionally, when a sharp change of camber deflects the car slightly; because of its low gearing, quite a large movement of the wheel is then necessary for correction. Normally it is sufficiently positive and responsive to feel higher geared than it really is; it is also light, except when parking in very confined spaces when it becomes heavy enough to indicate that higher gearing would not really be practical. Roadholding on bumpy corners is good, the tyres squeal very little, roll and lurch are well below average for a car of this size and kind, and side winds rock the car but do not deflect it badly. You can, in fact, drive it all day at moderately fast speeds on dry roads and have

The front seats recline; the rear seat, with the central armrest folded away, has more than enough width for three people.

Continued on the next page

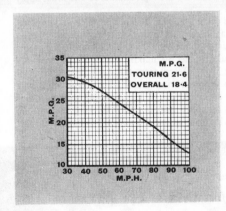

M.P.G.
TOURING 21·6
OVERALL 18·4

Brakes

Pedal pressure, deceleration and equivalent stopping distance from 30 m.p.h.

lb.	g	ft.
25	0.26	115
50	0·55	55
75	0.80	37½
100	0.92	32½
120	0.96	31
Handbrake	0.34	88

Fade test

20 stops at ½g deceleration at 1 min. intervals from a speed midway between 30 m.p.h. and maximum speed (= 66 m.p.h.)

	lb.
Pedal force at beginning	40
Pedal force at 10th stop	40
Pedal force at 20th stop	40

Clutch

Free pedal movement . . . . = ¼ in.
Additional movement to disengage clutch com-
pletely . . . . = 4 in.
Maximum pedal load . . . . = 32 lb.

Weight

Kerb weight (unladen with fuel for approximately 50 miles) . . . . 25.9 cwt.
Front/rear distribution 58½/41½
Weight laden as tested . . . . 29.6 cwt.

Parkability

Gap needed to clear a 6 ft. wide obstruction parked in front

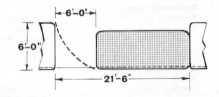

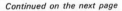

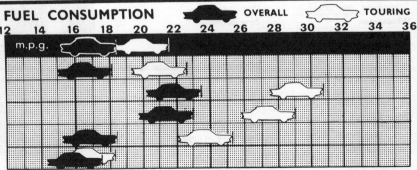

FUEL CONSUMPTION

0-50   20-40 IN TOP   OVERALL   TOURING
12 10 8 6 4 2 0 12 14 16 18 20 22 24 26 28 30 32 34 36
m.p.g.

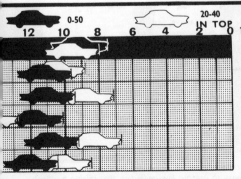

Ford Zodiac Mk. IV
continued

no serious criticisms except for a tendency to wander over white lines and longitudinal ridges.

If, on the other hand, you are in the habit of entering corners extremely fast, either deliberately or by misjudgement; if you are the sort of person to whom high speed emergencies happen; if you drive on wet and slippery roads, the picture is less satisfactory. It is possible on a dry corner to lift the inner rear wheel right off the ground but even before this stage the onset of wheelspin can give a reduction in cornering power which brings the tail round rather sharply. Even on bends of the 80 m.p.h. variety we encountered this condition when a bump or wave in the road surface raised the tail and increased the camber angle of the rear wheels. On wet roads, and particularly on wet, greasy London roads, the throttle must be treated delicately (which was difficult) to avoid wheelspin under acceleration and with even more care on corners to avoid losing the back—it is not always easy to recover it quickly.

Some of this may be blamed on a weight distribution which puts only $41\frac{1}{2}$ per cent of the unladen load on the driving wheels but most of it, we thought, on a roll centre too high at the back giving excessive weight transfer from the inner wheel on corners and also some of the "jacking" effect of simple swing-axle geometry.

The all-disc braking system was slightly on the heavy side but otherwise very satisfactory. Our fade test had virtually no effect at all; a few stops from really high speeds provoked some rumble and judder but without perceptible effect on their power. The water-splash affected braking ability only for a few seconds and then there was a rapid return to normal. Water affected the engine rather more—it cut dead momentarily and then gradually picked up.

An under-facia pull-out handbrake to the left of the steering column passed all objective tests satisfactorily—it held the car on a 1-in-3 gradient and it locked the back wheels from 30 m.p.h. to give a satisfactory emergency stop. Beyond this, it aroused no enthusiasm at all because of its spongy, springy feel and rather stiff release action.

This friction locking lever below the facia (above) allows the steering column to be raised and lowered.

Door handles (left) are recessed so that they cannot be caught accidentally in loose clothing.

Comfort and control

Until springs which compensate automatically for height and load become more common, it will always be difficult for a designer to decide whether to optimize the ride for light or heavy load conditions. We formed the impression that the Zodiac was designed (successfully) for the latter; when driving with only the front seats occupied the rear springs feel rather firm—the net result is comfortable but not exceptional by the high standards one must apply to this class of car.

At very low speeds there is a good deal of thumping and banging from the suspension as the wheels cross pot-holes and cats-eyes—fortunately this diminishes quickly as the speed rises and the whole car becomes very quiet up to 80 m.p.h. which is a deceptively effortless gait, feeling little different from 60 m.p.h. The absence of quarter lights helps to suppress wind noise and conversation is easy at the higher cruising speed. Above 80 m.p.h., wind noise becomes more prominent but certainly not loud unless there is a strong wind blowing. Such wind roar as there is appears to be admitted by

Safety check list

1	**Steering assembly**	
	Steering box position	Near rear of engine. Very well protected.
	Steering column collapsible?	No
	Steering wheel boss padded?	No
2	**Instrument panel**	
	Projecting switches etc.?	Toggle switches and heater control partly recessed inside hard frame. Radio controls, ashtray handle, handbrake and ignition key project.
	Sharp instrument cowls etc.?	Main cowl padded but has thin edge
	Effective padding?	Good padding in front of passenger
3	**Ejection**	
	Anti-burst door latches?	Yes
	"Child-proof" door locks?	On rear doors
4	**Windscreen**	Zone toughened
5	**Door structures**	
	Interior door handles	Good, recessed
	Window winders and quarter light catches	Winders project. No quarter lights
6	**Back of front seat**	Metal frame very heavily padded with high back
7	**Windscreen pillar**	No padding, but no sharp edges
8	**Driving mirror**	
	Framed?	Metal Frame
	Collapsible?	Detachable on impact
9	**Safety harness**	
	Type	3-point with locking reel
	Pillar anchorage	Well placed
	Floor anchorage	Well placed

Boxes totalling no less than 12.5 cu. ft. in volume were stored in the very wide boot. The jack is easy to use but low-geared so that raising a wheel off the ground takes a considerable time.

imperfect door seals and by stuffing these gaps it can be reduced to a very low level at any speed.

Some large cars look roomy inside and turn out not to be—the Zodiac genuinely is. The rear seat will easily take three people and the leg room is very generous. The front seats have a large range of adjustment, quite adequate for tall people and, in addition, their back rests are adjustable for rake—they won't fold quite flat because they rest on the front edge of the back seat. The upholstery is firm but by general agreement all the seats were rated comfortable for long journeys, though several people would have liked more support in the small of the back. Also by general agreement, the most tiring feature of the car on long runs was considered to be the lack of side support which means that a continuous muscular effort must be made, particularly by the front occupants, just to stay upright.

There were few complaints about the driving position. Pedals are well-placed and the steering wheel position allows most people to stretch their arms if they wish to. The column is not telescopically adjustable but a release lever alongside the column allows height adjustment through a range of 1¼ in. Our first impression was that nobody would ever want it anywhere but in the top position (when the wheel is still quite low) but we found one member of the staff who preferred it down.

Forward visibility is surprisingly good considering the size of the long, flat bonnet, which at least makes the width of the car obvious. In wet weather there are rather large unwiped portions in the upper corners of the screen. Visibility to the rear is spoiled by large quarter panels; the mirror could, with advantage, be a little bigger and the tail, although fortunately short, is completely invisible below the bottom edge of the rear window when parking. The headlights are probably the best fitted to any production car with the possible exception of certain Citroen models.

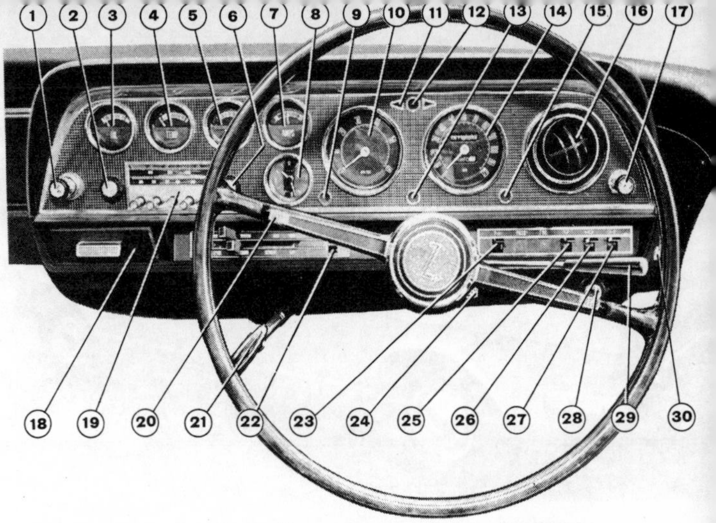
1
2
3
4
5
6
7
8
9
10
11
12
13
14
15
16
17
18
19
20
21
22
23
24
25
26
27
28
29
30

1, cigarette lighter. 2, radio. 3, oil pressure gauge. 4, water temperature. 5, fuel gauge. 6, radio. 7, ammeter. 8, clock. 9, handbrake warning light. 10, rev. counter. 11, indicator warning lights. 12, main beam warning light. 13, side/head warning light. 14, speedometer. 15, ignition light. 16, Aeroflow vent. 17, panel/interior lights. 18, ashtray. 19, radio. 20, horn bar. 21, handbrake. 22, two-speed heater fan. 23, parking lights. 24, steering column adjustment lever. 25, windscreen wipers. 26, screen washers. 27, head and side lights. 28, ingition/starter. 29, indicators/headlamp flasher. 30, speedometer trip.

First-class heating and ventilation is something one expects in modern Fords. There are two sliding levers one controlling air temperature, the other its distribution to car or screen; when the latter is moved beyond its normal left-hand position it progressively opens the Aeroflow ducts which can be adjusted to direct cold air in

Continued on the next page

Specification

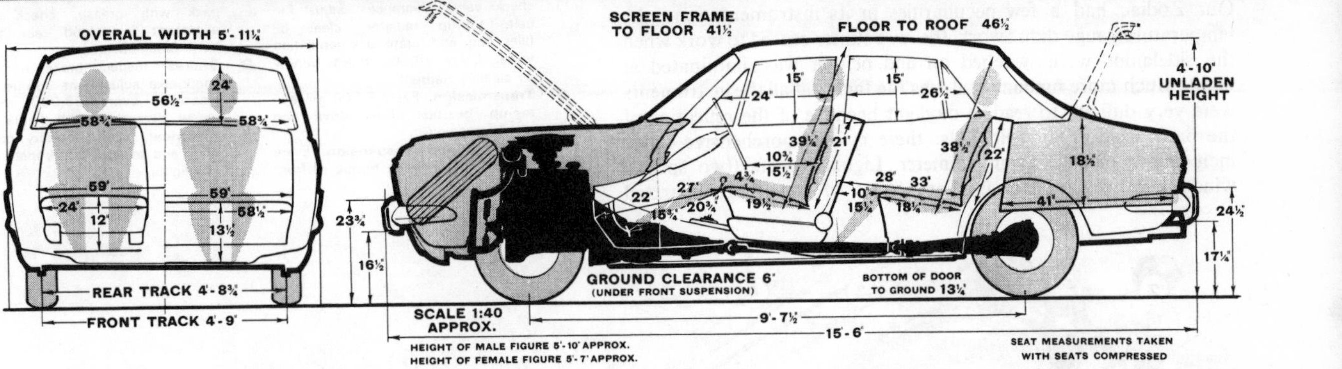
OVERALL WIDTH 5'-11¼
24"
56½"
58¾"
58¾"
59"
59"
24"
12"
13½
58½"
REAR TRACK 4'-8¾
FRONT TRACK 4'-9"
SCREEN FRAME TO FLOOR 41½
FLOOR TO ROOF 46½
4'-10" UNLADEN HEIGHT
15"
15"
24"
26½
39¼
21"
10¾
15½
38½
22"
18½
4¾
27"
22"
15¾
20¾
19½
28"
33"
10"
15½
18¼
41"
24½"
23¾
16½
17¼
GROUND CLEARANCE 6" (UNDER FRONT SUSPENSION)
BOTTOM OF DOOR TO GROUND 13¼
SCALE 1:40 APPROX.
9'-7½"
15'-6"
HEIGHT OF MALE FIGURE 5'-10" APPROX.
HEIGHT OF FEMALE FIGURE 5'-7" APPROX.
SEAT MEASUREMENTS TAKEN WITH SEATS COMPRESSED

Engine

Cylinders	60° V6
Bore and stroke	93.663 mm. x 72.415 mm.
Cubic capacity	2,994 c.c.
Valves	overhead (push rods)
Compression ratio	8.9:1
Carburetter	Weber 40 DFA twin choke d/d
Fuel pump	AC mechanical
Oil filter	Full flow
Max. power (installed)	128 b.h.p. at 4,500 r.p.m.
Max. torque (installed)	176 lb. ft. at 3,000 r.p.m.

Transmission

Clutch	
Top gear (s/m)	1.000
3rd gear (s/m)	1.412
2nd gear (s/m)	2.214
1st gear (s/m)	3.163
Reverse	3.346
Final drive	3.7 hypoid
M.p.h. at 1,000 r.p.m. in:—	
Top gear	19.7
3rd gear	14.0
2nd gear	8.9
1st gear	6.8

Chassis

Construction	All-steel unitary

Brakes

Type	Girling discs with vacuum servo
Dimensions	9.63 in. front, 9.91 in. rear discs
Friction areas:	
Front	20.8 sq. ins. of lining operating on 214 sq. ins. of disc
Rear	14.0 sq. ins. of lining operating on 139 sq. ins. of disc

Suspension and steering

Front	MacPherson struts with anti-roll bar
Rear	Independent by semi-trailing single wishbones each side and coil springs
Shock absorbers:	
Front and rear	Telescopic
Steering gear	Re-circulating ball worm and nut
Tyres	6.70-13 Goodyear G8
Rim size	4½J-13

Coachwork and equipment

Starting handle	No
Jack	Screw pillar type
Jacking points	2 each side under door sills
Battery	12-volt negative earth, 53 amp. hours capacity
Number of electrical fuses	10 plus 2 spare holders
Indicators	Self-cancelling flashers
Screen wipers	Twin-blade electric
Screen washers	Trico electric
Sun visors	2
Locks:	
With ignition key	Front doors and boot
Interior heater	Fresh-air type with two-speed fan and additional Aeroflow cold air ventilation
Extras	Automatic transmission, Laycock overdrive, leather upholstery, steering column lock. Other extras available for export models, including protective undershields and heavy-duty suspension
Upholstery	Cirrus vinyl
Floor covering	Cut pile carpet
Alternative body styles	None

Maintenance

Sump	8 pints S.A.E. 10W/30 (plus 1½ pints in filter)
Gearbox	3¼ pints S.A.E. 80
Rear axle	3 pints S.A.E. 90
Steering gear	S.A.E. 80
Cooling system (including heater)	19½ pints (drain taps 2)
Chassis lubrication	None
Minimum service interval	6,000 miles
Ignition timing	12° before t.d.c. static
Contact breaker gap	.014-.016 in.
Sparking plug gap	.023-.027 in.
Sparking plug type	Autolite AG 22
Tappet clearances (hot)	Inlet 0.010 in.; Exhaust 0.018 in.
Valve timing:	
inlet opens	20° b.t.d.c.
inlet closes	56° a.b.d.c.
exhaust opens	62° b.b.d.c.
exhaust closes	14° a.t.d.c.
Front wheel toe-in	0.21 in. (All at normal laden height)
Camber angle	1° positive (All at normal laden height)
Castor angle	Zero (All at normal laden height)
Kingpin inclination	7° (All at normal laden height)
Tyre pressures	24 lb. all round normal 28 lb. all round for sustained high speed

Bumpers are well wrapped round the body corners and have rubber inserts in the overriders. Twin reversing lights are standard.

Ford Zodiac Mk. IV
continued

any direction. A two-speed fan can be used to maintain the air flow when the car is moving slowly; this is tolerably quiet at its lower speed but very noisy in the high-speed position. The system is completed by air extraction grilles in the rear quarters (with non-return flap valves which sometimes rattle in gusty weather) so there should never be any need to open the windows.

Fittings and furniture

Our Zodiac had a few peculiarities in its instrumentation—the temperature gauge didn't work, the rev counter ceased to work when the sidelamps were switched on and neither was illuminated at night. Much more fundamental was the fact that all the instruments were very difficult to read in daylight because of the reflection of the back window in their dials; there is a comprehensive range including a clock and an ammeter. Lights, wipers (two speed), windscreen washer and auxiliary lights (if fitted) are operated

by a row of rather small toggle switches which must be memorized—although they are identified by symbols, these are difficult to see even when stationary let alone when moving.

One might reasonably expect more parcel and map stowage places inside the car. There are no pockets in the doors or seat backs and there is no parcel tray below the facia. There is a small but useful box with a hinged lid between the front seats and a much larger downward-opening locker below the facia on the passenger's side with a rather strong closing spring—two people complained that their wives or children had been trapped by it.

Standard fittings include a headlamp flasher, reversing lights, a cigarette lighter, coat hooks and a vanity mirror behind the passenger's sun visor. The seats and interior surfaces are trimmed in Cirrus black vinyl giving an effect which most people liked.

Servicing and accessibility

There is a good deal of space round the compact engine and all the components requiring periodic checks, adjustment or replenishment are very accessible. This applies to the spare wheel as well—since it lies under the bonnet there is never any question of removing the luggage to uncover it. The jack is easy to use but it takes a long time to raise the car high enough to get the wheels airborne.

All the chassis components, including the differential, are lubricated for life. The gearbox oil is changed at 3,000 miles but never again; the engine oil and filter are changed at the same time but, thereafter, only at 6,000 mile intervals. The brakes and clutch are entirely self-adjusting.

Maintenance chart
(After the 3,000 mile service)

A Engine. Every 6,000 miles—change oil, renew filter, adjust and lubricate distributor, adjust sparking plugs, clean fuel filter, clean air filter, check valve clearances, adjust fan belt, top-up radiator, clean oil filler cap and crankcase ventilation valve. Every 18,000 miles—renew air cleaner element.

B Transmission. Every 6,000 miles—top-up gearbox, final drive and clutch reservoir.

C Steering and suspension. Every 6,000 miles—check torque of front cross member retaining bolts, check gaiters on steering and suspension joints, top-up steering box. Every 18,000 miles—remove front hub assemblies wash bearings and re-pack with grease, check wheel alignment front and rear, top-up front shock absorbers.

D Brakes. Inspect brake pads and handbrake adjustment, top-up brake reservoir. Every 36,000 miles—renew all seals and hydraulic fluid.

E Electrical. Check battery connections and top-up, check instruments and lights.

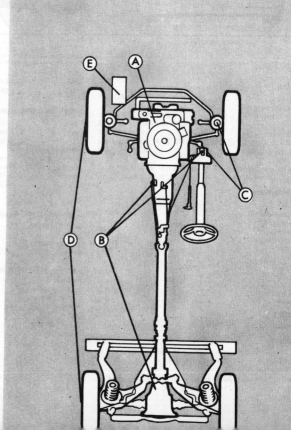

1, distributor. 2, brake reservoir. 3, clutch reservoir. 4, fuses. 5, jack and wheelbrace. 6, petrol pump. 7, battery. 8, dipstick. 9, radiator cap. 10, oil filler cap. 11, washer bottle.

MAKE Ford; MODEL Zodiac Mk. IV; MAKERS Ford Motor Company Ltd., Dagenham, Essex.

ZEPHYR 6 Mk IV 2,495 c.c.

AT A GLANCE: New 5-seater replacement for Mark III Zephyr with smooth vee-6 engine. Sensitive fade-free disc brakes on all four wheels. New independent rear suspension behaves better laden than with the driver only on board. High levels of wind and road noise, but engine very quiet. Comfortable seats and lots of room inside, but larger external dimensions and very heavy steering when parking. A worthwhile improvement on the previous model.

MANUFACTURER:
Ford Motor Co. Ltd., Warley, Essex.

PRICES
Basic	Not available
Purchase Tax	when these
Total (in G.B.) ..	pages closed for press. See first

EXTRAS (inc. P.T.)
	page of News
Ford push-button radio	and Views later
Ford inertia-reel seat belts	in this issue.
Bucket seats	

PERFORMANCE SUMMARY
Mean maximum speed ..	96 m.p.h.
Standing start ¼-mile ..	19·6 sec.
0–60 m.p.h.	14·6 sec.
30–70 m.p.h. (through gears)	15·8 sec.
Overall fuel consumption ..	19·4 m.p.g.
Miles per tankful	290

FORD (in this country, at least) are not a company to make changes purely for the sake of change. A new Ford model, therefore, is a new car which warrants the fullest treatment we can give it and this issue contains drawings and technical information on all details of the new Mark IV saloons, except its performance on the road; that is the purpose of this test.

We chose what we considered to be potentially the most popular version of the new range, a Zephyr 6 with floor-change manual gearbox and bucket front seats. With its close-to-£1,000 price tag all in, this is the Ford that most firms would choose for their junior executives and for family men with a lot to carry. It is one of the largest cars, size for price, available today.

The Zephyr 6 has a 2½-litre version of the new vee-6 engine with bore and stroke identical with those of the 1700 V-4 Corsair. It develops 112 b.h.p. net at 4,750 r.p.m., which is 14 b.h.p. more than the previous Zephyr in-line six and 3 b.h.p. more than the previous Zodiac. Maximum torque is practically the same as the old Zodiac's with 137·5 lb.ft. at 3,000 r.p.m. The new car has put on a bit of weight—it is larger overall—and turns the scales at 25·8 cwt ready for the road, about 1¼ cwt heavier than the last Zephyr 6 we tested almost

exactly two years ago on 10 April 1964.

Bearing these figures in mind, one might expect the new car to perform about as well as a Mark III Zodiac, but it is difficult to verify this because we have only tested the automatic versions in recent years. Compared with the previous Executive Zodiac, the new Mark IV Zephyr is much more sprightly. From rest, 60 m.p.h. is reached ½ sec earlier in 14·6 sec and 80 m.p.h. comes up 3·2 sec sooner in 28·7 sec. Maximum speed was a regular 96 m.p.h. mean for several laps of the M.I.R.A. banked circuit with 102 registered on our electric fifth-wheel speedometer over the most favourable quarter-mile.

In its performance characteristics the new engine feels much like that of the 2-litre V-4 Corsair GT we tested recently. There is a lot of bottom-end punch, and although the engine can be run up to almost 6,000 before valve bounce sets in, it does not pay to go more than a couple of hundred r.p.m. beyond the peak of the power curve (4,750) for maximum acceleration.

During this testing we were impressed with the quietness of the engine, for it never made itself heard except at the very top end; the only noise was the whoosh and roar of well-muffled intake and exhaust. In terms of smoothness there are no noticeable vibration periods, yet the

▶

MAKE: **Ford**

TYPE: **Zephyr 6 Mk IV**

Speed range and time in seconds

m.p.h.	Top (3.90)	Third (5.50)	Second (8.63)	First (12.32)
10—30	—	7.4	4.4	3.3
20—40	9.5	6.1	4.4	—
30—50	9.7	6.8	5.6	—
40—60	10.7	7.8	—	—
50—70	12.0	11.6	—	—
60—80	16.5	19.2	—	—
70—70	26.4	—	—	—

WEIGHT

Kerb weight (with oil, water and half-full fuel tank): 25·8cwt (2,896lb-1,317 kg)
Front-rear distribution, per cent F. 57·5; R. 42·5
Laden as tested .... 28·8cwt (3,232lb-1,471kg)

TURNING CIRCLES

Between kerbs .. L, 37ft 5in.; R, 38ft 7in.
Between walls .. L, 40ft 4in.; R, 40ft 7in.
Steering wheel turns lock to lock .. 5·5

PERFORMANCE DATA

Top gear m.p.h. per 1,000 r.p.m. .. .. 19·4
Mean piston speed at max. power 1,880ft/min.
Engine revs at mean max. speed .. 4,950 r.p.m.
B.h.p. per ton laden 78

OIL CONSUMPTION

Miles per pint (SAE 10W/30) 2,000

FUEL CONSUMPTION

At constant speeds

30 m.p.h.	..	..	..	..	30·5 m.p.g.
40 m.p.h.	..	..	..	..	28·8 m.p.g.
50 m.p.h.	..	..	..	..	26·6 m.p.g.
60 m.p.h.	..	..	..	..	23·3 m.p.g.
70 m.p.h.	..	..	..	..	20·1 m.p.g.
80 m.p.h.	..	..	..	..	17·5 m.p.g.
90 m.p.h.	..	..	..	..	14·6 m.p.g.

Overall m.p.g. 19·4 (14·6 litres/100km)
Normal range m.p.g. 17-25 (16·6-11·3 litres/100km)
Test distance .. .. 872 miles
Estimated (DIN) m.p.g. 18·3 (15·5 litres/100km)
Grade .. .. Premium (96·2-98·6 RM)

TEST CONDITIONS

Weather .. Cloudy with 5-10 m.p.h. wind
Temperature .. 6 deg. C. (43 deg. F.)
Barometer .. .. 29·7in. Hg.
Surfaces .. Dry concrete and tarmac

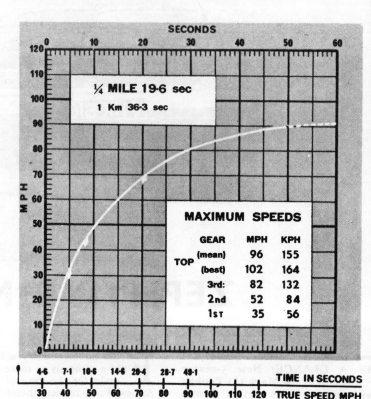

¼ MILE 19·6 sec
1 Km 36·3 sec

MAXIMUM SPEEDS

	GEAR	MPH	KPH
TOP	(mean)	96	155
	(best)	102	164
	3rd:	82	132
	2nd	52	84
	1ST	35	56

TIME IN SECONDS	4·6	7·1	10·6	14·6	20·4	28·7	49·1				
TRUE SPEED MPH	30	40	50	60	70	80	90	100	110	120	
INDICATED MPH	32	42	51	60	70	79	88	97			

BRAKES

(from 30 m.p.h. in neutral)	Pedal load	Retardation	Equiv. distance
	25lb	0·25g	120ft
	50lb	0·58g	52ft
	75lb	0·80g	38ft
	90lb	1·00g	30·1ft
Handbrake		0·30g	100ft

CLUTCH Pedal load and travel—30lb and 4·5in.

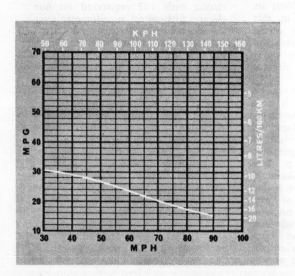

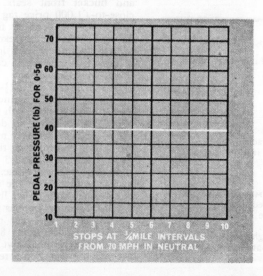

STOPS AT ¼ MILE INTERVALS
FROM 70 MPH IN NEUTRAL

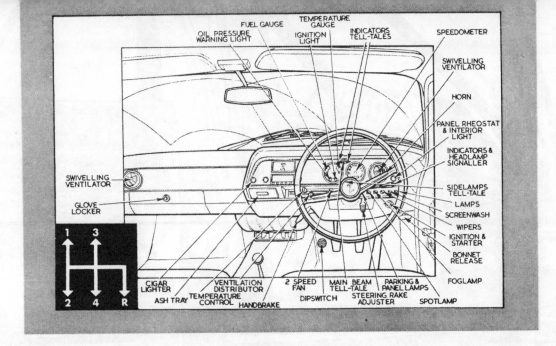

FUEL GAUGE · TEMPERATURE GAUGE · OIL PRESSURE WARNING LIGHT · IGNITION LIGHT · INDICATORS TELL-TALES · SPEEDOMETER · SWIVELLING VENTILATOR · HORN · PANEL RHEOSTAT & INTERIOR LIGHT · INDICATORS & HEADLAMP SIGNALLER · SIDELAMPS TELL-TALE · LAMPS · SCREENWASH · WIPERS · IGNITION & STARTER · BONNET RELEASE · FOGLAMP · SPOTLAMP · PARKING & PANEL LAMPS · STEERING RAKE ADJUSTER · MAIN BEAM TELL-TALE · DIPSWITCH · 2 SPEED FAN · HANDBRAKE · TEMPERATURE CONTROL · ASH TRAY · VENTILATION DISTRIBUTOR · CIGAR LIGHTER · GLOVE LOCKER · SWIVELLING VENTILATOR

sweetness of a straight six has been lost somehow particularly at the top end of the rev range.

Acceleration figures for each gear show the torque curve to be very flat with almost equal times for each 20-m.p.h. increment. First and second feel rather low compared with third, which has a very flexible range from 10 to 80 m.p.h. if required, although it is better not to go beyond 70 before changing into top. This makes it an ideal ratio for sweeping through the twisty bends of a country lane or surging past the inevitable 30–40-m.p.h. heavy lorries on trunk roads; each time we changed down again into second when baulked, we realized third would still have been adequate.

Gearbox

The gear-change is well up to the high standards set by smaller Fords, and in many ways it works and feels just like that of a GT Cortina. Reverse is over to the right beyond top, with a strong spring guard, and a key to the positions is moulded in the knob. The synchromesh is light and completely effective on all four ratios. The indirect gears run quietly with only a very faint, subdued whine that would never normally be noticed.

Despite being ½in. bigger in diameter and using higher spring clamping pressures, the clutch now needs a pedal load of only 30lb. instead of 50, while the travel has been cut by one inch to 4½in. There is an over-centre diaphragm spring which causes a rather abrupt take-up, but we were able to spin the back wheels on dry concrete without clutch slip. No hot smells or loss of efficiency resulted from easing the car from rest on a 1-in-3 test hill.

Ford still use Girling brakes with servo assistance, but discs are now fitted at the back as well as at the front; the entire system, including the handbrake, is self-adjusting for wear. Tested in neutral from 30

m.p.h., the brakes showed slightly better sensitivity than those of the previous model, with the rear wheels starting to lock at 75lb on the pedal and an easy 90lb giving 1g retardation. During fade tests from 70 m.p.h. there was no loss of braking power at all, quite the opposite in fact, with the driver having to lift off from 45 to 35lb during each stop to maintain 0·5g on the Mintex gauge (our chart shows the mean value of 40lb). There was, however, some slight unevenness as temperatures increased, which made itself felt as a twitching through the steering wheel; occasionally we encountered this on the road as well. Stability during braking was excellent, with barely any slewing.

The handbrake is worked by a T-handle on the left of the steering column under the facia. It is easy to reach with seat belts fastened and

will fly off rather noisily by twisting the handle and letting go. Tested on its own from 30 m.p.h. it proved easily able to lock the back wheels (0·3g) and held facing up or down a 1-in-3. However, we were surprised to find that when pulled really hard, as it needed to be, the handle came out a good 6in. beyond its more usual "on" position as something in the mechanism stretched. We would be worried about leaving the car parked like this, in case it caused some permanent set.

In one aspect the new big Ford has stolen a march on its competitors in the 2½-3-litre class by including independent rear suspension in its specification. The system used is a new and unusual one with articulated fixed-length drive shafts and semi-trailing alloy wishbones. It is designed to give controlled camber and toe-in angle changes to the wheels to

The spare wheel is mounted in the nose of the car to leave the boot area clear. Radiator header tank, battery and screen washer bottle are all easy to fill and the dipstick is tucked away near the top radiator hose

▶

Doors open very wide and each has an armrest-cum-door-pull; the interior release handles are recessed into rectangular openings below the window winders. Front-seat backrests are fixed but the steering wheel is adjustable for height

Ford Zephyr 6 Mk IV . . .

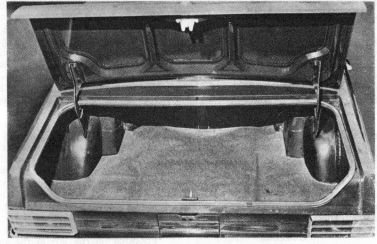

The boot is deep and roomy with no spare wheel to steal the space from luggage. Its lid is countersprung but there is a high sill to lift cases over

compensate for the weight distribution differences between the driver-only and fully-laden conditions. With passengers in the back it is most effective and the previous tail-swing and poor steering response when carrying a load is effectively eliminated.

In this loaded state there is an initial stable understeering tendency as the corner is entered which decreases towards the apex, so that the car seems to follow round without any further correction. With only two in the front there is a big difference. As the car goes into the turn it feels just the same until the lateral forces reach the tail, which rolls appreciably and causes very definite oversteer. During fast laps of a closed test circuit we lifted the inside rear wheel at this point, and rather than be caught out by sudden breakaway, we preferred to flick the tail round in stages by sawing at the steering wheel.

On ordinary roads, of course, one never reaches this point and the Zephyr can be thrust through fast bends, leaning hard but holding a very stable line. The liveliness of the previous beam axle is all gone, and we were able to patter over a level crossing diagonally without the tail tramping sideways.

Unfortunately, the new Zephyr has more weight in the nose (the spare wheel has been moved up front) and although the steering ratio is slightly lower, wheel effort has increased. We measured 5½ turns between locks on a 38ft turning dircle, although practically half a turn of this seemed to be springiness in the mounting of the mechanism. There is a very strong self-centring action which does not decrease much with speed, and manoeuvring to park the car calls for beefy muscular effort. We feel this would be beyond the strength of most women and any family man whose wife likes to drive should seriously consider the optional power assistance.

Despite its extra weight and bulk,

the new Zephyr returned an overall fuel consumption of 19·6 m.p.g., which is slightly better than before. Big Fords always seem to have a dip in their steady speed fuel graphs around 70 m.p.h., so our estimated (DIN) figure is for once unrealistically low. On a run we found 20 m.p.g. quite easy to get, although cruising at near 90 m.p.h. gives only 15 m.p.g. At this speed the engine is revving at 4,650 r.p.m., with a very low mean piston speed of 1,830 ft/min, well within its potential.

At speed the Zephyr runs more true than its predecessor, and showed remarkably little deviation when buffeted in gale-force winds across the downs behind Beachy Head. On motorways it runs straight right up to the maximum speed and there is no delay to steering movements when changing lanes.

One of our criticisms of the last Zodiac was the loud wind roar from the front door edges above 75 m.p.h. and despite fixed front quarterlights

Tested before its announcement, the Zephyr 6 was disguised with masking tape over the name plates. There are no over-riders and the twin reversing lamps under the bumper are extra

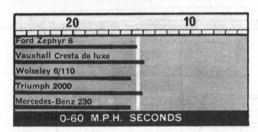

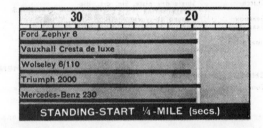

	MAXIMUM SPEED (mean) M.P.H.
TOTAL Approx £1,000	Ford Zephyr 6
PRICE £1,162	Vauxhall Cresta de luxe
£1,180	Wolseley 6/110
£1,119	Triumph 2000
£2,355	Mercedes-Benz 230

STANDING-START ¼-MILE (secs.)

HOW THE FORD ZEPHYR 6 Mk IV COMPARES:

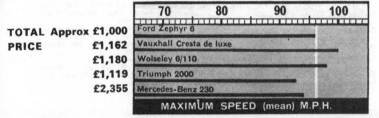

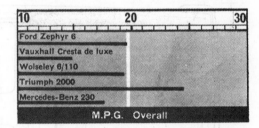

0-60 M.P.H. SECONDS

M.P.G. Overall

there has been no improvement. With the radio speaker on the rear shelf we had trouble hearing it unless the volume was turned well up for motorways.

Another aspect where the car disappoints is in the comfort of the suspension. The ride is harsh and decidedly noisy, every dip and ridge seeming to thump through the body, first at the front and then the back. Taut springs and firm damping give good resistance to pitching and the Zephyr ran across our close-set concrete waves in a most impressive and level manner. The washboard corrugations were completely ironed out from 40 through to 60 m.p.h., but the *pavé* track caused a lot of rattles and disturbing bangs as the wheels bounced about on the uneven slabs.

The tyres, too, make a lot of noise at times, whining on some types of road dressing and growling deeply on others. All the time it feels as if they have been inflated too hard, and although we started the test at 28 p.s.i. all round for our performance

work, there was no improvement when we later let them down to the normal pressure of 24.

For the first time these British Fords are fitted with an automatic starting device on the carburettor and it worked perfectly throughout the test. Hot or cold, one just touched the accelerator, turned the key and the engine started. Always it would pull away smoothly without any hesitation and idled smoothly. Within a mile from leaving home in the morning the heater blows out warm air.

Aeroflow ventilation of a type is fitted to the new Mark IV cars, but it is not as good as the system used on the Cortina and Corsair. There are extractor grilles on the rear quarters which dispense with the need to open a window for a through flow, and face-level ventilators each side of the facia. However, the temperature control proved very insensitive, switching itself suddenly from hot to cold over less than half an inch of its 4·5in. range and spoiling the effectiveness of the sensibly planned dis-

tribution valve. On the credit side, back seat passengers receive a good flow round their feet and at the same time those in the front can arrange for a refreshing cool stream to blow at face level.

The optional bucket seats are good, with much better springing than in the past. All the occupants sit high and have good visibility, so there is no disadvantage on this score in having to travel in the back. Lengthening the wheelbase by 8in., plus the shorter engine, have improved legroom by at least as much and the driver can now get well back from the pedals if he has long legs. In the back it is possible to stretch out, cross the knees and move around to prevent getting stiff on long runs.

An innovation is the vertical adjustment for the steering wheel which raises or lowers its rim by 1·5in. and is released and locked by a quick acting lever below the facia on the right.

In front of him the driver sees a small circular speedometer, accurate in the middle of its range and (even

▶

more unusual) pessimistic at the top end; there is a total mileage recorder (with 10ths) only, and this too is dead accurate. On the left is a matching dial containing a steady and accurate fuel gauge with water thermometer alongside and two warning lights below. To the right of the column is a row of piano-key switches for the accessories, all labelled and illuminated at night to match the instruments.

Most features of the new Ford show considerable improvements over the Mark III models. It is a bigger car overall, with much more room inside and considerably better and more comfortable furniture. There is a substantial performance increase, better braking, less heavy fuel consumption and the roadholding (especially with the car laden) has been made safer. The comfort of the suspension and general noise level seem less good comparatively, but the price is a competitive one in a very tough sector of the big-car market.

SPECIFICATION : FORD ZEPHYR 6 Mk IV, FRONT ENGINE, REAR-WHEEL DRIVE

ENGINE

Cylinders ..	6, in 60 deg. vee
Cooling system ..	Water; pump, fan and thermo-stat
Bore ..	93·7mm (3·69in.)
Stroke ..	60·3mm (2·38in.)
Displacement ..	2,495 c.c. (152·2 cu. in.)
Valve gear ..	Overhead, pushrods and rockers
Compression ratio ..	9·1-to-1
Carburettor ..	Zenith 38 IVT
Fuel pump ..	AC mechanical
Oil filter ..	Full-flow, renewable element
Max. power ..	112 b.h.p. (net) at 4,750 r.p.m.
Max. torque ..	137·5 lb. ft. (net) at 3,000 r.p.m.

TRANSMISSION

Clutch ..	Single dry plate, 9in. dia., diaphragm spring
Gearbox..	4-speed, all synchromesh
Gear ratios ..	Top 1·0, Third 1·41, Second 2·21, First 3·16, Reverse 3·35
Final drive ..	Hypoid bevel, 3·9 to 1

CHASSIS AND BODY

Construction ..	Integral with steel body

SUSPENSION

Front ..	Independent MacPherson struts with co-axial coil springs and dampers, anti-roll bar
Rear ..	Independent, semi-trailing arms, coil springs, telescopic dampers

STEERING

Type ..	Recirculating ball
Wheel dia. ..	16·5in.

BRAKES

Make and type ..	Girling discs front and rear
Servo ..	Girling vacuum type
Dimensions ..	F, 9·6in. dia.; R, 9·9in. dia.
Swept area ..	F, 214 sq. in.; R, 139 sq. in. Total 353 sq. in. (245 sq. in. per ton laden)

WHEELS

Type ..	Pressed steel, 5 studs, 4·5in. wide rim
Tyres ..	Goodyear, Firestone or India tubeless (Goodyear G.8 on test car), 6·70–13in.

EQUIPMENT

Battery ..	12-volt 53-amp. hr,
Generator ..	Lucas C40L 300 watt d.c.

Headlamps ..	2 Lucas sealed-beam 50—40-watt
Reversing lamp ..	Extra
Electric fuses ..	10, including circuit breakers
Screen wipers ..	2-speed, self-parking
Screen washer ..	Standard, electric
Interior heater ..	Standard, fresh-air type
Safety belts ..	Extra, anchorages built in
Interior trim ..	P.v.c. seats, p.v.c. headlining
Floor covering ..	Looped-pile carpets
Starting handle ..	No provision
Jack ..	Screw pillar
Jacking points ..	2 each side under sills
Other bodies ..	None

MAINTENANCE

Fuel tank ..	15 Imp. gallons (no reserve) (68 litres)
Cooling system ..	19·5 pints (including heater) (11 litres)
Engine sump ..	9·5 pints (5·4 litres) SAE 10W/30. Change oil every 5,000 miles. Change filter element every 5,000 miles.
Gearbox ..	3·25 pints SAE. Change oil after first 5,000 miles only.
Final drive ..	3 pints SAE 90. No change necessary
Grease ..	No points
Tyre pressures ..	F and R, 24 p.s.i. (normal driving); F and R, 28 p.s.i. (fast driving)

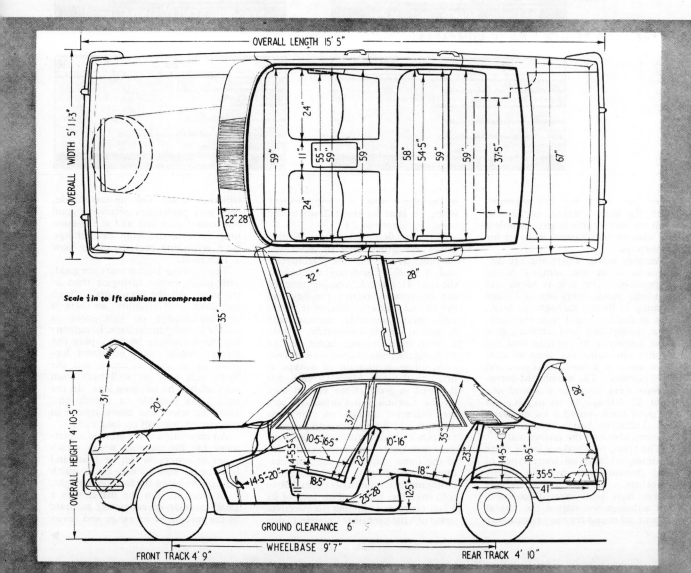

This is the automatic version of the new Zodiac. There is a rev counter, separate gauges for fuel, oil pressure, water temperature and battery current, and the speedometer has a trip mileage recorder. Reclining front seats are standard

Zephyr 6 we drove in Tunis had plenty of performance and would also top the 100 m.p.h.

Both Zodiacs and Zephyrs were very stable directionally and neither camber nor ridges along the road edges caused the cars to wander, and the strong winds scarcely affected them. What we at first took for directional vagueness proved to be an impression gained from the low-geared steering which has a sloppy feel around the centre point, with too much ineffectual movement of the steering wheel. Towards the locks the steering quickens and when taking a positive steering action the car controlled quite precisely.

The present sealing of the doors and windows is perfectly satisfactory for its primary purposes, but is thought to be responsible for the external wind noise, which becomes too loud at high cruising speeds. Otherwise, the Zodiacs in particular were a lot quieter than the models they replace.

Comfort is noticeably improved, too; the Zodiac seats are thickly padded and " dead " sprung so the ride was smoother, apart from the fact that the new suspension gave more level progress. The absence of roll and of sideways movements of the tail over rough roads contributed a lot to the stability and comfort of

Zodiac Automatic   2,994 c.c.   *DRIVING IMPRESSIONS—By THE EDITOR*

ONE way of getting to know a new car is to pound it south over the not-always good roads extending from Tunis on the Mediterranean coast of Africa to the edge of the desert proper, and back again. This we did with the new 6-cylinder Fords, covering some 630 miles in two days. The few main metalled roads have long undulating straights with unmade edges; while we were there, they were buffeted by fierce winds. Storms and wind together caused wash-outs where normally dry stream beds crossed the road and there were some sand-drifts. There is practically no traffic, and we were able to hold over 90 m.p.h. for long periods on some desert roads, both Zephyr and Zodiac showing how rapidly they can cover long distances. Our first car was a Zodiac with automatic transmission, export suspension and tyres blown up to 28 p.s.i. for fast, hot driving. Only recently run-in, it was less lively than we had expected and would not reach 100 m.p.h. The automatic changes were smooth and sweet, and the maximum kick-down speed was only 54 m.p.h. We decided that this car was not representative from the performance point of view and that the hard tyres

and stiffer suspension were detracting from the ride and causing vibration through the body. The engine was always smooth and mechanically quiet, such sound as was heard at high r.p.m. seeming to come from the fan and perhaps the air intake. A gentle, easy-going engine, this three-litre was over its power peak and beginning to run out of breath well before the red section of the r.p.m. indicator was reached.

Full throttle acceleration in D1 gave change-up speeds of about 22 and 55 m.p.h. These are below the designed figures, which should be 32-36 and 60-64 as confirmed by other automatic Zodiacs in the group taken to Tunisia. The kick-down speeds at full throttle should be about 2 m.p.h. below the maximum change-up speeds. The gear-selector on our car could have been more positive.

When we changed to a manual Zodiac we found it was faster and accelerated better than the automatic one. It reached 102 m.p.h. quite quickly and pulled really hard in the middle r.p.m. range. In this respect the advantage of the extra half-litre as compared with the Zephyr 6 engine could be felt. Even so, the

the occupants. For the first time also there is leg- and foot-room to spare in the back of a big Ford.

One or two sections of road in Tunisia were still being made up and it was over these that the real advantages of the i.r.s. became apparent. The cars held a straight course, hands-off, with no hopping about at the back, with pretty good suspension damping, and at no time did our car bottom (carrying three people and luggage).

Although North Africa was not hot three weeks ago, there were sufficient heat and humidity to exercise the ventilation system. Below 40 m.p.h. there is little ram effect but the rather noisy booster fan (fast or very fast) churns the air through the ducts very well. At higher speeds plenty of fresh ram air floats through the face-level ducts. The screen wiper blades are long and efficient and gave a clean sweep and even pressure at over 80 m.p.h.

We finished our days of driving fresh and relaxed, which speaks well for the cars. There were no breakdowns in over 15,000 miles of communal driving and no single car used more than one pint of oil during the two days of testing.

Zephyr and Zodiac go V6

MICHAEL COTTON

Compact V6 engines available in Ford's new Zephyr and Zodiac Mark 4s

COMPACT V6 engines of 2.5 and 3.0 litres capacity have been developed by Ford of Britain to power their new Mark 4 Zephyr and Zodiac range. The cars feature an ingenious independent rear suspension, servo-assisted (and self-adjusting) disc brakes on all four wheels, and new automatic or four-speed shift transmissions with an added option, Laycock overdrive. The many refinements include Aeroflow ventilation, an automatic choke, adjustable steering column rake, and for the Zodiac, an alternator and sporting instrumentation.

Every single component, right down to the doorhandles, has been specially prepared for the Mark 4s during a five-year, £28 million development programme which culminated with an elaborate preview in Tunisia for distributors, dealers, and Press. On the fast, but not always smooth African roads the Fords were shown off to very good effect—maximum speeds of around 100 mph can be maintained indefinitely, while braking, handling and ride all reach extremely high levels.

Some fresh thinking has been put into the body design. The V6 engines are eight inches shorter than the in-line sixes they replace; some of the benefit has been passed on to the passengers, but instead of economising on overall length the designers have placed the spare wheel in the nose, ahead of the engine. The "nose" area is a steel pressing, with cooling air ducted to the radiator from an intake beneath the

bumper bar. This arrangement has made possible an unobstructed, deep boot area which appears to be very short (due partly to the blended roof styling) but is in fact more roomy than on the Mark 3.

For the passengers, there is more shoulder, head and legroom within overall dimensions which are only slightly greater. The total length, for instance, is 15 ft 6 ins (an extra three inches), but front legroom is increased by 2.5 ins and at the rear by 1.5 inches. This incidentally is despite extremely thick seat cushions which are bound to reduce the space available. Shoulder room is increased front and rear by five and two inches respectively, while the overall width, 5 ft 10.6 ins, is up by only one inch. The Mark 4 is an inch higher than the Mark 3 but headroom is increased by that much.

Traditionally the power units have much in common with others in the Ford range, in this case the V4s. A common bore of 93.66 mm is used throughout, coupled with a stroke of 60.3 mm on the Zephyr 6 (2495 cc) and 72.41 mm on the Zodiac (2995 cc). In fact, the respective stroke measurements are the same as on the 1.6 and 2.0 litre V4 engines in the Corsairs, capacities increasing by half with two extra cylinders. Additionally, the two-litre V4 unit is fitted in the Zephyr 4 which, in its new form, continues to offer ample passenger and load capacities with the economy of a smaller engine.

Thus the Zephyr 4, which cost £933 including tax, has 88 bhp at hand and a maximum speed of 88 mph. The Zephyr 6, costing £1005, develops 112 bhp net and will reach 97 mph, while the Zodiac, costing £1220, develops 136 bhp and will attain 102 mph.

Power line

The main problem in designing a V4 engine is overcoming a characteristic firing imbalance, requiring a counterbalance shaft running parallel with the crankshaft. Fortunately the V6, in this case built with a 60 degree bore angle, is inherently smooth-running and the balance shaft is not needed. Design detail is almost exactly the same as on the V4s but the Zodiac has proportionally more power with better manifolding and a twin-choke Weber carburettor. Valvegear, employing hollow cylindrical tappets and short tubular pushrods, also follows the established principles; the conventional rocker shaft is replaced by individual stud mountings for each valve rocker, keeping the noise level down and making for easier adjustment. Crossflow cylinder heads are fitted and the combustion is entirely within the piston crown.

Standard equipment on the Zephyr 6, identified by more simple frontal styling, a single-headlamp system and individual rear lighting clusters, is bench seating at the front with a column change for the new, four-speed all-synchromesh gearbox. Individual seats and a floor change are optional, but standard fittings on the Zodiac. Laycock overdrive working on third and top gears is also available, and drive is transmitted through a nine-inch diaphragm clutch.

Alternatively, Ford have developed a new three-speed automatic transmission, the C4 unit, with a three element hydraulic torque converter. Cased in an aluminium housing, the total weight of the unit is only 168 lb. Placing the lever in D1 gives the driver control over the three gears, and Low position locks first gear. The D2 position, recommended for normal touring, confines all forward running to intermediate and high gears.

Final drive on the Zodiac is a 3.7:1 ratio, giving a running speed of 20.06 mph per 1000 rpm in top—thus at maximum speed the engine is running at 5100 rpm, even though it can go up to 5500 rpm sustained in safety. The Zephyr 4 also has a 3.7 axle, though with wider gearbox ratio spacings, but the Zephyr 6 has a 3.9 axle, giving 18.98 mph per 1000 rpm in top and again, an engine speed of 5100 rpm at the maximum speed of 97 mph.

One of the most interesting features of the new range is the independent rear suspension, which avoids the snags of other designs while offering the expected advantages. A form of triangulated location is arranged with the hubs carried by wishbone-shaped aluminium die-cast trailing links, and a shackle from the inner part of the link across to the nosepiece of the final drive. Side forces are resisted by the fixed-length driveshafts, each of which has two universal Hooke joints. The result of this is a suspension which offers either wheel fully independent action without resorting to splines or "doughnuts" to cater for track variation; neither do the wheels swing in a large arc about the differential, but rather in a much more limited way about a point just inside the hub. Even when the car is fully laden there is less than two degrees of negative camber, so tyre wear is unlikely to be abnormal, but cornering power is said to be even better.

A modified form of MacPherson strut, as expected, is fitted at the front on the pattern introduced last Autumn for the V4 Corsairs. The damper and its upright coil spring are eccentric so as to counteract side thrusts, and frictionless surfaces in the sliding parts overcome initial resistance to wheel movement.

An all-disc braking arrangement is fitted in conjunction with a Girling servo. The brakes are self-adjusting and the handbrake also adjusts itself. Steering, through a worm and nut box, has an overall ratio of 20.6 with 4¼ turns of the wheel from lock to lock.

Speed with comfort

Body design is inevitably a matter of taste and in such a project the stylists had to decide three years ago not only what would be fashionable today, but what would retain its appeal for another five years to come. It should be pointed out straight away that Ford did not intend to present a compact car, and the fact that Vee engines had been developed was not intended to influence the overall length of the Zephyr and Zodiac. If in the design stage the opportunity to utilise a short

bonnet had been accepted then the spare wheel would have been left in the boot and the hind-part would have been unproportionally long, so by a majority decision the spare wheel was mounted at the front. The bonnet is therefore dominant, and the Mark 4s are reminiscent of, if anything, the Mustang.

Interior space has been a prime objective, though the luxury of thick seating has slightly reduced the legroom advantage. Side windows are curved to give maximum shoulder room, and without doubt the new range will seat five or six people in great comfort. With independent rear suspension the differential is in a fixed position, so the propshaft tunnel can be kept low as it does not have to leave room for clearance as it would if the differential was rising and falling with the wheels.

The Zodiac is well equipped with individual front seats, an excellent floor gearchange, and a range of instrumentation including speedometer (with trip) and revcounter, petrol and ammeter gauges, an oil gauge and an electric clock; a neat row of tumbler switches is mounted on a sub-panel to the right of the fascia and the Aeroflow vents are positioned at the extreme ends of the fascia.

Also on the Zodiac, and optional on the Zephyr 6, the backrests of the front seats have full reclining mechanisms which, in conjunction with the steering wheel height —but not reach—adjustment should enable most people to make themselves comfortable. The pull-out handbrake is placed beneath the fascia.

Most of our testing was done on a four-speed Zodiac which revealed itself as a splendid long-distance car. Even up to maximum speed the engine is working well within its limits. Above all, the engine was extremely quiet and remote at all times, delivering a very smooth flow of power from low speed. Gearbox ratios are well spaced to give maxima of 34, 52, and 80 mph in the intermediates and 102 mph in top, observing a 5500 rpm rev limit. Performance figures taken on this car show that it will reach 50 mph in 8.5 seconds, 70 mph in 17.9 seconds, and 90 mph in 39 seconds. The Zephyr 6 is very little slower up to 70 mph, with its lower overall gearing, and as with the V4 units the smaller engine seemed to be the more willing although with less low-down torque and power at the top end of the range. Without a rev-counter one tends to rev the Zephyr 6 harder, and the speeds in the gears were about the same as with the Zodiac.

With Aeroflow ventilation the quarterlights are fixed and this allows good window sealing which keeps the wind noise down. The level seemed to vary from car to car but generally it was acceptably low at maximum speed. In crosswinds, which were heavy at times, the cars were quite stable and did not get knocked about too badly by heavy gusts.

The independent suspension is as good as on any saloon car we have driven. The test cars all had export suspension, which is harder sprung, and at low speed the ride in the back seat felt quite firm. As the speed increased the ride got better and the Fords can, in fact, be driven at maximum speed on quite bumpy roads without any discomfort. Even in places where the road had subsided, a frequent hazard in

Tunisia, the cars could be driven through quickly without bottoming the suspension. Through fast bends and slow corners alike the cars remain absolutely stable, with just a little initial roll and a trace of understeer. Flinging the Mark 4 round a sharper corner will bring the tail round slowly and controllably.

Braking is impressive, especially with the light pressures required with the servo unit helping. Altogether the Zephyr and Zodiac range offer light and easy control throughout the speed range, although to achieve this the steering has a low ratio requiring nearly five turns of the wheel from lock to lock. A parking manoeuvre calls for quite a lot of wheel-turning, but we will reserve judgment on this until we can test the car in England, a known environment. We may expect to hear soon of a power-assisted arrangement which raises the ratio to 3½ turns of the wheel.

In every respect the Mark 4 range is a great improvement on the Mark 3, especially regarding noise and comfort levels, handling, visibility, and braking. They succeed in Ford's philosophy of "taking established customers up a level each time a new model is introduced," and even at higher prices should gain an even wider following.

SPECIFICATIONS

Ford Zodiac Mk 4 (Zephyr 6)

ENGINE
Six cylinders, 60 deg V; bore 93.66 mm, stroke 72.41 mm (60.3 mm). Cubic capacity 2994 cc (2495 cc). Compression ratio 8.9 (9.1). Maximum bhp (net) 136 (112) at 4750 rpm; maximum torque (net) 181.5 (137.5) lb ft. at 3000 rpm. Overhead valves, pushrod operated. One Weber 40 DFA (Zenith 38 IVT) carburettor, AC mechanical fuel pump. Tank capacity 15 gallons. Water cooling with pump, fan and thermostat, Sump capacity 10 pints. 12V 53 amp/hr battery.

TRANSMISSION
Four speed all-synchromesh, floor or column change. Gearbox ratios: 1st—3.16; 2nd—2.21; 3rd—1.41; 4th—1.00. Optional Laycock overdrive, 0.82 ratio, on third and top. 9 in. diaphragm spring clutch, final drive by hypoid bevel gears, ratio 3.7 (also Zephyr 4) or 3.9 (Zephyr 6). Optional Ford C4 three-speed epicyclic gear automatic gearbox with torque converter.

CHASSIS
Integral construction. Suspension, front: MacPherson strut, co-axial telescopic dampers and coil springs; rear, independent, triangulated trailing arms, telescopic dampers and coil springs. Girling hydraulic disc brakes, with servo—front discs 9.6 in dia, rear 9.9 in dia. Recirculating ball steering, overall ratio 20.6. Steering wheel 16½ in. dia, 4½ turns. Pressed steel disc wheels; tyre size 6.70—13.

DIMENSIONS

	ft.	ins.
Wheelbase	9	7.25
Track, front	4	9
Track, rear	4	9.25
Overall length	15	5.8
Overall width	5	10.6
Overall height	5	6.6
Ground clearance		6
Turning circle	36	0
Kerb weight		25.7 cwt
Zephyr 6		25.2 cwt
Zephyr 4		24.2 cwt

PERFORMANCE

(Zodiac)	secs
0—30	3.8
0—40	6.5
0—50	8.5
0—60	13.1
0—70	17.9
0—80	26.2
0—90	39.0
Maximum speed	102 mph

ENTER THE V-6

RIGHT: *Zephyr corners in Tunisia's Australian-style conditions. FAR RIGHT: Ford's new independent rear suspension gives "highway" ride anywhere.*

47 او العربيتى

MOULARES 47

O N April 20 Ford of Britain introduced what I believe could cause almost as much of a revolution in the world car industry as Henry's original model T.

They introduced a new — completely new — Mark IV Zephyr and Zodiac series. Outwardly they look very much like the new Falcons to be introduced on the Australian market in August — but underneath the long, long bonnet is a technically brilliant V6 engine, and below the stubby tail end is an equally brilliant independent rear suspension system.

Between them is a compact, yet very roomy, five-six seater which is going to make the rest of the automotive world sit up and take notice.

Australia won't see the new cars for a while — they would be much too competitive for the straight-six Falcons. But the big boys at Broadmeadows must be thinking ahead about eventually incorporating some of the technically advanced specifications — especially that impressive rear end, which seems at first glance tailor-made for Australia's rough conditions.

I ought to know. I've just spent 750 wearing miles in Tunisia, at Ford's invitation, driving almost every variation in the range. I drove over fast roads, bumpy roads, dusty roads, wet roads, flooded roads, high roads, low roads, and sometimes twisty roads — conditions that weren't very very like Australia.

My findings? We'll get to them in a minute. First let's take a thorough look at the specifications.

Mechanicals

The Mark IVs are brand new from the tip of the rooflines to the tips of their tyres on the 13in. wheels.

Wheelbase goes up 8in. from the Mark III figures to 11in. and overall length 4in. to 186.8in.—but 3in. of this finds its way into extra legroom for passengers.

Width goes up 1½in. to 70.6in. and rear track 4½in. to 58.4in. Height is up 1¾in. to 56.2in., but so is interior headroom.

Under the bonnet are those V6s of either 2.5- or 3-litre capacity (or a 2-litre V4 from the Corsair range available for the Zephyr). There are disc brakes all-round and a boot free of spare wheel (that item goes, Citroen-fashion, up front, forward of that stubby V6 power unit).

The new cars have aeroflow and fresh air face ventilation (both tried out on other models in the Dagenham range and the brainchild of Australian Ken Teasdale, now Ford safety manager).

There are anti-burst door locks for safety in accidents. There's an adjustable—for rake—steering column, which to my mind is a victory of commonsense over the take-it-or-leave-it steering position of the past. And there are fully reclining front seats which, together with that 1½in. adjust-able column, provide a right-for-any-one steering position.

Underside there's a choice of three transmissions—a four-speed standard all-synchromesh box with column or floor shift, a four-speed box with overdrive on third and top; or a new fully automatic three-speed box with over-riding control on first and second gears.

The Zodiac gets a four headlamp system (a whopping 250watts on main beam) and the Zephyr the normal single dip headlights. The Zodiac has an alternator, the Zephyr the old-type generator-charging unit.

Engine in detail

These two new power units are 8in. shorter, 18-20lb. lighter, 32 percent more powerful and 17½ to 20 percent greater in capacity than the straight sixes they replace, but Ford claim they are just as economical.

The marker is the Zodiac with the 60 degree V6 in 3-litre form and producing a useful 144 bhp (136 bhp nett) at 4750 rpm on an 8.9:1 compression ratio.

The Zephyr has a 2.5-litre version producing 118.5 bhp (SAE), 112 bhp nett, at the same revs but on a 9:1 compression ratio.

Both engines share the bore of 3.6875in. (93.663mm) — identical to the V4s introduced last year.

Only the stroke changes — 2.851in. in the 3-litre and 2.376in. in the 2.5-litre.

Maximum torque comes in at 3000 rpm: for the 3-litre it is 192ft./lb. (181.5ft./lb. nett) and for the 2.5-litre it's 145ft./lb. (137.5ft./lb. nett).

Only other major difference in the cast-iron engines is in carburetion and manifolding. The engines are fairly compact and light — they measure 17.68in. long, 15.66in. wide and 12.12in. high.

The unit walls are generally less than one-fifth of an inch thick, so that the cast weight is only 170lb. which is reduced to 135lb. when fully machined. Dry weight is 379 and 377lb. respectively.

The four-bearing long crankshaft (9½in. shorter than on the previous straight six) rests on steel-backed copper-lead or alternative aluminium-tin bearings.

The camshaft, cast in "K" alloy, is gear-driven from the front of the engine, but does not run directly in the casting. It is supported in detachable and renewable steel-backed babbit bearings, identical with those on the earlier Corsair V4s. The bowl-in-piston combustion chambers are used.

A three-branch cast-iron exhaust manifold is bolted on either side of the head, and there is a water-heated, six branch intake manifold which, on the 2.5-litre, has a Zenith 38 IVT downdraught carburettor and on the 3-litre a single, twin-choke Weber. More engine power has meant a

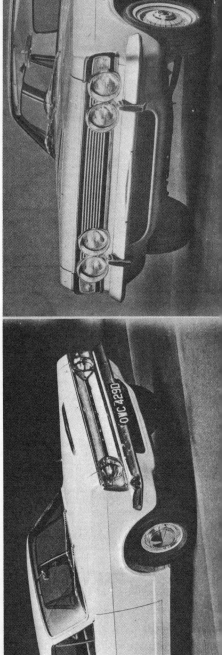

FOUR-HEADLAMP system identifies more powerful Zodiac version. Note engine air intake under bumper.

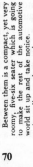

NEW Zephyr body is similar to Australian Falcon to be released in August—the big differences are underneath.

ENTER THE V-6

"MOST comfortable Ford seats yet," says enthusiastic Dvoretsky after trying Zodiac's buckets. Zephyr benches weren't so good.

new torque, and this is fed through a 9in. diameter diaphragm spring-type clutch, which needs no adjustment throughout its life. Operation is hydraulic and foot pressures are much less than on the Mark III range — 30lb. as compared with 44lb.

Hypoid bevel gears give the Zodiac a road speed at peak of the torque curve of 60.2 mph (3,000 rpm) and 95.3 mph at the top of the power curve (4,750 rpm). At that speed piston speed is 2,120ft./min. Top speed of the Zodiac is in excess of 95 mph.

Final drive ratios are 3.7:1 for the Zodiac and 3.9:1 for the Zephyr. Overdrive will reduce engine speeds by 18 percent.

The new automatic, called the Ford C4, weighs only 168lb. including flywheel and torque converter. The engine drives a three-element torque converter with an internal impeller fixed to a curved back plate of the main housing and revolves around a fixed sleeve called the stator support.

Ford claim that at a little more than 60 mph in top gear the device (their word, not mine) functions as a 98 percent efficient fluid coupling (they're saying it). The two-train epicyclic box automatically changes gear above 7-9 mph and below 67 kiph depending on throttle opening. Kick-down to lower gear from third to second is between 60-30 mph and from second to first at 30 mph and below.

That suspension

Front suspension is the now well-known MacPherson-type struts which in the Ford system are connected to a stabiliser bar. This, say Ford, allows in addition to the normal vertical movement, a degree of fore-and-aft deflection, and is a great absorber of impact shock as the wheels encounter bumps.

But it is the rear independent suspension that draws attention. Mounted on a sub-frame (an innovation for the real mass-produced market) it is a semi-trailing arm type with coil springs and telescopic dampers.

I imagine the patent covers a unique shackle mounting of the suspension arm to allow correct wheel articulation without sliding friction.

The brakes are Girling discs with servo assistance, and cables to the rear calipers from an umbrella-type handbrake. The front discs are 9.63in. diameter and the rears 9.91in., giving a front pad area of 28.8 sq. in. and a rear pad area of 14 sq. in. Swept friction area is 53 sq. in. (front), 34 sq. in. (rear).

On the road

So much for the specifications. How does it all work out on the road?

During Ford's special pre-release tryout in Tunisia, I drove one-up, two-up, three-up, four-up, five-up and six-up and spent many miles as passenger in the back seat with three or four aboard.

That new suspension works like a charm. It makes rough roads seem like super highways. When Ford go over to radials (they've a new rim coming out specially for them) the road-holding should be really exceptional.

Of course there are some "buts." But they are mostly of a minor nature, and can be corrected fairly easily as production gets really under way.

From the first glance I liked the stubby-looking tail and the unclut-tered big boot. I DON'T like the squarish bonnet which has the same "get-up-and-go" look as the new Australian Falcons pictured in last month's Modern Motor.

Frankly I would have preferred a sloping bonnet which would not only have cut down wind resistance (and hence fuel consumption), but would have made for (to my mind) a sleeker looking car.

But, overall, the general appearance is satisfying. The Zodiac four-headlight system (the first car in the world to use real big 7in. lamps for all four heads) looks right, and the twin-headlight system of the Zephyr is pleasing enough.

The doors are big and open wide for very easy entry. The seats (with the possible exception of the bench seat version of the Zephyr four and six) are the most comfortable Ford have ever turned out. The bucket seats of the Zodiac (and they're available for the Zephyr) are superb.

The steering position is magnificent and again the best ever from Ford. Adjustment for rake on the steering column combined with adjustable squab rake on the front seats provides a position to satisfy the most fastidious. About time, too.

At first the almost five turns lock-to-lock steering seems a bit spongy and I really was never completely satisfied. It's light enough for parking, and correction for normal running is little more than my Falcon Futura of a few years back in Australia.

In other words-it's not right; you really need power steering with fewer turns from lock-to-lock — but you get used to it.

Certainly if you overdo it (and overdoing it takes some doing in the dry, seldom in the wet and mostly on slippery gravelly surfaces) correction isn't that difficult, even for the mug. The wheel is big enough to get control quickly and efficiently.

Turning circle of 36ft. isn't too good, though.

The dashboard layout is one of the best. In the Zodiac you get the lot, though I would prefer instruments to carry well-marked figures on their gauges instead of this futuristic line stuff that leaves you wondering. Reflection in the dials is a problem if you drive long-arm.

The aeroflow ventilation system isn't as good as I would like. To get the aeroflow face vents (which are better placed on the new series than on most others) working properly it was necessary to keep a quiet blower fan turned on.

It seems that the "get-up-and-go" look obscures the intake near the screen and prevents an adequate supply of air to be pushed through.

Now, after so many miles the observant reader may think I could give full judgment on the handling

few extra miles on the first day, but this was due to careless navigation, not to any ambiguity in the painstakingly detailed route instructions.

The route was well-chosen, conditions varying from fast bitumen highways to dirt and gravel roads, with a fair proportion of twisty mountain-climbing. Here's how it went.

FIRST DAY: 474 miles from Bendigo (Vic.) to Orange (N.S.W.), to be covered in 11 hours 38 minutes— an average just under 41 mph; 236 miles of good, fast bitumen along the Midland, Goulburn Valley, and Newell Highways to the lunch stop at Narranwera, a mixture of gravel and bitumen for 120 miles from there to Forbes, then bitumen to Orange.

No problems — except for Firth's Cortina, which bottomed on a gravel heap, cracking its fuel line and losing that precious gallon of petrol.

SECOND DAY: 365 miles to Taree, to be done in 9h. 42m. (about 37.6 mph). A good deal of mountain running from Lithgow through the Kurrajongs and Colo, then over the Putty Road to Singleton for lunch, and on to the Pacific Highway at Hexham.

A thunderstorm with very heavy downpours and winds that strewed the road with broken branches livened things up on the last 30-mile stretch into Taree, but there were no incidents.

THIRD DAY: 388 miles to Surfers' Paradise, to be done in 9h. 48m. (just under 40 mph). Winding roads and pleasant coastal scenery, a detour inland through Casino after the Grafton lunch stop, then back to the Pacific Highway at Byron Bay and on into Queensland.

Plain sailing, on the face of it; yet the teenagers' Renault wasted some fuel due to a jammed throttle cable, the manual Valiant developed a leaking diff seal, and the Mustang went off the road at a T-junction near Lismore luckily without damage.

FOURTH DAY: 345 miles to Bundaberg, to be done in 8h. 30m. (40.6 mph), with a lunch stop at Gympie; following the Pacific and Bruce highways, with detours to coastal holiday resorts at Redcliffe, Caloundra, and Tewantin. Main hazards: traffic hold-ups — and police traps.

This year there were few changes of placings in the various classes from day to day. Of the ten eventual class winners, eight emerged as leaders on the first night and maintained their supremacy to the end.

Only fluctuations were in classes D and J. The Triumph 2000 led Class D on the first night out, then dropped behind the Peugeot 404 — only to come out on top again at the finish. While in Class J (for teenage drivers) each of the three entries led in turn, the prize finally going to the Mini-Minor.

WHAT all the fuss is about—Ford's compact, lively V-6, is a controversial point—but leaves boot uncluttered for luggage.

V6 ZODIAC with MEISSNER V camshaft

* Just one new feature adds 24 b.h.p. to that Zodiac powerhouse — and Ford backs it with a warranty!

A CAR ROAD TEST

THE new trend in car tuning is: no need to go to the speedshops — the local car dealer stocks the goodies, and knows how to use them!

First off the shelf (since the Ford "Performance-Plus" kit for the Anglia a few years back) is a very special camshaft for the new V6 Zodiac, and it is as easily obtainable from Amalgamated Motors, Knysna, as from Grosvenor Motors, Johan-nesburg — at a fixed price, with a standard fitting charge, and subject to the full Ford Parts Warranty. It can also be used in the Zephyr Mk. 4.

The camshaft is a special one developed by tuner Willie Meissner for the new Ford V4 and V6 engines, with lubrilised lobes to give extra value in engine performance, without any roughness.

AVAILABLE IN QUANTITY

The camshafts have been processed in quantity, brand-new from the Ford engine plant at Port Elizabeth, and by the time this appears in print they should be available off the shelf from any of the main Ford dealers in the Republic.

Standard price of the camshaft is R55.00, and fitting charge (labour, gaskets and timing adjustment included) is recommended at R27.24

The whole conversion is this business-like camshaft, with dull sheen denoting that it has been lubrilised for durability. It is available from Ford dealerships at a standard price.

so the total cost is R82.24, and the complete operation is carried out inside a working day.

An attractive new "Meissner Conversion" transfer is included with every pack.

We tested the camshaft in the same Zodiac used for our Road Test of the new model last month, and the results are quite dramatic for such a small change and outlay.

EXTRA 24 B.H.P.

The camshaft gives an extra 24 b.h.p. net (calculated) and, as the tables and graphs illustrate, gives a very clear improvement in all-round performance

The torque peak moves up a bit, but the car remains fully flexible right down to 25 m.p.h., and once 3,500 r.p.m. is passed it fairly streaks away from the standard model, notching 105 top speed on a level road.

QUIET IDLING

There is no trace of fussiness, the engine idling at 600 r.p.m. and registering 47·5 decibels on idle, which is very, very good!

There is no increase at all in noise levels, and a bonus feature is that fuel economy is improved from 60 m.p.h. up, and right through the cruising range.

In fitting, the only adjustment is that timing should be advanced an extra 5 deg., and plugs changed to one stage cooler (Champion N4, for instance, as used in the Cortina GT, are suitable). Tappet clearances remain untouched.

FULL WARRANTY

Final plus feature is that the modification has Ford approval, and that the camshaft is subject to the full Ford Parts Warranty, and a new car warranty is not affected by the modification.

For the man who wants an inexpensive, invisible and warranted performance-plus feature, freely available and without fitting snags, this is the answer.

It immediately starts paying for itself in open-road economy, and puts the Zodiac right near the top in terms of saloon car performance! ●

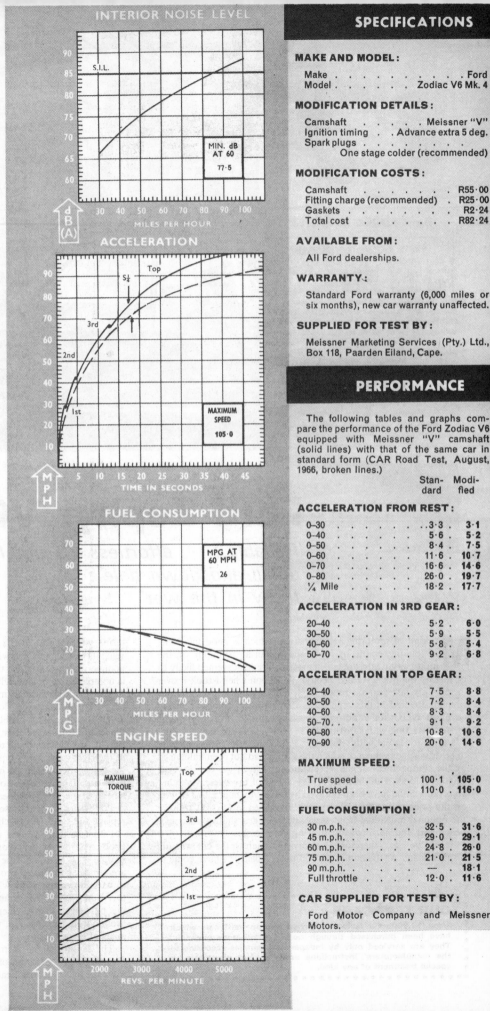

SPECIFICATIONS

MAKE AND MODEL:

Make . . . . Ford
Model . . . . . . Zodiac V6 Mk. 4

MODIFICATION DETAILS:

Camshaft . . . . . Meissner "V"
Ignition timing . . Advance extra 5 deg.
Spark plugs
     One stage colder (recommended)

MODIFICATION COSTS:

Camshaft . . . . R55·00
Fitting charge (recommended) . R25·00
Gaskets . . . . R2·24
Total cost . . . . R82·24

AVAILABLE FROM:

All Ford dealerships.

WARRANTY:

Standard Ford warranty (6,000 miles or six months), new car warranty unaffected.

SUPPLIED FOR TEST BY:

Meissner Marketing Services (Pty.) Ltd., Box 118, Paarden Eiland, Cape.

PERFORMANCE

The following tables and graphs compare the performance of the Ford Zodiac V6 equipped with Meissner "V" camshaft (solid lines) with that of the same car in standard form (CAR Road Test, August, 1966, broken lines.)

	Standard	Modified
ACCELERATION FROM REST:		
0–30	3·3	3·1
0–40	5·6	5·2
0–50	8·4	7·5
0–60	11·6	10·7
0–70	16·6	14·6
0–80	26·0	19·7
¼ Mile	18·2	17·7
ACCELERATION IN 3RD GEAR:		
20–40	5·2	6·0
30–50	5·9	5·5
40–60	5·8	5·4
50–70	9·2	6·8
ACCELERATION IN TOP GEAR:		
20–40	7·5	8·8
30–50	7·2	8·4
40–60	8·3	8·4
50–70	9·1	9·2
60–80	10·8	10·6
70–90	20·0	14·6
MAXIMUM SPEED:		
True speed	100·1	105·0
Indicated	110·0	116·0
FUEL CONSUMPTION:		
30 m.p.h.	32·5	31·6
45 m.p.h.	29·0	29·1
60 m.p.h.	24·8	26·0
75 m.p.h.	21·0	21·5
90 m.p.h.	—	18·1
Full throttle . . .	12·0	11·6

CAR SUPPLIED FOR TEST BY:

Ford Motor Company and Meissner Motors.

Not the ideal car for urban running in Little Britain, but it has a surprisingly compact turning circle for a 15 ft. 5 in. car.

Ford Zephyr V6

"Reliable . . . effortless 70 m.p.h. uphill and down dale . . . tricky in the wet"

by J. A. Kyd

MY kind of motoring requires a car which is good in traffic, nimble on remote by-roads and restful at 70 m.p.h. on the motorway. Only the last-named requirement seemed likely to be met by the Mk. IV Ford Zephyr V6 saloon when I took it over in mid-July last year on return from holiday; the 12,000 miles of running covered in this report was thus almost wholly conducted on business, but for a motoring journalist this involves every type of road, starting with farm tracks.

I came to the car with reluctance. Predominantly, I was unhappy to be driving something of which the styling had not been influenced by the compactness of the V6 engine so that, of the car's overall length of 15 ft. 5 in., some 8 ft. lay ahead of my eyes. My other objections could have been resolved by the payment of £24 11s. 8d., on the price of £1,005 (subsequently increased to £1,023), to have the optional individual front seats and floor gearshift in place of a bench-seat and an unwieldy steering column gear lever.

It will be clear, therefore, that my approach to the car was not dispassionate. At the end of 12,000 miles I believe I have come to

terms with it, and this is due partly to respect for the complete reliability of what is a newly engineered car and partly to surprising manoeuvrability in close traffic conditions when the road surface is completely dry; the slightest moisture on the highway makes the Zephyr V6 awkward to manage in braking, accelerating and cornering when it is easily "lost" in the most trivial circumstances.

This is not just a problem of poor weight distribution; in fact, the first time it rained after I had taken over the car was on Romney Marsh by-roads en route to Dover when it went straight on at one of the right-angle turns typical of that area. I was wondering about the tyres when I stopped in the cart track that served as an escape road and I have been wondering about them ever since. People have told me that Goodyear have thought again but the Ford main dealer where the car is serviced knew nothing about an offer to replace the tyres free of charge.

I confess that my first impressions from the driver's seat were good. The doors shut completely with a quality clunk, without any need to slam, and the draught sealing is so effective that you are almost completely protected from the noise of other traffic—to wind down the window in a London street is like adding sound to vision on TV. The sound proofing between the engine bay and the passenger compartment is not effective enough to stifle the pronounced tappet noise, which is absent for only the first 1,000 miles after servicing.

The layout of the instruments and switches is good with the exception that operation of the traffic indicator stalk tends also to work the lightly loaded headlamp flasher with which it is combined;

Ford Zephyr V6
12,000 mile report

this traffic indicator stalk is also apt to select opposite turn instead of cancelling when the steering wheel is straightened up rapidly, as in traffic driving.

The simple rake adjustment for the steering column provides a pleasantly low wheel position for those with reasonably proportioned thighs, and the bench seat can be pushed back as far as most people will need. It is also comfortable over a very long journey although this may be partly because of the side location offered by a seat belt. The great omission is lack of somewhere for odds and ends wanted on a long journey; the locker in front of the passenger is too far away from the driver. Cars with individual front seats have a box beneath the armrest between the seats.

The Aeroflow ventilation is excellent in theory and pretty good in practice. The temperature control lever gives an easily controlled range of temperatures (it takes three miles running to get working on a 40 deg. F. morning) and the distribution control lever directs the air where it is wanted. The low boost fan is required at speeds under 30-40 m.p.h. and high-boost (which is noisy) for demisting in cold rain. In traffic the booster fan seems to take in exhaust fumes from other vehicles and after the car has been parked for some time on a windy, dusty day, the first fan-boosted waft from the eyeball vents is apt to contain impurities, and if the vents are directed towards your face the dust gets in your eyes.

The ability to have fresh, cool air from the eyeball vents to keep one's head clear while the lower parts of the body are kept comfortably warm seems to me an important contribution to road safety; in practice I have found it best to direct the cool air to a point below my chin—I have also found that the right hand on the wheel is usually kept uncomfortably cool.

The V6 Zephyr is a wonderful starter. Even at the end of the 6,000-mile interval between servicing it will fire at the first touch—when cold the accelerator is depressed once to trigger the automatic choke. The unwieldy column gear change, coupled with rather long clutch pedal travel and no apparent cushioning in the transmission, make the car difficult to drive smoothly; after 12,000 miles I have not mastered it completely.

Synchromesh is exceptionally obstructive in downward changes and unless great strength is employed it is necessary to double de-clutch in dropping to second and first at speeds near the maximum for these ratios. Great strength is also required to apply the handbrake which has a very strong spring.

The engine is less smooth than the "old" straight-six Zephyr unit and while it confers a reasonably lively performance on the car

its principal merit is the ability to drive the car effortlessly at 70 m.p.h. up hill and down dale; the calm is broken only by considerable wind noise from the roof drain channels. Second gear is a useful ratio in town, quickly squirting the car up to 30 m.p.h. when it is convenient to change direct into top. "Squirting" is the operative word because high revs are accompanied by the sound of hydraulic disturbance from the heating system.

The good manoeuvrability in traffic mentioned earlier is a product of a surprisingly compact turning circle (34-35 feet) for a 15 ft. 5 in. car, but with five turns of the wheel from lock to lock you have to work for it. When the roads are wet the situation is trickier; it is possible in the dry (thanks to the independent rear suspension) to accelerate hard round a corner from a near standstill without the inside rear wheel lifting, but try it in the wet and the rear end slides with exceptionally little provocation. This aspect of the car has removed much of my pleasure in motoring; except in completely dry weather it is never possible to be certain that halfway round a sweeping open-road bend there may not be a patch of dew on the road and this is all the car needs to slide bodily sideways. On the straight, the tyres, which are undoubtedly the cause of this uncertain handling, are exceptionally prone to deflection caused by often unseen longitudinal ridges on the road surface.

This is all a pity because on a dry, country road the handling of the car is both certain and pleasurable—probably above average for a big family car having no pretence of being a Grand Tourer. Some may find the suspension harsh when the car is lightly loaded but it is such that with a full load it continues to be completely controllable at speed.

As one who cleans his car himself, I find the Zephyr V6 gets its rear flanks very dirty very quickly and it is a tedious task washing it. To do the job properly needs 1½ hours but it continues to come up clean and reasonably new looking, except for some of the chromium at the rear which is rust spotted.

Faults and failures

On delivery
Wheels out of balance
Loose section of facia
Fuel gauge
Temperature gauge
Instrument light   } inoperative
Near side tail and side lights
Short from trafficator stalk
Sticking headlamp flasher

Subsequently
Intermittent fault in washer motor
Loose gearbox support
Faulty starter connection
Automatic choke linkage detached
Rust pitting on rear bumpers

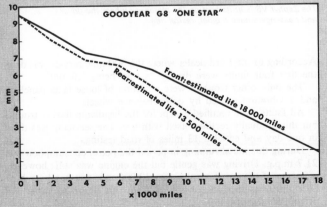

Up to 9,000 miles, the tyres remained in their original positions, the dealer having been told not to switch as recommended in the service schedule. They were, however, switched at the 9,000-mile service, with which a puncture had coincided, and the part of this graph subsequent to 9,000 miles is an estimate of the wear had the tyres remained in their original positions.

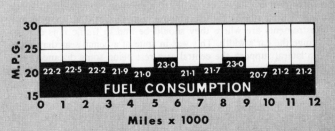

Apart from the two 23.0 m.p.g. peaks, the fuel consumption shows a remarkable consistency. The peaks coincide with periods during which a more-than-average amount of motoring was done on open roads. The low 20.7 m.p.g. was recorded during the latter half of December when urban traffic is always at its slowest.

The jack is excellent. The handle requires very little effort to turn, and the car rises quickly.

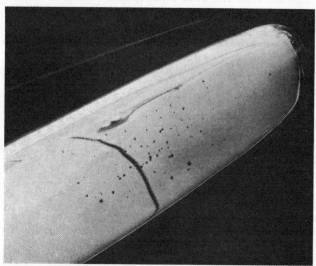

Rust spots on the side sections of the rear bumper. This area gets very dirty and it probably had more than a normal spattering of salt from winter roads.

The Zephyr V6 is at its best on the motorway where the driver and passengers have a quiet, restful ride.

Delivery and running-in

I see from my diary that my first impression from driving the car was that I immediately felt at home in it. In short, the controls and instruments are where they should be and in traffic it is easy to gauge the car's width. This was in spite of a bench seat that offers no lateral support, the central arm rest being some distance away from the driver.

On delivery the faults were almost wholly confined to the electrics, so that:—

(a) The fuel gauge didn't work.
(b) Ditto the temperature gauge.
(c) Ditto the instrument light.
(d) Ditto the near-side tail and side lamps.
(e) Sparks sometimes jumped from trafficator stalk to steering column surround.
(f) Headlamp flasher tended to jam "on".

According to the Ford dealer where the 600-mile service was done the first four faults were due to "a fuse being left out".

The only other troubles were a section of loose facia panelling and a vibration caused by out-of-balance wheels.

All faults were rectified except for the headlamp flasher trouble but this gradually rectified itself with use. The servicing was done in one day and entailed 13 miles of road testing.

During this initial running-in period the petrol consumption was 21.7 m.p.g. Driving was gentle but the engine was stiff; however, a feature of the car throughout its 12,000-mile test has been how little the consumption has varied from this figure whatever the driving conditions.

With the completion of **2,000 miles** in the first month, a poor August had shown that the automatic choke had been set too weak for starting in cool weather; the engine would not pull until it had

Ford Zephyr V6
12,000 mile report *continued*

warmed up for about five minutes on fast-idle. It was also found that the windscreen washer motor was uncertain in action and even now, in spite of attention, it has to be tapped to bring it to life after a period of inactivity. Night driving brought praise for the restful green lighting for the instruments and switches but showed that it is virtually impossible to read the mileage recorder except by day-light.

Oil consumption was around 1,000 miles to the pint at this stage and has subsequently become even lower. For the 1,400 miles following the 600-mile service petrol consumption was 21.2 m.p.g. The car was not yet being fully extended but it was already evident that some premium petrols (97-98 octane) were only just good enough for it, slight pinking being heard after fill-ups from certain pumps.

The Zephyr V6 is serviced at 6,000-mile intervals commencing at **3,000 miles.** Points requiring attention were:—

(a) Lazy windscreen washer motor.

(b) Too weak automatic choke.

(c) Sticky throttle.

(d) Vibration (from prop shaft?) at around 50 m.p.g. in top and third.

Again this service was done promptly (it was necessary to book a week ahead) and efficiently except that the windscreen washer motor remained uncertain in action. The vibration was cured by tightening a gearbox support and, surprisingly, new contact breaker points were fitted. The tappets had been very noisy before the service but were now quiet.

Checking my diary again I see the entry at **4,000 miles,** "tappets getting noisy again", and later experience has shown that they make themselves heard some 1,000 miles after servicing and become progressively noisier until, before the next service is due, the tick-over sounds like a diesel.

A hot spell in September caused the suspension joints to creak when starting away from rest and this continues to happen whenever the air is dry, but disappears with exercise. It was soon cold weather again; cold enough for the heater to be used for the first time and my first experience of the sound of hydraulic disturbance in the water system mentioned earlier. It happened when accelerating in third gear to get past a motorway coach, which was slowly building up to its 70 m.p.h. cruise after a temporary slackening due to road works, and it sounded like the initial stages of clutch disintegration. I'm quite used to it now, but it sometimes frightens a passenger.

Motorway cruising is the Ford's strong point. It needs only a small throttle opening to maintain 70 m.p.h., is not greatly affected by a gusting side wind, blows fresh air on the driver's face to relieve the soporific effect of unreasonable restraint and uses the same amount of petrol as for any other form of motoring. Nor does oil consumption rise; over some 1,000 miles, most of it done during a motorway survey, less than a pint was used.

Between **5,000 and 6,000 miles,** the one failure to start occurred —there was a fully charged battery but no response to the starter switch; no jammed pinion trouble either so it was clearly a faulty connection and a shove on the connecter to the solenoid mounted on the nose of the starter cured the fault.

At **6,000 miles,** prior to the intermediate performance testing, the car was given a Crypton check. All was found in good order but the distributor dwell angle was 42° and was altered to the specified 34°, and there was a 3° error in the ignition timing.

Before the performance testing, which involves a fair amount of running at top speed, I raised the tyre pressures by 3 lb. to give 28 lb. all round. This made the ride harsher than the normal firmness and resulted in the filaments of three of the four tail lamp bulbs failing; the replacements have kept going in spite of other periods of above-standard tyre pressure.

Calibration of the speedometer showed the mileage recorder to be 5% fast (the necessary corrections have been made in the fuel consumption figures quoted) and the speedometer read about 8%

Disc brakes are easily checked for wear. At 12,000 miles the rear ones shown here looked good for another 10,000 miles.

This amount of leverage was needed to shift the wheel nuts after the wheels had been switched round at 9,000-mile service.

What it cost

	£	s.	d.
Price of car	1005	0	0
Approximate resale value	750	0	0
Approximate depreciation	255	0	0
Running costs:			
Servicing: 3000 miles	8	13	3
9000 miles	8	7	3
Three tail lamp bulbs		7	6
Tyre wear—mean of 80% on four tyres	28	0	0
563.5 gal. petrol at 5s. 7d. a gal.	157	6	2
9 pints oil between changes	1	5	9
Road fund licence	17	10	0
Insurance (Group 4 tariff rate for Home Counties outside Metropolitan area)	60	0	0
Total running cost	281	9	11
Grand total	536	9	11
Cost per mile excluding depreciation			5.63d.
Cost per mile including estimated depreciation			10.73d.

Some of the Motor *readers who own this model criticize the short tail because they can't see where it is when reversing; others praise this lack of rear overhang as giving stable caravan towing.*

Performance comparisons

This model of Ford has not been road tested by *Motor* so we are unable to follow our usual 12,000-mile test practice of quoting figures taken during road test to supplement those of the 12,000-mile car.

	At 6,000 miles		At 12,000 miles (Gusty day)	
MAXIMUM	94.4 m.p.h.		93.2 m.p.h.	
MAXIMILE	92.6 m.p.h.		91.0 m.p.h.	
ACCELERATION (in secs.)	Top	Third	Top	Third
10-30 m.p.h.	—	6.4	—	—
20-40 m.p.h.	8.7	6.3	9.5	6.4
30-50 m.p.h.	9.4	6.7	10.1	6.9
40-60 m.p.h.	10.8	8.3	11.1	8.0
50-70 m.p.h.	12.8	11.0	14.1	11.9
60-80 m.p.h.	17.7	—	21.8	—
FUEL CONSUMPTION				
at 30 m.p.h.	28.8 m.p.g.		28.6 m.p.g.	
at 40 m.p.h.	29.0 m.p.g.		29.4 m.p.g.	
at 50 m.p.h.	26.3 m.p.g.		26.3 m.p.g.	
at 60 m.p.h.	23.0 m.p.g.		23.1 m.p.g.	
at 70 m.p.h.	20.1 m.p.g.		21.1 m.p.g.	
at 80 m.p.h.	17.2 m.p.g.		18.9 m.p.g.	
at 90 m.p.h.	14.0 m.p.g.		—	

fast meaning that I was within the law at an indicated 76 m.p.h. The results of the testing are shown in the accompanying table but it is interesting to note that the steady speed fuel consumption figure at 70 m.p.h. is very close to the overall fuel consumption figure achieved and that every 10 m.p.h. reduction in steady speed accounts for a 3 m.p.g. improvement in fuel consumption down to 40 m.p.h., below which the consumption worsens.

Between **6,000 and 12,000 miles** (the latter figure attained on February 1) the only untoward happening was the failure of the automatic choke caused by the linkage attached to the body of the carburetter coming adrift. This would have been easy enough to put right if the handbook had presented even a sketch or photograph of the assembly. Without any guidance it was a trial and error job to reassemble. The tool kit, incidentally consists of a wheel brace—no more, so the owner who normally expects to get himself out of the inevitable, trivial breakdown, must assemble his own tool kit.

It takes many thousands of miles before some qualities and applications of a car become evident. As the Zephyr ran up the miles it became clear that here was a car that had no body rattles; the doors, the seats, the trim and the facia assembly, in addition to the mechanical components, neither rattled nor squeaked when the car was driven over rough moorland tracks. On the other hand I found myself avoiding these narrow roads simply because of the difficulty in passing other cars; the Mk. IV Zephyr is, at 5 ft. 11 in., the same width as the Rolls-Royce Silver Shadow and is thus somewhat anti-social in the lanes.

Just before the **9,000 miles** service the engine began to misfire slightly at peak r.p.m. and the off-side headlamp tended to extinguish itself in high beam; the gear change also showed itself to be slightly out of adjustment. These three faults were corrected

More corrosion on the trim around the rear lamps.

Ford Zephyr V6
12,000-mile report *continued*

satisfactorily, new points were fitted again but the original sparking plugs (Autolite) were considered good for another 6,000 miles.

A puncture had occurred just prior to the service and this was repaired too. This puncture had served to demonstrate how efficient the jacking arrangements are; the complete operation of changing the wheel took about 12 minutes and no effort was required to work the wind-up jack. It was fortunate that the puncture did not occur in some remote place *after* the servicing, because they had switched the wheels round and done the nuts up absurdly tight. This I found out when removing a wheel to inspect the brake pads; it required double leverage, by fitting a ring spanner over the brace, to undo each nut and it would have been quite impossible to remove the wheel if a puncture had occurred out in the blue.

The switching of wheels during servicing had taken no account

Zephyr's horizontal styling theme accentuated by the City of London's new, towering office blocks.

of the previous balancing so vibration was evident again, this time at around 60-70 m.p.h.

The Zephyr ended its first **12,000 miles** with our normal performance tests preceded by a Crypton check. The latter showed that the timing was 3 deg. out again (this was corrected) and the plugs were not as good as new. The performance tests (see the accompanying table) showed a slight fall-off in performance possibly due to the plugs, but a useful improvement in fuel consumption at speeds over 60 m.p.h.

Second Opinion *by the Editor*

As luck would have it, it rained for the period of this second opinion test which amply confirmed the owner's remarks about wet road lack of adhesion. Nor was confidence improved by the low-geared, rather heavy steering, a bench seat which did nothing to secure the driver against roll on sharp corners and a tendency for the car to swerve sideways across white lines and ridges.

Since I last drove this Zephyr it had been serviced and the previous tappet clatter had disappeared entirely leaving a smooth, quiet and unobtrusive engine and gearbox. Mechanically, in fact, the whole car felt in first-class condition apart from a steering shimmy around 50 m.p.h. caused by an unbalanced front wheel, and criticism was aroused more by original design and styling features than by any deterioration due to age. One such source of irritation to the stranger is the layout of a facia in which the switches are identified by labels too small to be seen without close inspection and the instrument dials are almost completely obscured by reflection from the rear window.

Other owner's comments

ELECTRICAL and automatic choke troubles figured largely in the lists of faults on delivery experienced by *Motor* readers who drive Ford Zephy V6s. After these had been sorted out (not always completely in the case of the choke), there was very little consistency in the troubles encountered but they were generally comparatively non-crippling annoyances such as "anti-roll bar out of socket", "severe leak under scuttle" and "faulty windscreen washer motor". The most common faults mentioned were in connection with the automatic choke and rattles from the rear extractor vents. One owner was ill-fated, with three new gearboxes and the same number of replacement speedometers.

The owner with the greatest mileage (21,000) was the one with anti-roll bar trouble; he had also had a sheared generator flange (at 20,000 miles) and a blown

cylinder head gasket at 21,000 miles. His tyres lasted 20,000 miles and were then replaced with Michelin "X" which "appear to have improved things".

Only one person was dissatisfied with the Ford dealers' service, but several complained of lack of spares.

Comfort, spaciousness and effortless performance were the features of the car that appealed to owners. Dislikes which figured largely in replies to our questionnaire included the automatic choke, heavy steering in town and poor rearward visibility for reversing; there were a few complaints about harsh and/or noisy suspension, but only one complained bitterly of the handling—some had new tyres (two-star Goodyear G8s) fitted. Of those who had one-star G8s as original equipment, 40% had them replaced free by their Ford dealer, 30% remained on the

original tyres, 20% had replacement "two-stars" on a part-exchange deal with Goodyear and 10% were refused a change by the dealer.

Petrol consumption was usually quoted at between 20 and 22 m.p.g. although some owners were getting over 25 m.p.g. when touring.

Some 50% of the replies indicated that the owner would buy the same model again; others would do so if certain faults were rectified, and there were several who would buy another Ford, but not this one.

Manufacturer's comments

THE specification of the Goodyear tyres was changed in July, 1966, with the introduction of the 2-Star model. These tyres were immediately adopted by the Company and, in addition, 185 x 14 radial ply tyres on 14" wheels were introduced on the Zephyr V6 and Zodiac models as regular production options.

In October, 1966, Ford initiated a programme with its main dealers to change the tyres on early production models on receipt of customers' complaints. We can only assume the approach for the test car was made to the servicing dealer prior to the announcement of this programme.

The problem of tappet noise has been resolved by the introduction of a new adjusting nut with a flange.

As regards the heater intake drawing in exhaust fumes from other cars, we have not had this reported as a complaint and it is difficult

to see where the intake could be placed to avoid this. In front of the windscreen is usually considered to be the best place.

Recent minor design changes and revision of tolerances have much improved the precision and "feel" of the gearshift.

The hydraulic disturbances from the heater are undoubtedly due to bubbles in the system. The control valve has since been modified to reduce the chances of air getting in, but if the problem does occur the noise can be stopped by bleeding the system.

To counter comments on harsh suspension the road springs have been softened since model introduction.

The tool kit consists of a wheel-brace and jack not just a wheel-brace as mentioned in the text. **M**

Externally and internally, the Zephyr V4 is identical to the V6 model, with good front seats and plenty of rear leg room. The large boot has a very regular space, as the spare wheel is stowed at an angle just ahead of the engine block, which looks lost in the available space

Autotest

he Zephyr shape is individual, with long bonnet and short tail. There is no real difference externally etween the V4 and V6 versions

nder extreme cornering at the limit the inside ar wheel lifts high in the air as the outside one cks under. Even so the car remains controllable nd reasonably stable

AT A GLANCE: Smallest-engined version f Ford's Mk IV range. Performance good onsidering modest power-to-weight atio. Smooth engine except when pushed. oor steering. Comfortable ride. Near-fade-ree brakes. Roomy body but an awkward ar in towns. Good value.

MANUFACTURER

ord Motor Co. Ltd., Warley, Near Brentwood, ssex.

PRICES

Basic	.	.	£800	0s	0d
Purchase Tax	.	.	£222	4s	5d
Seat belts (pair)	.	.	£13	14s	9d
Total (in GB)	.	.	£1,035	19s	2d

EXTRAS (inc PT)

Radio	.	.	£23 10s	10d

PERFORMANCE SUMMARY

Mean maximum speed	.	95 mph
Standing start ¼-mile	.	20.3 sec
0-60 mph	.	17.7 sec
30-70 mph (through gears)	.	22.0 sec
Typical fuel consumption	.	25 mpg
Miles per tankful	.	375

AS far as engine size goes there are three models of the Ford Mk. IV. The biggest-capacity Executive (also available as the cheaper Zodiac) has a 3-litre V6 and in the middle comes the 2½-litre Zephyr V6. At the bottom is the Zephyr V4, an economy big car with 2-litre Corsair engine. Putting relatively small engines in big bodies does not usually make the best sort of motor car from anybody's point of view. Even if you drive with economy foremost in mind, you are likely to be disappointed as the small motor has to work much harder to move the car, and sometimes that uses more petrol. Despite all this, it is remarkable what this under-engined car—88 bhp for nearly a ton and half laden—can do.

Comparing performance figures with those for the Zephyr V6, the V4 takes 3.1sec longer to reach 60 mph (17.7sec) and 16sec longer to 80 mph (44.7sec). Up to 60 mph the Zephyr V4 can only just beat the Cortina 1300 (18.2sec) and falls a long way behind the more expensive Corsair 2000 (13.5sec). Overall fuel consumption during the 1,200 mile test period was 21.1 mpg (compared with 19.4 for the Zephyr V6), but we found it possible to obtain 25 mph on a typical touring country run. The 95 mph mean maximum speed is surprisingly high, all things considered, and suggests that that uncompisingly non-aerodynamic looking shape may not be as inefficient as it seems.

Highest cruising speed is about 80 mph which can be maintained up most motorway slopes. As well as a lot of motor car, the Zephyr also inherits a really useful-sized fuel tank from its big brothers—15 gallons—which gives a range of about 300 miles. Like the Cortina, the Zephyr at speed suffers from too much wind noise from around the fixed quarter-lights and back edges of the front doors. Towards maximum revs in 2nd, 3rd and top the gearlever chatters; this can be quelled with one's hand. Engine noise is acceptable unless one is accelerating hard.

Unusually for a contemporary Ford, we found that changing into 2nd and reverse gears was sometimes difficult and indefinite. As the performance figures show, the Zephyr is low geared which suits the large load-carrying capacity of which the car is capable. In ordinary use one tends to ignore bottom and start off in 2nd. Too many revs on starting from rest in 1st or 2nd produced clutch judder; we learnt to avoid this on the flat but it could not be

prevented during a hill start. At all other times, as on most cars with low power-to-weight ratios, it is very easy to drive the Zephyr smoothly, like a good chauffeur.

When the Escort was announced, Ford excused the lack of independent rear suspension by saying that, among other things, it was too noisy. It is interesting to note that they had already destroyed that argument by producing this inexpensive fully independent design which is very quiet in spite of being fitted with radial-ply tyres as standard. It also provides a comfortable ride, in a swooping, soft sort of way.

Since our criticisms of heavy steering on the original Zephyr V6, the ratio has been lowered so there are now 6.4 turns for a 38ft lock instead of 5.5. It lacks precision now with a vague, rubbery feel. There is nearly 1½in. of free play at the wheel rim in the straight-ahead position and then some "squodge" beyond that. Taking a simple bend (that is, one that doesn't change from left to right halfway through) even at moderate speeds, one has noticeably to anticipate it by beginning to turn the wheel earlier than usual. This is no problem unless one arrives suddenly at a more complicated situation involving an unexpected swerve or change of lock. At such moments, "slow" steering, even with good self-centring such as on this, can be untidy at best and often embarrassing. Straight-ahead stability is good until a breeze gets up, which the Zephyr notices and dislikes, or until a fast uneven road when there is some slight wandering.

Initially there is a lot of understeer which increases with cornering speed. As one corners faster the back wheels begin to tuck under until at the limit on a closed track we found the inside one lifted off the road under extreme roll. Normally the behaviour is reasonable, there being insufficient power to unstick the back end.

Brakes are nearly free from fade and are light and powerful, giving 1g braking for 90lb pedal load with all wheels on the point of locking. The handbrake is the umbrella type, not ideal to use but it did hold on the 1-in-3 hill.

Not only in outside appearance is the Zephyr a somewhat half-hearted take-off of its American cousins. Behind the big false nose one sits in a large comfortable seat close to the steering wheel, driving more from one's elbows than the shoulders. There is a small vertical adjustment for steering column height—a welcome feature. Pedals are well placed, the big organ treadle of the accelerator being especially so. Shorter staff-members thought the seating position a bit low which makes the wheel rim seem too high and the square bonnet even longer.

Instruments are clear and the Zephyr is an example to some other manufacturers on how to make finding the right switch easy at night—every one has a green-glowing label—eerie but very effective. Getting into front or back seats, one is aware that this is an unusually roomy car for five people, or six at a squash. As is generally acknowledged, in one respect the Zephyr beats all non-air-conditioned American cars—ventilation and heating. The fact that the quarter-lights are fixed does not matter except perhaps in tropical countries because, unlike most of Ford's European copiers, the Aeroflow ventilation system has enough capacity to give a good throughput even at low speeds. It was always cool driving the Ford, even on the hot days during the test period.

One or two petty economies betray the fact that you don't quite get everything for £942 (including delivery charges) in Great Britain. There's no trip mileometer and the horn—perhaps hooter is a better word—makes people look for an impudent van, not a big saloon. Nevertheless, the Zephyr V4 represents a great deal of car for your money even if you don't get as much engine.

PERFORMANCE

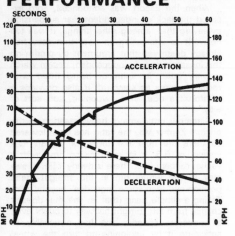

ACCELERATION

DECELERATION

MAXIMUM SPEEDS

Gear	mph	kph	rpm
Top (mean)	95	153	4,825
(best)	99	159	5,025
3rd	76	122	5,800
2nd	54	87	6,450
1st	29	47	6,450

Standing ¼-mile 20.3 sec 63 mph
Standing kilometre 39.6 sec 79 mph

MOTORWAY CRUISING

Error (ind. speed at 70 mph)	71 mph
Engine (rpm at 70 mph)	3,550 rpm
(mean piston speed)	1,403 ft/min
Fuel (mpg at 70 mph)	26.0 mpg
Passing (50-70)	14.8 sec
Noise (per cent silent at 70 mph)	55 per cent

TIME IN SECONDS	4.9	7.6	12.1	17.7	26.9	44.7	—
TRUE SPEED MPH	30	40	50	60	70	80	90
INDICATED SPEED	29	40	50	61	71	82	92

Mileage recorder 0.15 per cent under-reading.
Test distance 1,238 miles.
Figures taken at 4,600 miles by our own staff at the Motor Industry Research Association proving ground at Nuneaton.

SPEED RANGE, GEAR RATIOS AND TIME IN SECONDS

mph	Top (3.70)	3rd (5.57)	2nd (8.69)	1st (16.31)
10-30	—	8.6	5.2	
20-40	13.0	7.6	5.1	—
30-50	12.6	8.3	7.3	—
40-60	14.3	9.8	—	—
50-70	18.4	15.2	—	—
60-80	28.3	—	—	—

CONSUMPTION

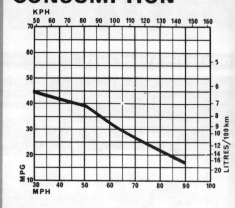

FUEL

(At constant speeds—mpg)	
30 mph	44.5
40 mph	41.2
50 mph	39.2
60 mph	32.0
70 mph	26.0
80 mph	21.5
90 mph	17.2

Typical mpg	25 (11.3 litres/100km)
Calculated (DIN) mpg	23.6 (12.0 litres/100km)
Overall mpg	21.1 (13.4 litres/100km)
Grade of fuel, Premium, 4-star (min 97RM)	

OIL

Miles per pint (SAE 10W/30)   600

HOW THE CAR COMPARES

Maximum Speed (mph)

70   80   90   100

- Ford Zephyr de luxe
- Humber Sceptre
- Jaguar 240
- Rover 2000 SC
- Vauxhall Victor 2000

0-60 mph (sec)

20   10

- Ford Zephyr de luxe
- Humber Sceptre
- Jaguar 240
- Rover 2000 SC
- Vauxhall Victor 2000

Standing Start ¼-mile (sec)

30   20   10

- Ford Zephyr de luxe
- Humber Sceptre
- Jaguar 240
- Rover 2000 SC
- Vauxhall Victor 2000

MPG Overall

10   20   30

- Ford Zephyr de luxe
- Humber Sceptre
- Jaguar 240
- Rover 2000 SC
- Vauxhall Victor 2000

Ford Zephyr de luxe	£1,021
Humber Sceptre	£1,259
Jaguar 240	£1,469
Rover 2000SC	£1,472
Vauxhall Victor 2000	£973

TEST CONDITIONS Weather: Cloudy dry. Wind: 5-10 mph. Temperature: 18 deg. C (65 deg. F). Barometer: 29.8 in. Hg. Humidity: 50 per cent. Surfaces: Dry concrete and asphalt

WEIGHT Kerb weight: 25.4 cwt (2,844lb-1,288kg) (with oil, water and half-full fuel tank). Distribution, per cent F, 55.6; R, 44.4. Laden as tested: 29.2 cwt (3,268lb-1,483kg).

TURNING CIRCLES
Between kerbs, L, 39ft 3in.; R, 36ft. 10in.
Between walls L, 41ft 9in.; R, 39ft 7in.
Steering wheel turns, lock to lock 6.4

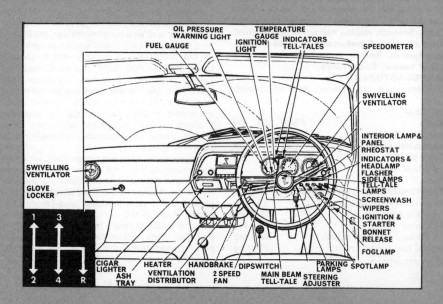

BRAKES

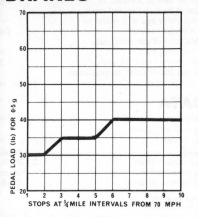

(from 30 mph in neutral)

Load	g	Distance
20lb	0.20	150ft
40lb	0.55	55ft
60lb	0.75	40ft
80lb	0.97	31ft
90lb	1.0	30.1ft
Handbrake	0.30	100ft
Max. Gradient	1 in 3	
Clutch Pedal 30lb and 4.2in.		

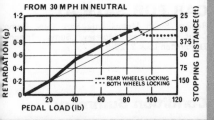

FROM 30 M PH IN NEUTRAL

---- REAR WHEELS LOCKING
······ BOTH WHEELS LOCKING

SPECIFICATION

FRONT ENGINE, REAR-WHEEL DRIVE

ENGINE

Cylinders	. .	4, in 60deg vee
Cooling system .		Water; pump, fan and thermostat
Bore . . .		93.66mm (3.69in.)
Stroke . . .		60.30mm (2.37in.)
Displacement .		1,996 c.c. (121.7 cu. in.)
Valve gear . .		Overhead pushrods and rockers
Compression ratio 8.9-to-1: Min. octane rating: 97RM		
Carburettor . .		One Autolite downdraught
Fuel pump . .		AC mechanical
Oil filter . . .		Fram full flow, renewable element
Max. power . .		88 bhp (net) at 4,750 rpm
Max. torque . .		116.5 lb. ft. (net) at 2,750 rpm

TRANSMISSION

Clutch . . .		Borg and Beck diaphragm spring, 8.0 in. dia.
Gearbox . . .		Four-speed, all-synchromesh
Gear ratios . .		Top 1.0
		Third 1.51
		Second 2.35
		First 4.41
		Reverse 4.66
Final drive . .		Hypoid bevel, 3.70-to-1

CHASSIS and BODY

Construction .		Integral, with steel body

SUSPENSION

Front		Independent, MacPherson struts, coil springs, bottom wishbones, telescopic dampers, anti-roll bar
Rear		Independent, semi-trailing arms, fixed length drive shafts, coil springs, telescopic dampers

STEERING

		Burman recirculating ball
		Wheel dia. . . 16.5in.

BRAKES

Make and type .		Girling discs front and rear
Servo . . .		Girling vacuum
Dimensions . .		F. 9.63in. dia.; R. 9.1in. dia.
Swept area .		F. 189.5 sq.in.; R. 146.8 sq.in.; Total 336.3 sq.in.

WHEELS

Type		Pressed steel disc, 5-stud fixing, 5in. wide rim.
Tyres—make .		Dunlop, Firestone, Goodyear or Pirelli; Firestone on test car
type .		F100 radial-ply tubeless
size . .		185-14in.

EQUIPMENT

Battery . . .		12 volt 53 Ah
Generator . .		Lucas C40L 25-amp d.c.
Headlamps . .		Lucas sealed beam 120/90-watt (total)
Reversing lamp.		Extra
Electric fuses .		10
Screen wipers .		Single speed, self-parking
Screen washer .		Standard, electric
Interior heater .		Standard, air-blending type
Heated backlight		Available from Triplex
Safety belts . .		Extra, anchorages built-in
Interior trim . .		Pvc seats, pvc headlining
Floor covering .		Carpet
Starting handle .		No provision
Jack		Screw pillar
Jacking points .		Two each side, under sills
Windscreen . .		Toughened
Underbody protection .		Phosphate treatment prior to painting

MAINTENANCE

Fuel tank . .		15 Imp. gallons (no reserve) (68 litres)
Cooling system		15.5 pints (including heater)
Engine sump .		7.5 pints (4.3 litres) SAE 10W/30. Change oil every 6,000 miles. Change filter element every 6,000 miles.
Gearbox . . .		3.3 pints SAE 80. Change oil once only at 3,000 miles.
Final drive . .		3 pints SAE 90. No change needed.
Grease . . .		No points
Tyre pressures .		F. 24; R. 28 p.s.i. (all conditions)
Maximum payload		1,075lb. (488 kg.)

PERFORMANCE DATA

Top gear mph per 1,000 rpm	19.7
Mean piston speed at max power	1,875 ft/min
Bhp per ton laden	60.3

STANDARD GARAGE 16ft x 8ft 6in.

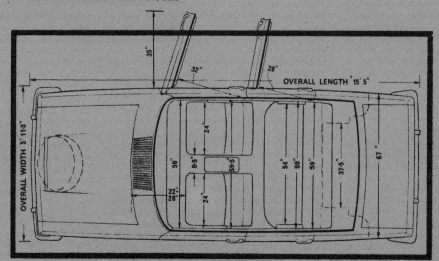

SCALE
3in. to 1ft
Cushions uncompressed

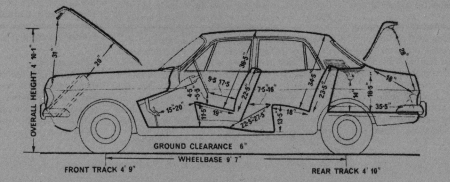

285: 1966 Ford Zephyr V4

PRICES

Car for sale at Molesey at £5
Typical trade advertised price
  for same age and model in
  average condition £6
Total cost of car when new
  including tax £9
Depreciation over 2½ years £3
Annual depreciation as proportion
  of cost new . . . . 14½ per c

DATA

Date first registered   27 April 19
Number of owners
Tax expires   30 November 19
M.o.T.   Not requi
Fuel consumption   21-24 m
Oil consumption   100 m
Mileometer reading   28,8

TYRES

Size: 6.40-13 in. Goodyear G8 whitewalls on
except left rear, for which a new whitewall is on orde
Approx. cost per replacement tyre £8 16s 6d (tubeles
Depth of original tread 9 mm; remaining tread dep
6 mm at front, and left rear; 2 mm on right rear, 1 m
on spare.

TOOLS

Jack and wheelbrace in position under bonnet. I
handbook.

CAR FOR SALE AT:

Ramsay Smith Motors Ltd., Park View, Hampt
Court Road, East Molesey, Surrey. Telephor
TEDdington Lock 2128-9.

PERFORMANCE CHECK

(Figures in brackets are those of the Autotest, published 15 August 1968)

			In top gear:		
0 to 30 mph	5.3 sec	(4.9)	20 to 40 mph	11.9 sec (13.0)	
0 to 40 mph	8.5 sec	(7.6)	30 to 50 mph	12.0 sec (12.6)	
0 to 50 mph	13.1 sec	(12.1)	40 to 60 mph	14.2 sec (14.3)	
0 to 60 mph	19.0 sec	(17.7)	50 to 70 mph	19.4 sec (18.4)	
0 to 70 mph	29.0 sec	(26.9)	60 to 80 mph	32.5 sec (28.3)	
0 to 80 mph	48.2 sec	(44.7)	Standing km	40.1 sec (39.6)	
Standing ¼ mile	21.2 sec	(20.3)			

EXACTLY three years ago in this series we tested a 1963 Ford Zodiac III, age at the time a few months more than the 2½ years of this Zephyr IV. The price asked then was £685, so the £595 which will buy this Zephyr IV seems very reasonable, particularly if allowance is made for the improved specification and the way costs generally have risen in the past three years. The car is also in outstandingly good condition all round, with all the evidence of very careful use. The high oil consumption is the only weak point.

It's not long since we published the *Autotest* on the Zephyr V4, and comparisons are interesting. This used example, with 28,000 miles behind it, still performs almost as well. Front tyre pressures were 6 psi high when the car was collected, and adjustment transformed the ride comfort. It really is a most comfortable car. The engine pulls smoothly at low revs and, as found in the *Autotest*, the acceleration is quite good, with none of the sluggishness which one might expect of a 2-litre engine in such a large body. Quite relaxed cruising at up to 80 mph is possible. However, the engine is harsh under power, and it is best when driven gently and without high revs. There is a great deal of tappet noise at tickover, but we were warned before taking the car away that the vendors are having the tappets adjusted before selling the car.

An automatic choke is standard, and ensures instant starting and snatch-free performance immediately after a cold start, but some over-richness occurs in the next few minutes before it cuts out. Clutch take-up is smooth, provided first gear is used for starts from rest.

Mounted on the column, the gear change is a little stiff into the lower gears, and has to be used rather roughly to obtain reverse, but other gear lever movements are light and reasonably positive. First and second gears are nearest the driver, and the lever is spring-loaded to drop naturally into the third-fourth plane. Floor mounted gear change was, of course, optionally available, as fitted to the car used for the later *Autotest,* and with the column change goes a bench front seat. Synchromesh is still effective on all four gears, and there is little gear noise in the indirect ratios.

From the driving seat, which seems to have sagged slightly, giving an even lower sightline than standard, the Zephyr feels every bit as big as it is, and is a rather embarrassing car to drive in confined quarters. The car feels very bulky indeed, and this impression is not helped by steering which is fairly heavy, low geared and rather vague. Directional stability at speed is fair, and the car is enjoyed far more on the open road.

As well as independent suspension, the other important development on Ford's Mk IV range was the use of servo-assisted disc brakes all round. Response is very good. Firm braking from high speed brings a lot of tyre shriek, but really good stopping power is available. The handbrake, with pull-out lever in the lower part of the facia, has to be pulled really hard, but then holds effectively on a reasonable gradient.

Apart from the slightly looser and more rattly behaviour of the car over poor surfaces, this Zephyr has really lasted extremely well and is in most respects almost indistinguishable from new. In some ways it is an uninspiring car, designed to be driven in lazy and unhurried fashion; yet the generously big six-seater carrying capacity in relation to low price and the promise of moderate running costs are the things to consider. Seen this way it is undoubtedly a good used car buy and represents even better value than that Zodiac of three years ago.

Condition Summary

BODYWORK

It is fair to expect a car to be in very goo condition after only two-and-a-half years an less than 30,000 miles; even so the maroo finish is outstandingly well preserved. There no rust at all, even on the front apron and alon the sills. Because the finish is so good we ha to look hard for traces of any repainting, b every indication is that this is still the origin paintwork. The chromium is unmarked and th interior condition is also to a very high standar The black PVC upholstery and carpets sho little wear and the roof lining also is clea Underbody examination revealed that a n rear silencer box has been fitted and traces ca be seen of a thin bitumastic material, evident painted on and successfully inhibiting corrosio The underbody is exceptionally free from rust.

Equipment

Thermometer and cigarette lighter are no working. Other equipment including the wind screen wipers and washers, parking lam provision and lamps are working correctly. Th only other possible exception is the horn, whic works but gives a rather anaemic note. Th efficient and controllable ventilation system including one way valves in the extractors o the rear quarters, is also working properly.

Accessories

For those who like them, two headrests hav been added, one for each side of the benc front seat; and the car has been fitted wit reflective number plates. A radio is include with the sale, but the set was away for repa while we had the car for test. Lap and diagon

We have to go back nearly a year to match the beautiful condition of this Ford Zephyr IV. On opening the bonnet (left) the first impression is that the engine must have fallen out on to the road, but in fact all is there, though rather buried away. Interior condition (right) is again outstanding but the steering wheel needs to be reset on the splines

USED CAR TEST ZEPHYR 4 . . .

safety belts have been fitted to comply with the legal requirement for them. There are also fog and reversing lamps.

About the Zephyr 4

Ford's policy, dating back to first introduction of the Zephyr for the 1950 Earls Court Motor Show, has always been to offer alternative engines in the same body shell. In those early days, of course, the four-cylinder version was offered in the cheaper model known as the Consul, but with introduction of the Mk III range in April 1962 the name Zephyr was used for both versions. The four-cylinder was still the 1,703 c.c. engine previously fitted in the Consul Mk II.

The new body style for the Mk IV range was introduced in April 1966, and production of the 1,703 c.c. unit was abandoned, its place being taken in the Zephyr by the 2-litre V4 unit as fitted in the then-current Ford Corsair GT. Corsairs still use the V4 engine.

Capacity is 1,996 c.c., and the cylinder bore at 93.7 mm is standardized throughout the Zephyr Zodiac range. Stroke is 72.4 mm, the same as in the 3-litre Zodiac, this engine having identical dimensions but two extra cylinders. Compression ratio is 8.9 to 1 and peak power of 88 bhp net is produced at 4,750 rpm. Four-speed gearbox with floor or column change, or Ford C4 automatic, were transmis-

sion options, and Laycock de-Normanville overdrive working on third and top gears was available for the first time on any Ford. Other major departures from previous models were the use of disc brakes all round with servo, and independent rear suspension using semi trailing arms and coil springs.

In production there have been a number of modifications including redesigned valve gear to eliminate the frequent need for tappet adjustment on the earlier engines. Because of criticisms of steering heaviness, the steering ratio was lowered, increasing the already high number of turns from lock to lock from 5.5 to 6.4. The range continues in production and spares are readily available. ☐

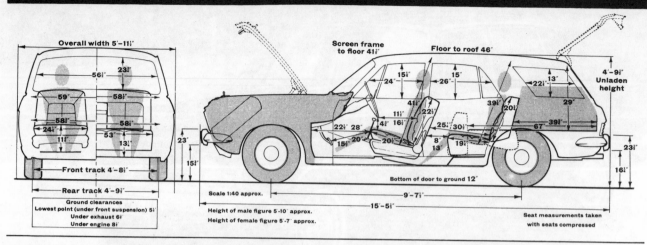

Front engine rear wheel drive with all-independent suspension

Engine

Block material	Cast iron
Head material	Cast iron
Cylinders	60° V-6
Cooling system	Water
Bore and stroke	93.67 mm. (3.96 in.) 72.42 mm. (2.88 in.)
Cubic capacity	2.994 c.c. (183 cu.in.)
Main bearings	4
Valves	Pushrod o.h.v.
Compression ratio	8.9:1
Carburetter	Weber 40 DFA twin-choke downdraught
Fuel pump	AC mechanical
Oil filter	Full flow
Max. power installed	128 b.h.p. at 4,500 r.p.m.
Max. torque installed	176 lb.ft at 3,000 r.p.m.

Transmission

Clutch	9 in. s.d.p. diaphragm
Internal gearbox ratios	
Top gear	1.000
3rd gear	1.412
2nd gear	2.214
1st gear	3.163
Reverse	3.346
Overdrive top	0.82
Synchromesh	All forward gears
Overdrive type	Laycock
Final drive	Hypoid bevel 3.7:1
M.P.H. at 1,000 r.p.m. in:—	
O/d top gear	24.5
Top gear	19.7
3rd gear	14.0
2nd gear	8.9
1st gear	6.8

Chassis and body

Construction	All-steel unitary

Brakes

Type	Girling discs with vacuum servo
Dimensions	9.63 in. front, 9.91 in. rear discs
Friction areas:	
Front	20.8 sq.in. of lining operating on 214 sq.in. of disc
Rear	14.0 sq.in. of lining operating on 139 sq.in. of disc

Suspension and steering

Front	Independent by McPherson struts with anti-roll bar
Rear	Independent by semi-trailing single wishbones each side and coil springs
Shock absorbers:	
Front and rear	Telescopic
Steering type	Recirculating ball worm and nut with power assistance
Tyres	Goodyear G800 185 x 14
Wheels	Pressed steel disc
Rim size	5J x 14

Coachwork and equipment

Starting handle	None
Tool kit contents	Jack and wheelbrace incorporating hub-cap removers
Jack	Screw pillars
Jacking points	Two each side under sills
Battery	12-volt, negative earth 53 amp. hrs. capacity
Number of electrical fuses	10
Headlamps	4
Indicators	Self-cancelling flashers
Reversing lamp	2 automatic
Screen wipers	Electric two-speed self-parking
Screen washers	Trico electric
Sun visors	2
Locks:	
With ignition key	Front doors and tail-gate
With other keys	Underfloor compartment
Interior heater	Fresh air
Upholstery	Cirrus pvc
Floor covering	Carpet
Alternative body styles	Saloon
Maximum load	1,075 lb.
Maximum roof rack load	100 lb.
Major extras available	Automatic transmission

Maintenance

Fuel tank capacity	15 galls.
Sump	8 pints SAE 10W-30
Gearbox	3¼ pints SAE 80
Rear axle	3 pints SAE 90
Steering gear	SAE 80
Coolant	19½ pints (2 drain taps)
Chassis lubrication	None
Minimum service interval	6,000 miles
Ignition timing	12° before t.d.c. static
Contact breaker gap	.014-.016 in.
Sparking plug gap	.023-.027 in.
Sparking plug type	Autolite AG22
Tappet clearances (hot)	Inlet 0.010 in.; Exhaust 0.018 in.
Valve timing:	
Inlet opens	20° b.t.d.c.
Inlet closes	56° a.b.d.c.
Exhaust opens	62° b.b.d.c.
Exhaust closes	14° a.t.d.c.
Rear wheel toe-out	0.23 in.
Front wheel toe-in	0.15 in.
Camber angle	1° 33'
Castor angle	−0° 32'
King pin inclination	6° 27'
Tyre pressures:	
Front	24 p.s.i.
Rear	28 p.s.i.

Safety check list

Steering Assembly

Steering box position	Well back
Steering column collapsible	Yes
Steering wheel boss padded	Yes
Steering wheel dished	NO

Instrument Panel

Projecting switches	Yes
Sharp cowls	No
Padding	Yes

Windscreen and Visibility

Screen type	Zone toughened
Pillars padded	Yes
Standard driving mirrors	Interior
Interior mirror framed	Yes
Interior mirror collapsible	Yes
Sun visors	Padded

Seats and Harness

Attachment to floor	On slides
Do they tip forward?	No
Head rest attachment points	No
Back of front seats	Light padding
Safety harness	Lap and diagonal
Harness anchors at back	Yes

Doors

Projecting handles	Window winders only
Anti-burst latches	Yes
Child-proof locks	On rear doors

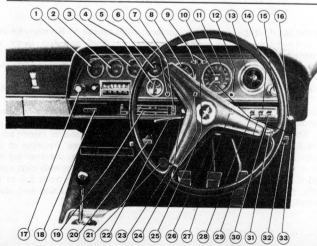

1, oil pressure gauge. 2, temperature gauge. 3, fuel gauge. 4, clock. 5, ammeter. 6, handbrake tell-tale. 7, boost fan. 8, rev counter. 9, direction indicator tell-tales. 10, distance recorder. 11, speedometer. 12, ignition warning light. 13, fresh air vent. 14, direction indicator/headlamp flasher/horn stalk. 15, panel/interior light control. 16, trip zero. 17, cigar lighter. 18, ashtray. 19, heater temperature and distribution slides. 20, handbrake. 21, dipswitch. 22, overdrive stalk. 23, radio speaker balance control. 24, sidelights tell-tale. 25, main beam tell-tale. 26, steering column vertical adjustment clamp. 27, parking lights. 28, wipers. 29, washers. 30, side and head lights. 31, ignition/starter key. 32, bonnet lock. 33, trip mileage recorder.

Freight Express

Coachbuilt conversion with ample if not optimum capacity for its size's modest payload; fair performance, relaxed cruising and quiet comfort for five passengers and loads of luggage; expensive compared with saloon

IT IS a characteristic of design that the useful capacity of an estate car is seldom proportional to the overall size, the ratio getting smaller as the car gets larger. Certainly this is so with the Ford Zodiac Estate, currently the largest, most expensive model in the British Ford range. Not that anybody is likely to find it lacking in room; unlatching the solid well-made tail-gate and lowering the rear seat squab provides what seems almost enough room to hold a party or carry all the hunting, shooting and fishing gear for the most elaborately equipped weekend's sport. But given such a large car to begin with designers do not seem to have gone to the same trouble to incorporate fully fold-down seat arrangements and make use of every nook and cranny as they do in the small cars.

Purely as a bulk load carrier the Zodiac hardly rates with the Cortina. It even has a lighter payload ($10\frac{1}{2}$ cwt.) and though it is 15 in. longer, 6 in. wider, 8 cwt. heavier overall, and getting on for twice as expensive, its maximum floor length is 6 in. shorter and the maximum unobstructed width (36 in.) just about the same. All this is rather academic for most purposes; it would swallow everything we required, including two armchairs, but for people who sometimes need to spend the occasional night sleeping in their car it is less suitable than several estate models with much more compact overall dimensions.

However, by making space secondary to luxury, Ford have produced a car more in keeping with the original concept of the wooden bodied shooting brake. Along with the Corsair it is one of two models still converted after partial completion by Abbot of Farnham which makes it nearly £460 more expensive than the Zodiac saloon. For this you get an extremely comfortable hold-all with none of the draughts, squeaks and rattles which go
continued

PRICE: £1,426 plus £435 14s. 6d. equals £1,881 14s. 6d.
Overdrive £58 15s. 1d.
INSURANCE: AOA group rating, 5; Lloyd's 5.

Ford Zodiac Estate
continued

with some of the less expensive car/van compromises and one which retains all the cosiness and amenities of a luxury saloon, right down to the security of a place to store valuable luggage invisible from outside.

As a car the Zodiac has been improved with development since we had several misgivings on initial appraisal in 1966. It is still very softly sprung which together with its size makes it a handful to drive fast on country roads but the larger wheels and increased negative camber at the rear have greatly improved roadholding and raised the speed at which the handling behaviour becomes unpredictable beyond the level which most owners would reach in normal motoring. The optional power steering takes all the effort out of manoeuvring and with overdrive the 3-litre engine combines a relaxed, almost fuss-free and deceptively rapid performance with a slightly better fuel

consumption than we managed last year on a $2\frac{1}{2}$ litre Zephyr saloon, albeit a non-overdrive model. As the price suggests it is an estate car in the grand manner and one likely to remain sufficiently uncommon to carry prestige appeal in addition to its considerable practical value.

Performance and economy

An automatic choke is standard with the V-6 engine. Once it is set with a dab of the throttle, the engine starts immediately and apart from a slight rise in idling speed there is little difference in performance cold or fully warm. Though not quite as smooth as the best in-line sixes the engine is almost silent up to around 3,500 r.p.m. when some harshness begins to intrude, but not to the same extent as it does with the $2\frac{1}{2}$ litre apart from a pronounced boom resonance at about 4,100 r.p.m. A feature of the unit is its flexibility and tractability in the lower and middle ranges which, thanks to the new throttle linkage fitted since we last tested a 3 litre, can now be exploited to full. It will pull comfortably from below 10 m.p.h. in top gear and with the

Performance

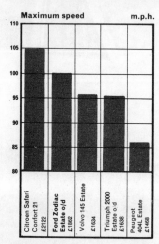

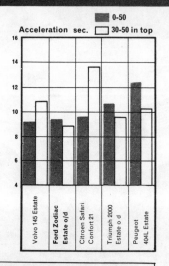

Performance tests carried out by *Motor's* staff at the Motor Industry Research Association proving ground, Lindley.

Test Data: World copyright reserved; no unauthorised reproduction in whole or in part.

Conditions
Weather: Warm and dry, wind 0-5 m.p.h.
Temperature: 66-74°F.
Barometer: 29.4 in. Hg.
Surface: Dry asphalt.
Fuel: 98 octane (RM) 4-star rating.

Maximum Speeds
	m.p.h.	k.p.h.
Mean lap banked circuit	100	161
Best one-way ¼-mile	103.3	166
3rd gear	77	124
2nd gear } at 5,500 r.p.m.	49	79
1st gear }	34	55

"Maxmile" speed: (Timed quarter mile after 1 mile accelerating from rest)
Mean	93.5
Best	98.7

Acceleration Times
m.p.h.	sec.
0-30	3.6
0-40	6.0
0-50	9.3
0-60	12.7
0-70	17.4
0-80	24.5
0-90	34.1
Standing quarter mile	18.8
Standing kilometre	35.1

	O/d			
	Top		Top	3rd
m.p.h.	sec.		sec.	sec.
10-30	—		—	6.2
20-40	11.6		8.7	6.0
30-50	12.1		8.8	5.7
40-60	12.2		8.7	6.1
50-70	12.6		8.8	8.0

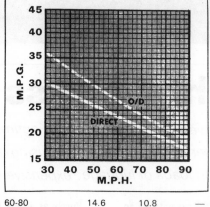

60-80	14.6	10.8	—
70-90	18.7	16.0	—

Fuel Consumption
Touring (consumption midway between 30 m.p.h. and maximum less 5% allowance for acceleration)
	23.8 m.p.g.
Overall	21.0 m.p.g.
	(=13.4 litres/100km)
Total test distance	1,122 miles

Brakes
Pedal pressure, deceleration and equivalent stopping distance from 30 m.p.h.
lb.	g.	ft.
25	0.45	67
60	0.92	33
75	1.0	30
Handbrake	0.39	77

Fade Test
20 stops at $\frac{1}{2}$g deceleration at 1 min. intervals from a speed midway between 40 m.p.h. and maximum speed (=70 m.p.h.)

	lb.
Pedal force at beginning	20
Pedal force at 10th stop	20
Pedal force at 20th stop	25

Steering
	ft.
Turning circle between kerbs:	
Left	33
Right	$36\frac{1}{4}$
Turns of steering wheel from lock to lock	$4\frac{1}{4}$
Steering wheel deflection for 50ft. diameter circle	1.3 turns

Clutch
Free pedal movement	= $\frac{1}{2}$in.
Additional movement to disengage clutch completely	= 2in.
Maximum pedal load	=30lb.

Speedometer
indicated	10	20	30	40	50	60	70
True	10	20	30	40	49	57	65
Indicated	80	90	100				
True	74	83	92				
Distance recorder					1% slow		

Weight
Kerb weight (unladen with fuel for approximately 50 miles) .... $27\frac{1}{2}$ cwt.
Front/rear distribution .... $56\frac{1}{2}$/$43\frac{1}{2}$
Weight laden as tested .... $31\frac{1}{4}$ cwt.

Parkability
Gap needed to clear 6ft. wide obstruction in front

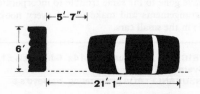

middle range ability to pull out of corners and climb hills up to 1-in-7 in top gear it is possible to cover long distances virtually without changing gear in open country. Through the gears, the extra 1½ cwt of the estate takes some of the edge off acceleration; the 0-60 m.p.h. times goes up from 11.0 s. to 12.7 s. which is still not exactly slow, and the maximum speed is still a comfortable 100 m.p.h.

More impressive than the actual figures is the car's ability to reach cruising speeds over 80 m.p.h. very quickly and hold them with an ease which makes the speed deceptive. The standard 3.7:1 axle ratio is not changed when overdrive is fitted, to give a cruising ratio equivalent to 24.5 m.p.h. per 1,000 r.p.m.—under 3,700 r.p.m. at 90 m.p.h.

Our top speed was achieved in overdrive; power tails off sharply towards the top end as the engine, though still smooth, becomes harsher. There is very little reason ever to exceed 5,000 r.p.m. during normal motoring, although the rev-counter is not red-lined until 5,500 r.p.m.

The overdrive, which operates very smoothly, has a worthwhile

effect on fuel consumption, our overall figure of 21 m.p.g. being nearly 3 m.p.g. better than the non-overdrive 3 litre saloon which itself was only slightly thirstier than the 2½ litre. Part of the improvement may be accounted for by different driving conditions during the tests for the margin on the estimated touring figure (one based on overdrive and the other on direct gearing) is only 2 m.p.g. But several times we recorded over 20 m.p.g. for journeys with a full load—very satisfactory for a car of this size and weight. With a tank capacity of 15 gallons the refuelling range could approach 300 miles, a distance which many drivers will often be quite content to cover between stops in Continental touring.

Transmission

The floor mounted gear lever has a fairly long travel but is light and pleasant to use, though some drivers criticized the spring-loading to the right which we have found is essential with this box to prevent chatter. Clutch travel appears to have been reduced—only 2 in. was required to free it on the test car—but

continued

The extended roof is pvc covered, the finished effect giving no indication that the car is converted after completion. Many people may prefer the estate car's long line to the saloon's "Manx" tail.

Dimensionally the interior space is not as great as some in relation to overall size but it swallows most normal household items. Rear lights intrude a little on the width of the loading step.

Rear quarter pillars from the saloon are retained to incorporate the ventilation extractors and relieve the boredom of an unbroken expanse of glass. Unfortunately much of the improved visibility to be gained from an estate design is sacrificed.

Ford Zodiac Estate
continued

bite is still concentrated at the top end and care is needed with the throttle when changing up not to let the revs fall too far before the bite point is reached if a jerk is to be avoided. This is particularly true of second gear, a ratio which feels altogether too low and too close to first so that it encourages starting in second, using first only for hill starts. As a result reluctant gear changers may be inclined to treat the box almost as a three-speed, but it is less satisfactory for drivers who enjoy stirring the lever.

Third, on the other hand, is a well chosen ratio, close enough to top to be of real use for steadying the car on fast sweeps and able to produce rapid acceleration for overtaking with a maximum of nearly 80 m.p.h. All gears have powerful synchromesh and apart from a slight whine on the overrun, probably from the final drive, the transmission on the test car was silent. It restarted quite easily on the 1-in-3 slope with a little clutch slip.

Handling and brakes

Power steering is standard on the Zodiac and generally well liked by our drivers. Requiring $4\frac{1}{4}$ turns from lock to lock, it still feels too low geared and calls for excessive winding in confined spaces; it does offer some resistance to wheel movement, which goes a long way to correct the sensation of insecurity engendered by the extreme lightness of some systems.

Sitting behind a vast expanse of bonnet, siting a bend through the bonnet motif like a snooker player surveying the table down his cue, the driver tends to be discouraged from fast cornering by the suspension softness and sheer size though, thanks to the larger wheels, radial tyres and the revised rear suspension camber settings, cornering power is now quite high and the car can be hustled round twisty roads briskly. Similarly, though, there is little precision in the handling: a single main road bend will not provoke excessive roll or tyre squeal, the steering remains directionally stable, and large independent wheel movement enables bumpy corners to be absorbed without any serious change of line. However, when caught out by a sudden change of camber or a succession of bends, it will begin to wallow and quite a lot of steering movement may be necessary to get the car back on line.

The once alarming tendency for the tail to slide when a bump or wave raised it and changed the camber angles has been reduced and was seldom noticed on the estate car, which carries more weight aft—nearly 44% over the driving wheels. The basic characteristics are little changed on wet roads except that it is once again possible to spin the inside wheel when accelerating hard out of a corner, a vice which now scarcely applies to the estate on a reasonably surfaced dry road.

The brakes are extremely good—powerful, light and progressive. Barely 70 lb. pressure was necessary for a straight line stop of better than 1g. The fade test produced only a slight rise in pressure towards the end and there was rapid return to normal after a soaking in the water splash. An under-facia pull-out handbrake on the left of the steering column was passed as being

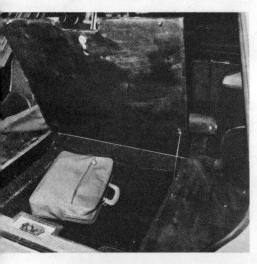

A lockable compartment under the floor enables valuables to be left in the car out of sight of passers-by.

Rear seat passengers lack nothing in comfort for the conversion; the seat is embracing and the back as high as on the saloon. Knee room could be improved, probably without loss of comfort at the front if the squabs were a little thinner.

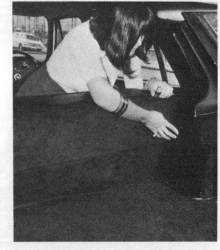

Conversion takes only seconds: the rear cushion hinges forward, two push-button catches release the squab which drops flat, held secure by metal latches in the base of the cushion.

Ford Zodiac Estate

satisfactory in effect if not in action. It locked the wheels on the 1-in-3 slope (though the car slid on the down slope) and was good enough for almost 0.4 g in an emergency stop from 30 m.p.h. Otherwise its stiff return action and insensitive springy feel evoked little enthusiasm.

Comfort and controls

We have previously suggested that the long rear spring travel of the Mk. 4 range makes it an ideal subject for self-levelling suspension; to compromise for a car with the vast variation in loading which applies to the Zodiac estate is virtually impossible.

Assuming, correctly we believe, that the most popular freight for an estate car of this class is more likely to comprise bulky but comparatively light items like fishing rods and golf clubs than heavy objects like bags of cement, Ford have made no changes to the suspension; a tail-heavy wallowing and marked nose-up attitude on the rare occasions when the back is loaded with the aformentioned cement is considered preferable to too much firmness with a light load. Certainly on one run with two passengers and accoutrements for a weekend's fishing the ride was judged about right for this class of car. Minor irregularities produce very little disturbance and pitch is well controlled but there is a tendency for the body to float over long wavelength undulations. Road noise is only prominent at very low speeds when there is the typical radial thump over pot-holes and Cat's Eye studs but this subsides as the speed rises until the car is very quiet and feels completely effortless at 80 m.p.h. The absence of quarter vents assists in the suppression of wind noise, which is generally low—just a few random whistles build up from less than perfect door and window seals towards maximum speed.

Conversion to an estate car makes no difference to the interior; it is still very roomy front and rear with ample space for three people across the rear seat, and plenty of legroom. Some drivers found the thick, deeply padded seats less comfortable than they looked, lacking lumbar support for a tall driver; almost complete lack of side support calls for a continuous effort from the occupants to remain in place on twisty roads. Otherwise the driving position is good, with a large range of fore-and-aft adjustment and squabs which recline. Pedals are well spaced and the steering wheel location allows a well stretched out position. The column is not telescopic but it does have an adjustment for height, though most of our drivers kept it firmly locked in the highest position and some thought this too low.

With the rear seat squab upright there is ample room behind for most touring luggage or a bag of golf clubs but, for larger loads, conversion to a flat floor takes only seconds. The seat cushion folds forward to stow upright and the squab folds down and locks against it on release of a push button safety-catch

at each side. The floor thus formed is completely flat for 67 in. and lushly carpeted like the sides and the rest of the car but there are no rubbing strips to prevent damage from sharp edged objects. Our only real criticism was the extent of the intrusion of the rear spring cases inside and above the wheel arches, removing much of the advantage of the car's overall width and restricting room for sleeping, or the carriage of bulky objects, to a width of 3 ft. The tail gate is solid, fits well, and the stout centre catch is well clear of the head when loading. An automatic switch illuminates the interior. Much appreciated by people who need to leave brief-cases, cameras and other valuables in their car is a concealed lockable compartment under the rear carpet which eliminates one of the shortcomings of most estate cars that anything too big to go in the glove compartment has to be left in full view as an invitation to larceny.

Apart from the size of the bonnet, which obscures the view when surmounting sharp brows, forward visibility is good and both front corners are clearly visible from the seat. The rear quarter panels of the saloon are retained as a styling feature and restrict rear visibility when pulling out of side turnings, and the mirror could give a wider view to advantage, as could the swept area of the windscreen, large unwiped portions being left in the upper corners. The headlights are excellent; possibly the best orthodox system we have encountered.

We have come to expect a powerful and versatile heating system on modern Fords and the Zodiac is no exception, two slides giving fairly sensitive control of temperature and distribution with the aid of a two-speed boost fan, rather noisy when on full. The face level vents are of the latest eye-ball type with built-in adjustment and aided by extractors in the rear side panels provide adequate flow even at low speeds in very hot weather.

Fittings and furniture

Though neat and comprehensive, the Zodiac's instrumentation is more a stylist's than an ergonomist's ideal; reflections make some of the dials difficult to read and important controls such as lights, wipers (two-speed), electric washers and the optional auxiliary lights are sited on a small panel tucked away to the right of the steering column where their labels are practically impossible to identify on the move. On the other hand, the comparatively little-used switch for interior and panel lighting (defunct on the test car) is most prominently displayed on the facia console.

Lights are dipped by a rather vintage style floor button but the flasher is a neat micro-switch behind the indicator stalk. A stalk on the other side controls the overdrive which was very smooth in its operation. Standard fitting include reversing lights, cigar lighter, electric clock, coat hooks, three ashtrays and vanity mirror. There are no door pockets, or parcel shelf, but a large downward opening locker below the facia and a useful box with a hinged lid forming the armrest between the seats should cope with most of the maps and leaflets which accumulate in a car.

The thickly padded, deep carpeted interior and thick quilted seats give the interior the desired impression of luxury and would help to cushion an unharnessed passenger in an accident. An additional safety measure included since our last Zodiac is the Capri-style safety steering wheel with its convoluted boss and padded spokes.

Service and accessibility

Regular maintenance is limited to changing the engine oil and filter and to the normal carburetter and ignition checks at 6,000 mile intervals. The gearbox oil is changed only once at 3,000 miles and chassis and differential are lubricated for life. There is plenty of room to work round the compact engine and most components are easily accessible including the spare wheel which, since it also lies under the bonnet, does not need luggage to be unloaded for access.

M

1, brake fluid reservoir. 2, clutch fluid reservoir. 3, radiator filler cap. 4, coil. 5, fuses. 6, washer reservoir. 7, battery. 8, alternator. 9, distributor. 10, fuel pump. 11, dipstick.

Make: Ford. Model: Zodiac Estate. Makers: Ford Motor Co., Ltd., Dagenham, Essex. Estate conversion by E. D. Abbott Ltd., Farnham, Surrey.

MOTOR TESTED

Ford's Status Symbol.

Spacious and well equipped; effortless transport if not pressed; smooth automatic gearbox; good driving position but poor seats.

The off-the-shelf personalised car—if you'll accept the contradiction in terms—is gaining popularity on the British motoring scene. Rootes joined the game with the Avenger, but the credit for fully exploiting it must go to Ford with their Capri custom packs and E versions of the Mark IV, Corsair and Cortina. Only the Mark IV E, however, gets the full Executive title. For £1846, the most expensive saloon in the Ford line-up, you get such a very fully equipped car that there is very little even the most fanatical accessory enthusiast could add.

The Mark IV range brought out in 1966 inherited only model names from its predecessor. It broke new ground for Ford of Britain with all-round independent suspension; their familiar MacPherson struts at the front, semi-trailing arms with coil springs (ingeniously mounted to accommodate fixed length drive shafts) at the rear. We said in our road test of the Zodiac (April 23, 1966) that the suspension had shortcomings when driving quickly because the nose-heavy weight distribution and a high rear roll centre gave too much weight transfer at the back and produced a jacking effect, characteristic of swing axle geometry.

In October 1967 a Mark Two version was announced incorporating, along with a number of other detail improvements, larger wheels and modified suspension geometry with more negative camber at the rear. Certainly the Zephyr V6 we tested in 1968 (August 10) had much improved handling but with the 2½-litre V6, instead of the Zodiac's 3-litres, we thought it rather gutless.

At the bottom of the range the Mark IV is virtually unrivalled in terms of metal-for-money, the 2-litre V4 Zephyr selling for £1071. At the top the Executive faces direct competition from the Austin 3-litre, Vauxhall Viscount and several Continental imports. Rootes have not had a car in this sector of the market since the demise of the large Humbers and we wonder whether the Mark IV's replacement will be such a large car. Perhaps Ford's product planners were too strongly influenced by the parent company when the Mark IV was conceived. Its size makes it rather unwieldy on our crowded roads—the BLMC 1800 manages to package similar interior dimensions into a smaller and more manageable car.

Nevertheless, the Executive looks imposing (or perhaps pretentious) with spacious accommodation; leather upholstery; genuine wood cappings on the doors and instrument panel; an impressive array of instruments and switches; a radio; sliding

PRICE: £1414 plus £432 1s. 2d. purchase tax equals £1846 1s. 2d.

roof; heated rear window; and wing mirrors—all in the standard specification.

The car behaves quite well but it still has limitations when extended. Performance is a bit disappointing with a maximum speed of only 95.4 mph and 0-50 mph in 9.3s; the manual Zodiac recorded 102.5 mph and 7.5s respectively. Smooth automatic transmission is standard in the Executive.

Performance and Economy

The engine started promptly when cold. Flooring the throttle and releasing it gently sets the automatic choke which makes the engine idle at around 1200 rpm until normal running temperature has been reached. The choke was reluctant to cut out on one of the two cars we tried—the heater delivered warm air some time before the engine idle returned to its normal 600-700 rpm. However, a quick dab on the throttle after two or three miles usually reduced the idling speed, suggesting some stickiness in the linkage—a common problem.

The engine pulled without hesitation from cold, but the fast idle caused the car to creep rather quickly. With an 8.9:1 compression ratio we used four star fuel and could detect no pinking, though the engine developed a curious "tinkle" when accelerating through 1500 rpm. This was also apparent on the second Executive at 2000 rpm.

The 3-litre 60° V6 Essex engine is not very highly stressed, producing 136 bhp DIN at 4750 rpm and maximum torque of 181.5 lb. ft. at 3000 rpm. Above 5000 rpm the engine becomes rough and obtrusively noisy but as the automatic changes up at 4500-4900 on full throttle, you don't often notice this shortcoming. Using the selector to hold first and intermediate gears at 5100 did not improve the acceleration times, so presumably the engine's breathing is none too efficient. Our maximum speed, timed over a lap of the MIRA banked track, of 95.4 is not very fast. Even downhill the car would not exceed 100 mph. (The Mark IV range suffers from a rather high drag coefficient of 0.47, probably due to its slab front.) In compensation, the maximum is reached fairly rapidly—witness our best maximile of 94.8 mph.

Acceleration from low speed is fairly brisk, with a 0–50 mph time of 9.3s but, on the road, where acceleration from 50 mph is useful for getting past a stream of traffic, the car has little in reserve even when using the kickdown. Our 50-70 mph time of 9.4s compares poorly with the 6.5s of the manual Zodiac in third gear. Most people, however, will probably find the performance quite adequate and should obtain a fuel consumption of 18-21 mpg.

PERFORMANCE

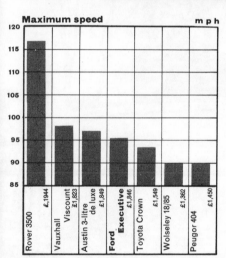

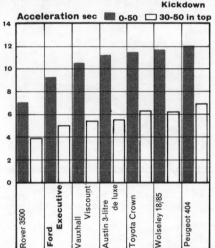

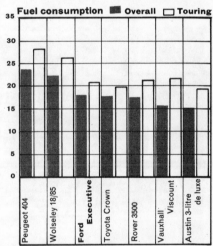

Performance tests carried out by *Motor's* staff at the Motor Industry Research Association proving ground, Lindley.

Test Data: World copyright reserved; no unauthorized reproduction in whole or in part.

Conditions
Weather: Cool and dry, wind 10-25 mph
Temperature: 36.5-43.0
Barometer: 29.67in. Hg.
Surface: Dry tarmacadam
Fuel: 98 octane (RM), 4 Star rating

Maximum Speeds
	mph	kph
Mean lap banked circuit	95.4	153.4
Best one-way ¼-mile	95.8	154.0
Top gear	80	128
2nd gear } at 4000 rpm	55	88
1st gear } at 4000 rpm	34	55
"Maximile" speed: (Timed quarter mile after 1 mile accelerating from rest)		
Mean	93.8	—
Best	94.8	—

Acceleration Times
mph	sec.
0-30	4.3
0-40	6.4
0-50	9.3
0-60	13.4
0-70	18.7
0-80	26.4
0-90	40.3
Standing quarter mile	19.3
Standing kilometre	36.0

mph	'Kickdown' sec.
20-40	3.9
30-50	5.0
40-60	7.0

50-70	9.4
60-80	13.0
70-90	21.6

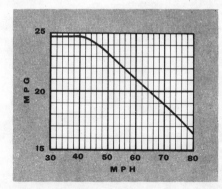

Fuel Consumption
Touring (consumption midway between 30 mph and maximum less 5% allowance for acceleration) 20.8 mpg
Overall 18.0 mpg
(=15.7 litres/100km)

Total test distance 2802 miles

Brakes
Pedal pressure, deceleration and equivalent stopping distance from 30 mph.
lb.	g.	ft.
25	0.47	64
50	0.69	43.5
75	0.92	33
80	0.98	31
Handbrake	0.30	100

Fade Test
20 stops at ½g. deceleration at 1 min. intervals from a speed midway between 40 mph and maximum speed (=66.4 mph)
	lb.
Pedal force at beginning	20
Pedal force at 10th stop	23
Pedal force at 20th stop	26

Steering
Turning circle between kerbs:	ft.
Left	37½
Right	33½
Turns of steering wheel from lock to lock	4.2
Steering wheel deflection for 50 ft. diameter circle	1.5 turns

Speedometer
Indicated	10	20	30	40	50	60
True	10.5	20.5	31	40.5	51	60.5
Indicated	70	80	90			
True	70	80	90			
Distance recorder accurate						

Weight
Kerb weight (unladen with fuel for approximately 50 miles) 27.4 cwt
Front/rear distribution 57/43
Weight laden as tested 31.1 cwt

Parkability
Gap needed to clear 6ft. wide obstruction in front

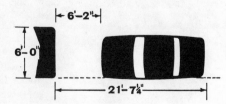

Transmission

The Executive uses the Borg Warner 35 three-speed gearbox and a torque converter which allows an easy start on the 1 in 3 test hill. The stiff but well placed tunnel-mounted selector works in a gate marked PRND 2 and 1. We would have preferred a more positive indication of the selector position, particularly at night. Engaging D from rest should produce a barely discernible jolt, though the first Executive we tried gave a pronounced lurch, particularly when the engine was cold and idling above its normal speed. Smooth take-offs were also easier to achieve in the second car—the throttle of the first was very sensitive in its initial movement, which made creeping in traffic rather tricky. Once away, however, changes up the box, even on full throttle, were commendably smooth on both cars. On part throttle the changes came at around 25 and 35 mph, with foot floored at 37 and 62 mph (4500 rpm). Some thought the kickdown too fierce—at any speed over 40 mph the downward change into intermediate produced a jolt and the resulting roar from the engine as the revs rose discouraged use of the kickdown. However, as the engine has excellent low-speed torque there is little need to use the kickdown. Around town, part throttle downchanges were unpredictable; this was particularly noticeable on right-angle turns when the gearbox would

The front seats recline but do not lie flush with the rear seat squab, above. An imposing slab front restricts the Executive's maximum speed to just over 95 mph, but it cruises effortlessly at 70, below. Wind noise is high.

EVX 485H

94

The seats are not as comfortable as they look and were unanimously criticized. They offer little lateral support and with the high roll angles the car adopts don't encourage brisk cornering (upper picture). Plenty of legroom in the back, and there is a reading light in the grab handles above the door (lower picture).

This lever unlocks the steering column rake adjustment. The row of switches on the right are obscured by the horizontal steering wheel spoke on a straight road (upper picture). Winder for the sliding roof, which was draught-free unless fully opened.

sometimes change in the middle of the turn, at others as the car accelerated away. Using the manual override to select a lower gear when, say, entering a roundabout, the downward change is very smooth.

Most owners will probably be content to leave the selector in D and let the automatic do the work smoothly and unobtrusively on its own. The gearbox and back axle were both quiet. An optional four-speed manual transmission with overdrive costs £45 less.

Handling and Brakes

Power steering ensures that the Executive is light to manoeuvre but the gearing (4.2 turns from lock to lock) is too low. One-and-a-half turns of the safety wheel are required to scribe a 50 ft. circle and this means a lot of wheel-whirling around town. Even so, the steering is fairly accurate and some resistance gives an impression of road feel. The steering of one car had more resistance than the other, neither gave much increase in effort as the cornering speed increased; this is usually a fair indication of the degree of feel given by a power steering system.

Wet or dry the Executive clings on remarkably well, helped no doubt by its fat 185 x 15 Goodyear G800 tyres. Unfortunately they squeal too readily and the body rolls a lot so brisk cornering is discouraged. The car wallows on entering a tight corner, which is rather uncomfortable for the passengers, but then stays on line with initial understeer changing to a gentle tail slide on the limit. Lifting off in mid corner had no dramatic effect on the car's line so evidently the earlier jacking effect has been eliminated by the revised rear suspension and larger wheels. The nose-heavy weight distribution, 57/43 front/rear, still exaggerates understeer but on main roads deceptively high average speeds are easily maintained, with the car holding the chosen line through fast open bends. Not the best of cars for quick town journeys, though, as its size and ponderous behaviour are not conducive to quick lane changes.

Pedal pressure for the servo-assisted disc brakes (on all four wheels) rose from 20 to 26lb. in our fade test. The servo is very sensitive so only a slight increase in pressure can lock the wheels. With a delicate touch, though, the brakes are very reassuring and we achieved 0.98 g with a pedal pressure of 80lb. The under-facia pull-out handbrake would not hold the car on the 1 in 3 hill—possibly with the handbrake better adjusted it would, since one wheel locked and slid down the concrete surface of the hill, while the other rolled. The handbrake's 0.3 g could also probably be improved. A really good soaking in the water splash had little effect on the brakes.

Comfort and Controls

For a large car weighing 27cwt we were not very impressed with the low-speed ride, particularly over small bumps which

The carpeted boot took 13.1 cu. ft. of our test luggage. The pillar jack did not feel very sturdy.

14x11x5

17½x13x6

21x15x7

24x18x8

28x21x9

produced a joggling motion in the body reminiscent of scuttle shake. This vibration is transmitted to the passengers through the seat rather than the body. However the Executive floats over long wave length irregularities with commendable ease, only a slight side to side motion of the bonnet and occasional rolling of the body indicating the workings of the suspension.

The leather-covered seats came in for unanimous criticism. They look impressive but offer no lateral support—perhaps with the optional cloth covering they might hold the occupants better. Poor support combined with lots of body roll means that passengers are thrown about even at low cornering speeds. Armchair seats like this are not suitable for cars, and the money spent on making them *look* impressive would be better spent providing them with more lateral and lumbar support. Ample leg room front and rear means that the chauffeur-driven executive will not be cramped, but because of the lack of side support most front-seat passengers preferred to have the seat well forward so they could brace their feet against the bulkhead.

The driving position is good; it needs to be with such a large bonnet. The steering wheel is adjustable for rake (there is a locking lever to the right of the column under the dashboard) but with the wheel in its near vertical position there is not a lot of clearance between the driver's thighs and the steering wheel rim. The organ throttle and large brake pedal are well placed and come complete with unnecessary chrome trimmings.

Minor controls are not so well laid out; their arrangement is probably more due to marketing requirements for an impressive array of switches than to engineering/ergonomic considerations. With the steering wheel in its straight ahead position the row of switches to its right and below the facia are neatly obscured by the horizontal spoke, so to operate the correct switch, the driver has to peer round the side of the wheel. Most of the auxiliaries are controlled from this panel, including the smeary two-speed wipers and electric washers, which on one of the cars we tried were "dribblers" and on the other gave a useful jet of water. The right-hand stalk operates the horn, and flashes the lights. Unlike most other current Fords the dipswitch is on the floor and this brings on all four headlamps which can be supplemented by the auxiliary tungsten spot and fog lamps (standard in the Executive specification); the auxiliaries are operated by a single switch. With everything on there is a good spread of light. Reversing lights are operated automatically by the gear selector. Rear visibility however is not very good and the rear corners of the car cannot be seen from the driving seat; blind rear three-quarters makes filtering into a traffic stream rather fraught though this shortcoming is compensated for by the wing mirrors which can be used truck-driver style for reversing. The day/night interior mirror does not provide such good visibility due to its rather odd shape.

As we have come to expect from Ford the heating and ventilation are first rate. Different combinations of the facia-mounted and easy to understand heater controls give cold, warm or hot air to the feet, the same temperature variations to the screen, and whatever the other settings variable amounts of cool air to the face from the well-sited eyeball vents at the ends of the facia. A noisy two-speed fan supplements the ram flow in traffic. A heated rear-window (an alternator is fitted to cope with the supply) ensures a clear rear window.

If engine noise at high revs is not one of the Executive's strong points then lack of road noise certainly is. There is very little radial thump from the wide tyres and only subdued bangs from the suspension over bad surfaces. This unfortunately tends to focus attention on the excessive wind noise which comes from the guttering round the screen, spoiling the otherwise extremely quiet and effortless high-speed cruising; some instability in cross-winds mars high-speed driving too.

Fittings and Furniture

The appointments of this big Ford are fully in keeping with its title. The comprehensive array of instruments is well sited in the driver's line of vision; unfortunately the glasses are at such an angle that the rear window is reflected in the face of the instruments, which makes the accurate speedometer difficult to read. The matching tachometer is of academic interest and most owners will find no use for it. None of our staff liked the chrome surrounds to the instruments; others disliked the walnut facia insert and door cappings though we appreciate that many people like this kind of embellishment.

Mounted each side of the instrument panel are two large knobs; that on the left is a cigar lighter, the other is a rheostat for the instrument illumination which also operates the front interior light. There are also courtesy switches on the front doors. The rear compartment is lit by two small lights integral with the grab handles (with magnifying inserts presumably for reading) which are operated both by courtesy switches on the rear doors and small switches on the door pillars. Fumbly door lock catches lie flush with the walnut cappings when depressed and lifting them to unlock the doors is a nail-breaking exercise. All door locks can be child-proofed, however, and we liked the interior door handles which lie within cavities in the door panel. The sliding steel roof, operated by a handle just above the screen, is draught free and produced no internal buffeting provided it was not fully opened. Even when ajar, however, it was not possible to listen to the Ford radio, even with the balance control adjusted to give full volume to the front speaker.

This is mounted on the front face of a central console, whose rear-hinged lid is difficult to open. Other stowage space is provided by a large lockable drop-down glove locker and a map pocket to the right of the driver's feet. A shelf behind the rear seats can also accommodate other items. Both the Executives we tried were finished in Aubergine—one had colour-keyed trim, and the other the alternative black which we thought much improved the car's interior. Full carpeting and door panels trimmed in a pale shade of purple are not to our taste.

The inertia reel belts are easy to use with the reservation that the short section tended to get lost behind the front seats. The enormous carpeted and illuminated boot took 13.1 cu. ft. of our test luggage.

Service and Maintenance

With such a long bonnet there is ample space around the short V6 engine to give easy access to all routine service points, though topping up the oil level is awkward due to the proximity of the huge air cleaner to the filler cap. The release catch for self-propping bonnet is located above the driver's right foot and when open the bonnet is illuminated. The tool kit contains only a jack and hub cap remover cum wheelbrace—presumably Ford consider that owners of their status car have passed the do-it-yourself stage. The jack works fairly well, but gives the uneasy feeling that it is about to seize; when not in use it is stowed above the spare wheel at the front of the engine compartment. The Executive needs servicing at 6000 mile intervals, or every six months, whichever comes first.

1 air cleaner. 2 windscreen washer reservoir. 3 coolant overflow container with filler cap. 4 battery. 5 brake fluid reservoir. 6 dipstick. 7 alternator. 8 distributor. 9 radiator pressure cap. 10 jack. 11 wheelbrace.

MAKE: Ford. MODEL: The Executive. Ford Motor Company Ltd., Warley, Essex, England.

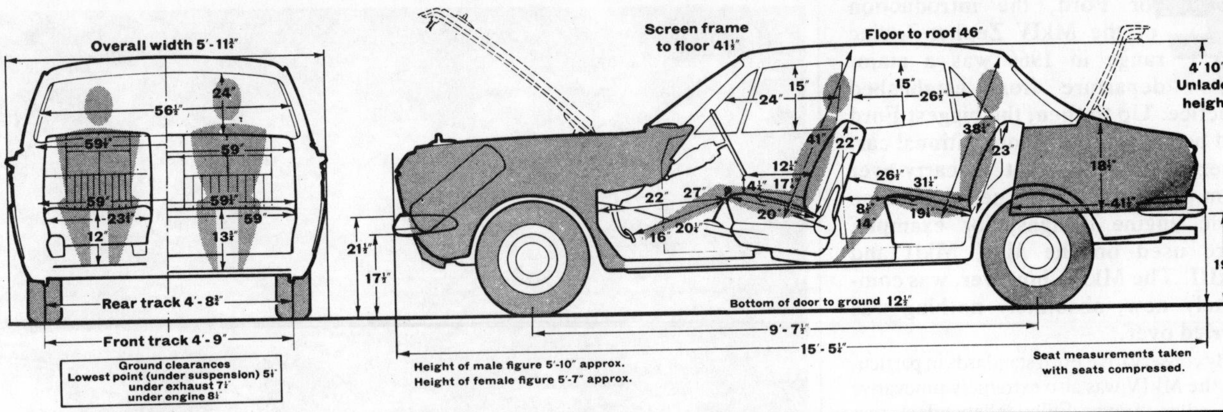
Overall width 5'-11¾"
24"
56½"
59¼"
59"
59"
59¼"
23¼"
59"
12"
13¾"
21½"
17½"
Rear track 4'-8¾"
Front track 4'-9"
Ground clearances
Lowest point (under suspension) 5¼"
under exhaust 7¼"
under engine 8¼"
Screen frame to floor 41½"
Floor to roof 46"
4'10" Unladen height
15"
24"
15"
26½"
41"
22"
38¾"
23"
18½"
12½"
4½"
17¾"
26½"
31½"
22"
27"
20"
8½"
14"
19¼"
41½"
16"
20½"
23½"
19½"
Bottom of door to ground 12½"
9'-7½"
15'-5¼"
Height of male figure 5'-10" approx.
Height of female figure 5'-7" approx.
Seat measurements taken with seats compressed.

Front engine, rear drive; three litre V6 engine; all independent suspension; disc brakes

Engine

Block material	Cast iron
Head material	Cast iron
Cylinders	V6
Cooling system	Water, semi-sealed
Bore and stroke	93.66 mm. (3.68in.) 72.42 mm. (2.85in.)
Cubic capacity	2994 c.c. (182.5 cu. in.)
Main bearings	4
Valves	Pushrod ohv
Compression ratio	8.9:1
Carburetter(s)	Weber twin choke
Fuel pump	AC mechanical
Oil Filter	AC or Fram full flow
Max. power (net)	136 b.h.p. at 4750 r.p.m.
Max. power (gross)	144 b.h.p. at 4750 r.p.m.
Max. torque (net)	181.5 lb.ft. at 3000 r.p.m.
Max. torque (gross)	192.5 lb.ft. at 3000 r.p.m.

Transmission

Borg-Warner Type 35 three speed automatic with torque converter

Internal gear box ratios	
Top gear	1.000
2nd gear	1.450
1st gear	2.393
Reverse	2.094
Final drive	Hypoid bevel 3.7:1
Mph at 1000 rpm in:—	
Top gear	20
2nd gear	13.8
1st gear	8.4

Chassis and body

Construction	Integral-all steel welded

Brakes

Type	Servo-assisted discs
Dimensions	Front 9.63 in. dia.; rear 9.91 in. dia.
Friction areas:	
Front	20.8 sq. in. of lining operating on 189.5 sq. in. of disc
Rear	14.0 sq. in. of lining operating on 146.8 sq. in. of disc

Suspension and steering

Front	Independent by Macpherson struts and coil springs with anti-roll bar
Rear	Independent by semi-trailing arms with swinging shackles and coil springs
Shock absorbers:	
Front, Rear	Telescopic, double acting
Steering type	Power assisted recirculating ball
Tyres	185R-14 Goodyear G800
Wheels	Steel disc
Rim size	5J

Coachwork and equipment

Starting handle	No
Tool kit contents	Jack & wheelbrace
Jack	Screw pillar
Jacking points	4—2 each side under sills
Battery	12 volt negative earth. 53 amp hrs capacity
Number of electrical fuses	10
Headlamps	Twin Lucas 7 in. round sealed beam 250/120 W
Indicators	Self-cancelling flashers
Reversing lamp	Yes
Screen wipers	Two-speed electric
Screen washers	Electric
Sun visors	2
Locks:	
With ignition key	Front doors and boot
Interior heater	Fresh air type, with two-speed fan and face level ventilation
Upholstery	Hide or cloth
Floor covering	Nylon cut pile carpet
Alternative body styles	None
Maximum load	1075 lb
Maximum roof rack load	100 lb
Major extras available	Manual gearbox with over-drive option

Maintenance

Fuel tank capacity	15 Imp galls
Sump	9.5 Imp pints SAE 10W/30 (including filter)
Gearbox	12 Imp pints SAE ESW/MZC 33F
Rear axle	3 Imp pints SAE 90 EP
Steering gear	0.7 pints SAE 90 EP
Coolant	21.8 pints (2 drain taps)
Chassis lubrication	None
Minimum service interval	6,000 miles
Ignition timing	12° B.T.D.C.
Contact breaker gap	0.025 in.
Sparking plug gap	0.023/0.027 in.
Sparking plug type	Autolite A.G. 32A
Tappet clearance (hot)	Inlet 0.010 in. Exhaust 0.018 in.
Valve timing:	
Inlet opens	20° b.t.d.c.
Inlet closes	64° a.b.d.c.
Exhaust opens	70° b.b.d.c.
Exhaust closes	14° a.t.d.c.
Rear wheel toe-out	$\frac{1}{16}$ in.
Front wheel toe-in	0-0.25 in.
Camber angle	1°
Castor angle	0°
King pin inclination	7°
Tyre pressures:	
Front	24 p.s.i.
Rear	28 p.s.i.

Safety Check List

Steering Assembly

Steering box position	On siderail to rear of engine and crossmember
Steering column collapsible	No (steering wheel hub collapsible)
Steering wheel boss padded	Yes
Steering wheel dished	No

Instrument Panel

Projecting switches	Yes
Sharp cowls	Yes
Padding	Yes—on top of facia

Windscreen and Visibility

Screen type	Zone toughened (laminated optional)
Pillars padded	Yes
Standard driving mirrors	1 interior; 2 on front wings
Interior mirror framed	Yes
Interior mirror collapsible	Yes
Sun visors	2

Seats and Harness

Attachment to floor	On slides
Do they tip forward?	No
Head rest attachment points	No
Back of front seats	Padded
Safety Harness	Lap and diagonal; inertia reel
Harness anchors at back	No

Doors

Projecting handles	Window winders
Anti-burst latches	Yes
Child-proof locks	Yes

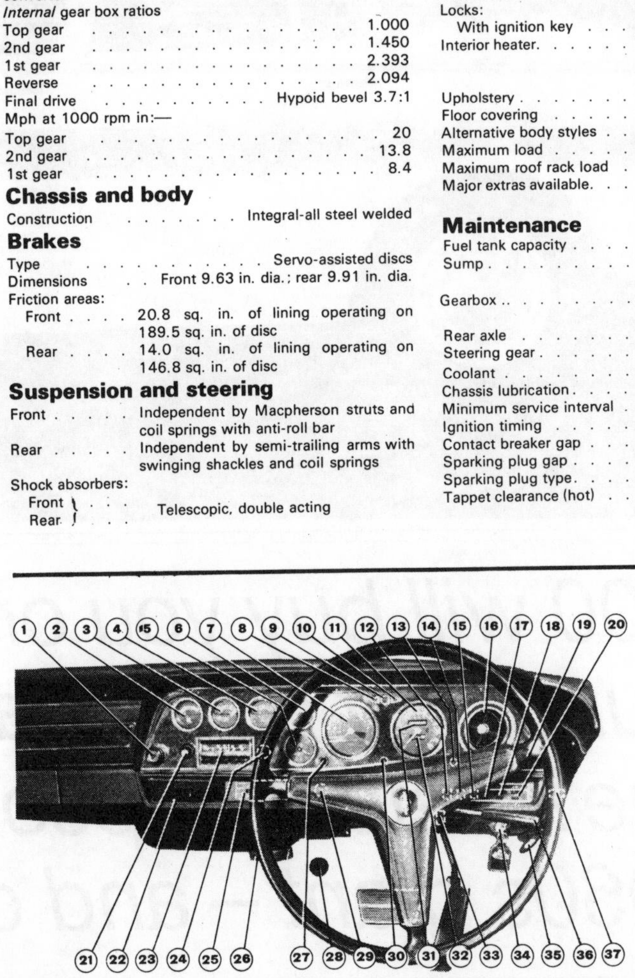
1 2 3 4 5 6 7 8 9 10 11 12 13 14 15 16 17 18 19 20
21 22 23 24 25 26 27 28 29 30 31 32 33 34 35 36 37

1 cigar lighter. 2 oil pressure gauge. 3 water temperature gauge. 4 fuel gauge. 5 clock. 6 ammeter. 7 tachometer. 8 and 10 indicator tell tales. 9 main beam tell tale. 11 speedometer. 12 parking lights. 13 ignition warning light. 14 heated rear window. 15 pass/fog lights. 16 fresh air vent. 17 wipers. 18 washers. 19 instrument panel/ interior light. 20 side and headlights. 21, 23 and 24 radio. 22 ashtray. 25 heater controls. 26 handbrake. 27 handbrake warning light. 28 dipswitch. 29 radio sound balance control. 30 side and headlights tell tale. 31 mileometer. 32 trip meter. 33 steering column adjustment lever. 34 ignition/starter. 35 bonnet release catch. 36 direction indicator/headlamp flasher/horn. 37 trip reset.

For Ford, the introduction of the MkIV Zephyr/Zodiac range in 1966 was a major departure from established practice. Up to then, the biggest Ford had been an entirely conventional car. There had been a lot of carry-over from one model to the next; the same basic engine designs, for example, were used on the MkI, MkII and MkIII. The MkIV, however, was completely new; absolutely nothing was carried over.

By conservative Ford standards in particular, the MkIV was also extremely innovative and adventurous. Fully independent rear suspension, disc brakes all round and, perhaps most significant of all, V configuration engines. The styling was also slap-bang up to the minute. Clean lines replaced the MkIII's tail fins and the MkIV's long nose and short tail made it instantly recognisable. The MkIV's shape has since become regarded as something to be either loved or loathed but there's no doubting that it was refreshingly different and gave the car a purposeful and powerful look. The simple, square and uncluttered frontal treatment also made the car look wider than it was. Unusually, the engine air intake was below the front bumper (the engine was mounted at the rear of its compartment with the spare wheel mounted at an angle in front; this helped direct the air on to the radiator). There was thus no need for an actual radiator grille and early Zephyrs did not have one – and that fitted to the other MkIVs was a fake, just there for styling and because people expected it to be!

From the start there were four MkIV mod-

Take three MkIVs. Zephyrs are instantly identifiable by having just two headlamps; Zodiacs and Executives had four. MkIVs were used by several police forces but the car in the foreground is unusual as it's fitted with Ferguson four-wheel-drive. Twenty-five were built and supplied for assessment to police forces throughout the country, this example going to Durham. It's the only known surviving roadworthy 4WD MkIV, although another exists in poor condition and a third car is rumoured in a west country scrapyard. It has been restored to full police specification.

els, all direct successors to cars from the MkIII range. The Zephyr Four had a 1996cc V4 engine, the Zephyr Six, Zodiac and Executive were all V6-powered with the Zodiac and Executive units being 2994cc and the Zephyr 2495c. As before, the Zodiac was a more upmarket version of the Zephyr. The Executive (a replacement for the short-lived MkIII Zodiac Executive) was the top of the range and featured as standard leather upholstery, wooden door cappings, factory-fitted sunroof, automatic transmission and auxiliary driving lights. Contrary to popular belief, the correct name of this model was not Zodiac Executive but just Ford Executive. It was, of course, the first of the 'E' models from Ford, a range that eventually included

Battleshi

£2000 will buy you on around; but does that value? Peter Simpson 1960s giant – and c

Bargain!

f the best MkIV Fords
present good classic
vestigates Ford's late
es away impressed.

the Cortina 1600E and 2000E MkIII, Escort 1300E, Corsair 2000E and Capri 3000E.

Power-steering and overdrive were available on all six-cylinder cars and automatic transmission and a factory fitted sunroof were available across the range. The Executive was officially available with manual as an option (at a slightly reduced price) but few if any Executive buyers opted for it. A steering column lock was also specified as an optional extra on all models but, from 1970, a security device was made compulsory on new cars sold in the UK and most, if not all post-1969 cars (and certainly all post 1970), had this as standard. Up to 1969 Zephyrs were normally supplied with column gearchange and a bench front seat; on Zodiacs the floor-change was standard but column change could be specified at extra cost.

As had by then become almost traditional for Ford, the Zephyr/Zodiac estate car was produced 'outside' by E.D. Abbots of Farnham, and it was a direct conversion from the saloon. The estate car, however, was given full manufacturer's approval; it featured in the brochures and was listed alongside the saloons in the price lists. Introduced a couple of months after the saloons, the conversion was quite expensive, adding £430 after tax (1966) to the saloon price and making the bottom of the range Zephyr Four estate £138 dearer than the Zodiac saloon! Relatively few were sold and surviving estate cars are now regarded as rare.

There was a mid-run update in 1969. From then on floor change and individual front seats became the norm for Zephyrs (although bench seats and column change was available as an option, few buyers wanted it) and there were also various trim and detail changes. The most significant change for Zephyrs was that they now also had 'proper' dummy radiator grilles between the headlamps! Production continued until 1972 when the MkIV, and the Zephyr and Zodiac model names that had been part of the Ford scene since 1951 and 1953 respectively, were discontinued. Several MkIV components, including the V4 and V6 engines, however, were used in the MkIV's replacement, the Consul/Granada range.

Nowadays, the MkIV has something of a mixed reputation. The six-cylinder cars are certainly fast and stable enough in a straight line but many people find that the ride is far too soft and wallowy; almost vomit-inducing according to some! Because of this the car has been given the perhaps slightly unfair nickname of 'flying pig'. The MkIV also acquired a reputation, probably quite justified, for rusting away vital structural members early in its life. Flaking-off undersealant didn't help matters. In 1975 (when the very oldest cars were just nine years old) the AA advised anyone considering buying a MkIV to 'inspect the belly thoroughly, ensuring that a screwdriver point cannot be pushed right through'. The cars seemed to rot everywhere, quite literally, from top to bottom! Additionally they started to look tatty outside after a few years. Ford went through a bad period for paintwork in the late sixties; metallic finishes in particular tended to fade and flake off; remember all those old Cortinas you used to see with huge patches of primer showing through? Depreciation was very rapid and many cars were scrapped without there being that much wrong with them; repair just wasn't justified in relation to the cars' value. I could have bought a not unpresentable F-reg Zephyr Six for £50 in 1976; but being too young to drive there wasn't a lot of point!

Buying guide

Given the widespread slaughter of MkIVs over the past few years, it perhaps isn't surprising that a high percentage of the survivors have had one (often elderly) owner for much of their life, the sort of person who keeps a car a long time and isn't that concerned about market value. Such cars often look very good from on top but it is still vital to inspect the underbody thoroughly. Lift the carpets, too, to check the floors for rust and, worse, holes. Sills also frequently rust, along with rear wheelarches, front wings around the headlamps, inner wings around the MacPherson strut turrets and door bottoms – all the usual places for Fords really! Bear in mind that virtually nothing is available in the way of new body panels. On the other hand the car's smooth lines can make fabricating repair sections easier than on many cars. Don't be too concerned if an originally metallic car has been resprayed; it's probably because the original paint fell off!

Turning to the mechanicals, it's generally accepted that the V6 engine is better than the V4, the latter being rather a noisy unit that also has to work very hard dragging the MkIV body along! Listen carefully for nasty rattles on starting and when pulling hard, and check that the oil light goes out as soon as the engine starts. The V6 is regarded as tougher but the same checks should also be carried out. Bear in mind that an engine rebuild isn't cheap, although there shouldn't be any difficulty getting the parts. A good secondhand unit may be a more attractive option but be certain that what you're putting in is good. Transmissions are generally good, particularly the Borg-Warner automatic for which parts are still available. One or two individual components for manual boxes are getting tricky but the units are generally reliable and careful adjustment and a few new bushes will usually cure any vagueness in the column change.

MkIV suspension is soft at the best of times but weak shock absorbers and a few perished rubbers will make the ride positively horrible! Even on a low mileage car you should expect to replace some of the bushes, particularly at the rear, where defects sometimes get past the MoT tester. Steering fluid leaks can be a problem; there are specialists who recondition pumps but their standard varies and it's probably best to use someone who is recommended.

Interior trim isn't that durable compared to other luxury cars and some items, particularly dash tops (which are prone to cracking) and injection-moulded trim panels, are extremely difficult to repair. Cars that are clean inside do turn up however and, although the interior obviously isn't as important as structural strength, good trim is definitely a plus-point.

It's not unknown for brake calipers (the system, incidentally is the same as on the P6

The underbonnet layout is unusual. The angled spare wheel helps direct air onto the engine. Inner wing rust, particularly along the seam where they join the outer, is a common problem. Check also the join with the bulkhead.

Typical late sixties Ford trim! Even the Zephyr was plush but the Zodiac and Exective were even plusher!

in!/continued

Estate cars are very usable. This 1968 Zephyr (with Zodiac mechanics and trim) started life with Massey Ferguson and is now on at least its third engine. The present owner (who uses the car daily for business) estimates its present mileage at over 300,000.

Front wing problems like this are common. Front and rear underwings should be hosed off regularly.

From the rear. Zodiacs and Executives had full-length rear reflectors as shown here; Zephyrs had just the tail lights.

Rover) to seize partially or completely, particularly on cars that are used only infrequently. Dismantling the caliper and fitting new rubbers often cures the problem. New calipers are expensive but available (try a Rover specialist). You'll need a special tool, incidentally, to change the rear pads; this is still available from Girling.

Spares availability

For most classic cars, the spares situation has got better over the past five years. For MkIVs it hasn't. There still isn't much in the way of remanufacturing and body panels, which could still be found with a little searching until quite recently, are now getting rare. Front wings are particularly scarce. Things are better on the mechanical side however. Many parts were used on the Consul/Granada and other later models; these are still available through Ford dealers and, in many cases, independent motor factors. Ford specialists such as Newford also supply MkIV parts. There are one or two curious shortages though; power-steering inner track rod ends for example – these were made by Ford themselves rather than an outside supplier and are now unobtainable. Although it doesn't offer a spares service as such the club do help members find parts.

What to pay

Prices vary from about £200 upwards for rough but running cars (model makes little if any difference at the bottom end) up to around £1600 for a low mileage condition one Zephyr, £1900 for a Zodiac and perhaps just over £2000 for an Executive. A presentable car capable of safe everyday use but with some external shortcomings should be available for around £800-£1000 but, if your ultimate aim is perfection, it's probably best to take time to find the best car possible. Despite their rarity estate cars aren't that much more valuable; add perhaps 10-20%. Limousine values are entirely dependent on

condition; a car that's too tatty to use for business has only curiousity value but a clean one is still usable to the 'matching and dispatching' trade and can be worth upwards of £3000. Because MkIVs aren't yet particularly fashionable, prices can fluctuate widely and one sometimes finds bargains priced at well below these figures. MkIVs are also occasionally overpriced by people who think any old car is worth a lot of money but we see no reason to pay more than our prices.

On the Road

I had driven a MkIV before; it was around 1979 when I was vaguely considering buying a £120 (I think) Zephyr Six. The lasting memory left by that car was not pleasant but, as it was a decidedly tired example, it is perhaps unfair to judge all MkIVs by that. Peter Barnes' 1972 Executive is an original, low-mileage car that he has kept up well and I was anxious to drive it. Inside, the car seemed enormous; the nearside of the dash was almost out of sight! Having owned and driven many sixties and early seventies Fords in the past I found many of the fixtures and fittings very familiar. That bonnet may look big from the outside – from behind the wheel it seems enormous; the square bonnet motif seems to be almost on the horizon! Once I'd remembered the handbrake (which is tucked away under the dash) we moved off down the dual carriageway. In a straight line the car was certainly fast and I appreciated the V6 burble almost as much as my Stag's V8 note. Steering? Well it was rather light for my liking but I'm sure I could get used to it given time and I certainly think I'd prefer a MkIV with power steering to one without!

I was keen to try the car around some country lanes. As I turned off the main road the car suddenly seemed very, very big! Although I wouldn't describe it as at all 'chuckable', I was very surprised to find that, for a car that's really best at high speeds, the MkIV was surprisingly nimble; cornering seemed quite acceptable and, while the ride is soft, I wouldn't describe it as unpleasant. As is so often the case, much of the MkIV's reputation comes from people driving bad examples; a good MkIV, although not perfect in these areas, is certainly acceptable. Now if I could get together £1500 I wonder what I could get.....

The writer wishes to thank Peter Barnes, John Glaysher and other members of the Ford MkIV Zephyr & Zodiac Owners Club for their help in preparing this feature.

Clubs

The **Ford MkIV Zephyr and Zodiac Club** are a small but very enthusiastic body with around 250 members. A good quality magazine is produced, events are held throughout the year and help is given with obtaining spares. Further details may be obtained by sending an sae to 94 Claremont Road, Rugby, Warwickshire CV21 3LU.

Executive Owners are also eligible to join the **Ford Executive Owners Register.** This body also cater for the Escort 1300E, Cortina 1600E, Cortina 2000E, Corsair 2000E and Capri 3000E, and details may be obtained by sending an sae to Mrs J. Whitehouse, 3 Shanklin Road, Stonehouse Estate, Coventry.

If you were successful in the mid-fifties, either a businessman or of independent means, chances are that you would have driven a Ford Zodiac. If you were in showbusiness or just plain flash, it may have been a convertible. The Mk2, launched in 1956, was undoubtedly right for the times; witness the range's impressive production total of 651,661 units in little over six years. But it was nevertheless rather basic in its interior appointments. With their ever-increasing affluence, the car buying public were beginning to demand more from their cars than just the bare minimum. This trend brought about the first Zodiac in 1953, but by the late fifties even the Mk2 was being left behind by its rivals in terms of interior specification. For a car in the Zodiac's class, painted metal finish to the doors and dashboard were definitely demodé.

In planning the Mk2 replacement, Ford decided to move even the entry model of the range more up-market, leaving the yet to be launched Consul Classic to take on the role of the Mk2 Consul. The Zodiac was to move even further up the luxury ladder, with unique interior finishes and its own distinctive profile.

In late 1959, it is believed, the first proposal for the Mk3 was built, not by Ford, but by the respected Italian firm of Frua. As can be seen from the accompanying pictures, Frua had already defined the Zodiac outline. Although the front was completely reworked, the rear remained largely intact.

With the complete takeover in late 1960 of Ford of Britain by the US parent, the Dearborn styling influence became stronger. Although not totally rejecting the Frua proposal, the decision was taken to 'corporatise' the styling. Canadian Roy Brown, who had come to Dagenham after his involvement with the Edsel, was charged with styling the Mk3. The decision not to proceed with the Frua proposal is summed up by an ex-employee of the time thus: "One could not, in retrospect, expect the US board to approve anything reflecting such good taste and sophistication; a case of club hammers versus scalpels as it were". Strong stuff indeed. Car styling is a very subjective and emotive topic, and Mk3 fans can decide for themselves which they prefer.

Drawing his corporate styling inspiration from the 1960 Falcon, Roy Brown quickly produced the Mk3 style with which we are all familiar. Some of the prototypes were certainly more styled than the production versions, notably in the bumper and lighting areas. The fully-integrated bumpers were no doubt rejected on grounds of cost, as would seem to be the case with the flush door handles seen on another Zodiac mock-up, unless these were dropped because they didn't work. Interestingly, as late as the spring of 1961, Ford were still undecided on what type of Zodiac they wanted. As can be seen, one proposal was for the 'traditional' Zodiac, this being merely a dressed-up Zephyr. The four-light

Z CARS

Darlings of the sixties
Motorway Age, a Mk3
Zephyr or Zodiac could be a
bargain 'pound of flash' today,
as Martin Rawbone explains

style only appeared once in the design stage, however, and was probably proposed as a cheaper alternative to the six-light style. At this late stage, the base model was still known as Consul. It was probably felt that Consul presented too down-market an image, as the name was now being applied to the smaller Fords. With the April 1962 launch date fast approaching, 'Styling' were still trying out different badges and trim.

In late 1961, 41 pilot-build Zodiacs were produced, these being to a finalised design. Serious production did not get under way until April '62, when the cars were launched. The Zodiac was first, debuting on April 13. *The Autocar* commented thus: 'The new MkIII Zodiac, which has been designed in its entirety at Dagenham (!), is not simply a replacement for the Mk2 model, as its manufacturers have raised their sights at a higher price market'. Including purchase tax, the new car, at £1136, was nine and a half

per cent dearer, although the buyer was getting substantially more car for his money. *The Autocar* found the styling 'international'; if only they had known!

Following the Zodiac by a fortnight were the Zephyrs, the surprises here being the different roofline and the dropping of the Consul nameplate. *The Sporting Motorist* commented: 'Outwardly the lines of all three cars are alike, although each has a different grille, only the Zodiac sporting four head-lamps, and the new Zephyrs also have an altered roofline which conveys a rather elegant squared-off effect to the back of the roof by incorporating a quarterlight in the rear door and bringing a wider roof panel down behind it'.

Mechanically, there were some worthwhile improvements, notably the four-speed, all-synchro-mesh gearbox, Ford's first all synchro 'box. Although by now not new to Ford, electric wind-screen wipers were making their first appearance on the big Fords, and most welcome they were too. Another notable feature, and claimed to increase shoulder room for the occupants, was the use of curved side-window glass. The braking followed established Ford practice (also established by just about every other manufacturer too) in having servo assisted disc and drum brakes. The engines, although virtually the same as those of the Mk2, were suitably modernised. Otherwise, the specification remained much as before, not only because the layout was tried and tested, but also to simplify the stocking of spare parts by Ford dealers.

Although Ford had moved the cars more up-market, many enthusiasts bemoaned the lack of a convertible version. The estate car was also absent from the initial line-up, but appeared in October '62 at the Earls Court Show. As with the Mk2, the estate was a conversion of the saloon by E.D. Abbott Ltd of Farnham, Surrey. Development work started early in 1962, and the first example was completed shortly after the launch of the saloons. This first prototype had a steel tailgate, with a pronounced hump to the design. Concurrently, Ford had produced a glass-fibre tailgate with less of a hump, and it was this design which was adopted for production. The estate was well received at the show and was certainly a more professional design than the Mk2, looking more like a factory-built car than a conversion. With the rear seat erect, the estate offered 29 cu ft of luggage space, which increased to 61 cu ft with the seat folded. These figures feature in all the early reports and brochures; later brochures quote 34.6 cu ft and 64.5 cu ft.

Coincident with the announcement of the estate car came news from Hooper Motor Services that they were to offer a super luxury version of the Zodiac. This featured a fully retrimmed interior, with hide upholstery, thicker pile carpets and extensive sound insulation. There was a choice of bench seat with split backrest or fully reclining Reutter seats.